An Inquiry Into The Nature Of Peace And The Terms Of Its Perpetuation

Thorstein Veblen

Contents

PREFACE 7
CHAPTER I INTRODUCTORY: ON THE STATE AND ITS RELATION TO ......
    WAR AND PEACE..9
CHAPTER II ON THE NATURE AND USES OF PATRIOTISM 30
CHAPTER III ON THE CONDITIONS OF A LASTING PEACE........................62
CHAPTER IV PEACE WITHOUT HONOUR...91
CHAPTER V PEACE AND NEUTRALITY..133
CHAPTER VI ELIMINATION OF THE UNFIT...172
CHAPTER VII PEACE AND THE PRICE SYSTEM..218

AN INQUIRY INTO THE NATURE OF PEACE AND THE TERMS OF ITS PERPETUATION

BY

Thorstein Veblen

PREFACE

It is now some 122 years since Kant wrote the essay, ***Zum ewigen Frieden***. Many things have happened since then, although the Peace to which he looked forward with a doubtful hope has not been among them. But many things have happened which the great critical philosopher, and no less critical spectator of human events, would have seen with interest. To Kant the quest of an enduring peace presented itself as an intrinsic human duty, rather than as a promising enterprise. Yet through all his analysis of its premises and of the terms on which it may be realised there runs a tenacious persuasion that, in the end, the regime of peace at large will be installed. Not as a deliberate achievement of human wisdom, so much as a work of Nature the Designer of things--Natura daedala rerum.

To any attentive reader of Kant's memorable essay it will be apparent that the title of the following inquiry--On the nature of peace and the terms of its perpetuation--is a descriptive translation of the caption under which he wrote. That such should be the case will not, it is hoped, be accounted either an unseemly presumption or an undue inclination to work under a borrowed light. The aim and compass of any disinterested inquiry in these premises is still the same as it was in Kant's time; such, indeed, as he in great part made it,--viz., a systematic knowledge of things as they are. Nor is the light of Kant's leading to be dispensed with as touches the ways and means of systematic knowledge, wherever the human realities are in question.

Meantime, many things have also changed since the date of Kant's essay. Among other changes are those that affect the direction of inquiry and the terms of systematic formulation. ***Natura daedala rerum*** is no longer allowed to go on her own recognizances, without divulging the ways and means of her workmanship. And it is such a line of extension that is here attempted, into a field of inquiry which in Kant's time still lay over the horizon of the future.

The quest of perpetual peace at large is no less a paramount and intrinsic human duty today than it was, nor is it at all certain that its final accomplishment is nearer. But the question of its pursuit and of the conditions to be met in seeking this goal lies in a different shape today; and it is this question that concerns the inquiry which is here undertaken,--What are the terms on which peace at large may hopefully be installed and maintained? What, if anything, is there in the present situation that visibly makes for a realisation of these necessary terms within the calculable future? And what are the consequences presumably due to follow in the nearer future from the installation of such a peace at large? And the answer to these questions is here sought not in terms of what ought dutifully to be done toward the desired consummation, but rather in terms of those known factors of human behaviour that can be shown by analysis of experience to control the conduct of nations in conjunctures of this kind.

February 1917

CHAPTER I
INTRODUCTORY: ON THE STATE AND ITS RELATION TO WAR AND PEACE

To many thoughtful men ripe in worldly wisdom it is known of a verity that war belongs indefeasibly in the Order of Nature. Contention, with man-slaughter, is indispensable in human intercourse, at the same time that it conduces to the increase and diffusion of the manly virtues. So likewise, the unspoiled youth of the race, in the period of adolescence and aspiring manhood, also commonly share this gift of insight and back it with a generous commendation of all the martial qualities; and women of nubile age and no undue maturity gladly meet them half way.

On the other hand, the mothers of the people are commonly unable to see the use of it all. It seems a waste of dear-bought human life, with a large sum of nothing to show for it. So also many men of an elderly turn, prematurely or otherwise, are ready to lend their countenance to the like disparaging appraisal; it may be that the spirit of prowess in them runs at too low a tension, or they may have outlived the more vivid appreciation of the spiritual values involved. There are many, also, with a turn for exhortation, who find employment for their best faculties in attesting the well-known atrocities and futility of war.

Indeed, not infrequently such advocates of peace will devote their otherwise idle powers to this work of exhortation without stipend or subsidy. And they uniformly make good their contention that the currently accepted conception of the nature of war--General Sherman's formula--is substantially correct. All the while it is to be admitted that all this axiomatic exhortation has no visible effect on the course of events or on the popular temper touching warlike enterprise. Indeed, no equal volume of speech can be more incontrovertible or less convincing than the utterances of the peace advocates, whether subsidised or not. "War is Bloodier than Peace." This would doubtless be conceded without argument, but also without prejudice. Hitherto the pacifists' quest of a basis for enduring peace, it must be admitted, has brought home nothing tangible--with the qualification, of course, that the subsidised pacifists have come in for the subsidy. So that, after searching the recesses of their imagination, able-bodied pacifists whose loquacity has never been at fault hitherto have been brought to ask: "What Shall We Say?"

* * * * *

Under these circumstances it will not be out of place to inquire into the nature of this peace about which swings this wide orbit of opinion and argument. At the most, such an inquiry can be no more gratuitous and no more nugatory than the controversies that provoke it. The intrinsic merits of peace at large, as against those of warlike enterprise, it should be said, do not here come in question. That question lies in the domain of preconceived opinion, so that for the purposes of this inquiry it will have no significance except as a matter to be inquired into; the main point of the inquiry being the nature, causes and consequences of such a preconception favoring peace, and the circumstances that make for a contrary preconception in favor of war.

By and large, any breach of the peace in modern times is an official act and can be taken only on initiative of the governmental establishment, the State. The national authorities may, of course, be driven to take such a step by pressure of warlike popular sentiment. Such, e.g., is presumed to have been the case in the United States' attack on Spain during the McKinley administration; but the more that comes to light of the intimate history of that episode, the more evident does it become that the popular war sentiment to which the administration yielded had been somewhat sedulously "mobilised" with a view to such yielding and such a breach. So also in the case of the Boer war, the move was made under sanction of a popular war spirit, which, again, did not come to a head without shrewd surveillance and direction. And so again in the current European war, in the case, e.g., of Germany, where the initiative was taken, the State plainly had the full support of popular sentiment, and may even be said to have precipitated the war in response to this urgent popular aspiration; and here again it is a matter of notoriety that the popular sentiment had long been sedulously nursed and "mobilised" to that effect, so that the populace was assiduously kept in spiritual readiness for such an event. The like is less evident as regards the United Kingdom, and perhaps also as regards the other Allies.

And such appears to have been the common run of the facts as regards all the greater wars of the last one hundred years,--what may be called the "public" wars of this modern era, as contrasted with the "private" or administrative wars which have been carried on in a corner by one and another of the Great Powers against hapless barbarians, from time to time, in the course of administrative routine.

It is also evident from the run of the facts as exemplified in these modern wars that while any breach of the peace takes place only on the initiative and at the discretion of the government, or State,[1] it is always requisite in furtherance of such warlike enterprise to cherish and eventually to mobilise popular sentiment in support of any warlike move. Due fomentation of a warlike animus is indispensable to the procuring and maintenance of a suitable equipment with which eventually to break the peace, as well as to ensure a diligent prosecution of such enterprise when once it has been undertaken. Such a spirit of militant patriotism as may serviceably be mobilised in support of warlike enterprise has accordingly been a condition precedent to any people's entry into the modern Concert of Nations. This Concert of Nations is a Concert of Powers, and it is only as a Power that any nation plays its part in the concert, all the while that "power" here means eventual warlike force.

Such a people as the Chinese, e.g., not pervaded with an adequate patriotic spirit, comes into the Concert of Nations not as a Power but as a bone of contention. Not that the Chinese fall short in any of the qualities that conduce to efficiency and welfare in time of peace, but they appear, in effect, to lack that certain "solidarity of prowess" by virtue of which they should choose to be (collectively) formidable rather than (individually) fortunate and upright; and the modern civilised nations are not in a position, nor in a frame of mind, to tolerate a neighbor whose only claim on their consideration falls under the category of peace on earth and goodwill among men. China appears hitherto not to have been a serviceable people for

1 A modern nation constitutes a State only in respect of or with ulterior bearing on the question of International peace or war.

warlike ends, except in so far as the resources of that country have been taken over and converted to warlike uses by some alien power working to its own ends. Such have been the several alien dynasties that have seized upon that country from time to time and have achieved dominion by usufruct of its unwarlike forces. Such has been the nature of the Manchu empire of the recent past, and such is the evident purpose of the prospective Japanese usufruct of the same country and its populace. Meantime the Chinese people appear to be incorrigibly peaceable, being scarcely willing to fight in any concerted fashion even when driven into a corner by unprovoked aggression, as in the present juncture. Such a people is very exceptional. Among civilised nations there are, broadly speaking, none of that temper, with the sole exception of the Chinese,--if the Chinese are properly to be spoken of as a nation.

Modern warfare makes such large and direct use of the industrial arts, and depends for its successful prosecution so largely on a voluminous and unremitting supply of civilian services and wrought goods, that any inoffensive and industrious people, such as the Chinese, could doubtless now be turned to good account by any warlike power that might have the disposal of their working forces. To make their industrial efficiency count in this way toward warlike enterprise and imperial dominion, the usufruct of any such inoffensive and unpatriotic populace would have to fall into the hands of an alien governmental establishment. And no alien government resting on the support of a home population trained in the habits of democracy or given over to ideals of common honesty in national concerns could hopefully undertake the enterprise. This work of empire-building out of unwarlike materials could apparently be carried out only by some alien power hampered by no reserve of scruple, and backed by a servile populace of its own, imbued with an impeccable loyalty to its masters and with a suitably bellicose temper, as, e.g., Imperial Japan or Imperial Germany.

However, for the commonplace national enterprise the common run will do very well. Any populace imbued with a reasonable measure of patriotism will serve as ways and means to warlike enterprise under competent management, even if it is not habitually prone to a bellicose temper. Rightly managed, ordinary patriotic sentiment may readily be mobilised for warlike adventure by any reasonably adroit and single-minded body of statesmen,--of which there is abundant illustration. All the peoples of Christendom are possessed of a sufficiently alert sense of nationality, and by tradition and current usage all the national governments of Christendom are warlike establishments, at least in the defensive sense; and the distinction between the defensive and the offensive in international intrigue is a technical matter that offers no great difficulty. None of these nations is of such an incorrigibly peaceable temper that they can be counted on to keep the peace consistently in the ordinary course of events.

Peace established by the State, or resting in the discretion of the State, is necessarily of the nature of an armistice, in effect terminable at will and on short notice. It is maintained only on conditions, stipulated by express convention or established by custom, and there is always the reservation, tacit or explicit, that recourse will be had to arms in case the "national interests" or the punctilios of international etiquette are traversed by the act or defection of any rival government or its subjects. The more nationally-minded the government or its subject populace, the readier the response to the call of any such opportunity for an unfolding of prowess. The most peaceable governmental policy of which Christendom has experience is a policy of "watchful waiting," with a jealous eye to the emergence of any occasion for national resentment; and the most irretrievably shameful dereliction of duty on the part of any civilised government would be its eventual insensibility to the appeal of a "just war." Under any governmental auspices, as the modern world knows governments, the keeping of the peace comes at its best under the precept, "Speak softly and carry a big stick." But the case for peace is more precarious than the wording of the aphorism would indicate, in as much as in practical fact the "big stick" is an obstacle to soft speech. Evidently, in the light of recent history, if the peace is to be kept it will have to come about irrespective of governmental management,--in spite of the State rather than by its good offices. At the best, the State, or the government, is an instrumentality for making peace, not for perpetuating it.

*   *   *   *   *

Anyone who is interested in the nature and derivation of governmental institutions and establishments in Europe, in any but the formal respect, should be able to satisfy his curiosity by looking over the shoulders of the professed students of Political Science. Quite properly and profitably that branch of scholarship is occupied with the authentic pedigree of these institutions, and with the documentary instruments in the case; since Political Science is, after all, a branch of theoretical jurisprudence and is concerned about a formally competent analysis of the recorded legal powers. The material circumstances from which these institutions once took their beginning, and the exigencies which have governed the rate and direction of their later growth and mutation, as well as the ***de facto*** bearing of the institutional scheme on the material welfare or the cultural fortunes of the given community,--while all these matters of fact may be germane to the speculations of Political Theory, they are not intrinsic to its premises, to the logical sequence of its inquiry, or to its theoretical findings. The like is also true, of course, as regards that system of habits of thought, that current frame of mind, in which any given institutional scheme necessarily is grounded, and without the continued support of which any given scheme of governmental institutions or policy would become nugatory and so would pass into the province of legal fiction. All these are not idle matters in the purview of the student of Political Science, but they remain after all substantially extraneous to the structure of political theory; and in so far as matters of this class are to be brought into the case at all, the specialists in the field can not fairly be expected to contribute anything beyond an occasional ***obiter dictum***. There can be no discourteous presumption, therefore, in accepting the general theorems of current political theory without prejudice, and looking past the received theoretical formulations for a view of the substantial grounds on which the governmental establishments have grown into shape, and the circumstances, material and spiritual, that surround their continued working and effect.

By lineal descent the governmental establishments and the powers with which they are vested, in all the Christian nations, are derived from the feudal establishments of the Middle Ages; which, in turn, are of a predatory origin and of an irresponsible character.[2] In nearly all instances, but more particularly among the nations that are accounted characteristically modern, the existing establishments have been greatly altered from the mediaeval pattern, by concessive adaptation to later exigencies or by a more or less revolutionary innovation. The degree of their

---

2 The partial and dubious exception of the Scandinavian countries or of Switzerland need raise no question on this head.

modernity is (conventionally) measured, roughly, by the degree in which they have departed from the mediaeval pattern. Wherever the unavoidable concessions have been shrewdly made with a view to conserving the autonomy and irresponsibility of the governmental establishment, or the "State," and where the state of national sentiment has been led to favor this work of conservation, as, e.g., in the case of Austria, Spain or Prussia, there the modern outcome has been what may be called a Dynastic State. Where, on the other hand, the run of national sentiment has departed notably from the ancient holding ground of loyal abnegation, and has enforced a measure of revolutionary innovation, as in the case of France or of the English-speaking peoples, there the modern outcome has been an (ostensibly) democratic commonwealth of ungraded citizens. But the contrast so indicated is a contrast of divergent variants rather than of opposites. These two type-forms may be taken as the extreme and inclusive limits of variation among the governmental establishments with which the modern world is furnished.[3]

The effectual difference between these two theoretically contrasted types of governmental establishments is doubtless grave enough, and for many purposes it is consequential, but it is after all not of such a nature as need greatly detain the argument at this point. The two differ less, in effect, in that range of their functioning which comes in question here than in their bearing on the community's fortunes apart from questions of war and peace. In all cases there stand over in this bearing certain primary characteristics of the ancient regime, which all these modern establishments have in common, though not all in an equal degree of preservation and effectiveness. They are, e.g., all vested with certain attributes of "sovereignty." In all cases the citizen still proves on closer attention to be in some measure a "subject" of the State, in that he is invariably conceived to owe a "duty" to the constituted authorities in one respect and another. All civilised governments take cognizance of Treason, Sedition, and the like; and all good citizens are not only content but profoundly insistent on the clear duty of the citizen on this head. The bias of loyalty is not a matter on which argument is tolerated. By virtue of this bias of loyalty, or "civic duty"--which still has much of the color of feudal allegiance--the governmental establishment is within its rights in coercively controlling and directing the actions of the citizen, or subject, in those respects that so lie within his duty; as also

---

3 Cf., e.g., Eduard Meyer, *England: its political organisation and development*. ch. ii.

in authoritatively turning his abilities to account for the purposes that so lie within the governmental discretion, as, e.g., the Common Defense.

These rights and powers still remain to the governmental establishment even at the widest democratic departure from that ancient pattern of masterful tutelage and usufruct that marked the old-fashioned patrimonial State,--and that still marks the better preserved ones among its modern derivatives. And so intrinsic to these governmental establishments are these discretionary powers, and by so unfailing a popular bias are they still accounted a matter of course and of axiomatic necessity, that they have invariably been retained also among the attributes of those democratic governments that trace their origin to a revolutionary break with the old order.

To many, all this will seem a pedantic taking note of commonplaces,--as if it were worth while remarking that the existing governments are vested with the indispensable attributes of government. Yet history records an instance at variance with this axiomatic rule, a rule which is held to be an unavoidable deliverance of common sense. And it is by no means an altogether unique instance. It may serve to show that these characteristic and unimpeachable powers that invest all current governmental establishments are, after all, to be rated as the marks of a particular species of governments, and not characteristics of the genus of governmental establishments at large. These powers answer to an acquired bias, not to an underlying trait of human nature; a matter of habit, not of heredity.

Such an historical instance is the so-called Republic, or Commonwealth, of Iceland--tenth to thirteenth centuries. Its case is looked on by students of history as a spectacular anomaly, because it admitted none of these primary powers of government in its constituted authorities. And yet, for contrast with these matter-of-course preconceptions of these students of history, it is well to note that in the deliberations of those ancients who installed the Republic for the management of their joint concerns, any inclusion of such powers in its competency appears never to have been contemplated, not even to the extent of its being rejected. This singularity--as it would be rated by modern statesmen and students--was in no degree a new departure in state-making on the part of the founders of the Republic. They had no knowledge of such powers, duties and accountabilities, except as unwholesome features of a novel and alien scheme of irresponsible oppression that was sought to be imposed on them by Harald Fairhair, and which they incontinently made it their chief and immediate business to evade. They also set up no joint or collective establishment with powers for the Common Defense, nor does it appear that such a notion had occurred to them.

In the history of its installation there is no hint that the men who set up this Icelandic Commonwealth had any sense of the need, or even of the feasibility, of such a coercive government as would be involved in concerted preparation for the common defense. Subjection to personal rule, or to official rule in any degree of attenuation, was not comprised in their traditional experience of citizenship; and it was necessarily out of the elements comprised in this traditional experience that the new structure would have to be built up. The new commonwealth was necessarily erected on the premises afforded by the received scheme of use and wont; and this received scheme had come down out of pre-feudal conditions, without having passed under the discipline of that regime of coercion which the feudal system had imposed on the rest of Europe, and so had established as an "immemorial usage" and a "second nature" among the populations of Christendom. The resulting character of the Icelandic Commonwealth is sufficiently striking when contrasted with the case of the English commonwealth of the seventeenth century, or the later French and American republics. These, all and several, came out of a protracted experience in feudalistic state-making and State policy; and the common defense--frequently on the offensive--with its necessary coercive machinery and its submissive loyalty, consequently would take the central place in the resulting civic structure.

To close the tale of the Icelandic commonwealth it may be added that their republic of insubordinate citizens presently fell into default, systematic misuse, under the disorders brought on by an accumulation of wealth, and that it died of legal fiction and constitutional formalities after some experience at the hands of able and ambitious statesmen in contact with an alien government drawn on the coercive plan. The clay vessel failed to make good among the iron pots, and so proved its unfitness to survive in the world of Christian nations,--very much as the Chinese are today at the mercy of the defensive rapacity of the Powers.

> And the mercy that we gave them   Was to sink them in the sea, Down   on the coast of High Barbarie.

No doubt, it will be accepted as an axiomatic certainty that the establishment of a commonwealth after the fashion of the Icelandic Republic, without coercive authority or provision for the common defense, and without a sense of subordination or collective responsibility among its citizens, would be out of all question under existing circumstances of politics and international trade. Nor would such a commonwealth be workable on the scale and at the pace imposed by modern industrial and commercial conditions, even apart from international jealousy and ambitions, provided the sacred rights of ownership were to be maintained in something like their current shape. And yet something of a drift of popular sentiment, and indeed something of deliberate endeavour, setting in the direction of such a harmless and helpless national organisation is always visible in Western Europe, throughout modern times; particularly through the eighteenth and the early half of the nineteenth centuries; and more particularly among the English-speaking peoples and, with a difference, among the French. The Dutch and the Scandinavian countries answer more doubtfully to the same characterisation.

The movement in question is known to history as the Liberal, Rationalistic, Humanitarian, or Individualistic departure. Its ideal, when formulated, is spoken of as the System of Natural Rights; and its goal in the way of a national establishment has been well characterised by its critics as the Police State, or the Night-Watchman State. The gains made in this direction, or perhaps better the inroads of this animus in national ideals, are plainly to be set down as a shift in the direction of peace and amity; but it is also plain that the shift of ground so initiated by this strain of sentiment has never reached a conclusion and never has taken effect in anything like an effectual working arrangement. Its practical consequences have been of the nature of abatement and defection in the pursuit of national ambitions and dynastic enterprise, rather than a creative work of installing any institutional furniture suitable to its own ends. It has in effect gone no farther than what would be called an incipient correction of abuses. The highest rise, as well as the decline, of this movement lie within the nineteenth century.

In point of time, the decay of this amiable conceit of *laissez-faire* in national policy coincides with the period of great advance in the technology of transport and communication in the nineteenth century. Perhaps, on a larger outlook, it should rather be said that the run of national ambitions and animosities had, in the eighteenth and nineteenth centuries, suffered a degree of decay through the diffusion of this sentimental predilection for Natural Liberty, and that this decline of the manlier aspirations was then arrested and corrected by help of these improvements in the technological situation; which enabled a closer and more coercive control to be exercised over larger areas, and at the same time enabled a more massive aggregate of warlike force to strike more effectively at a greater distance. This whole episode of the rise and decline of *laissez-faire* in modern history is perhaps best to be conceived as a transient weakening of nationalism, by neglect; rather than anything like the growth of a new and more humane ideal of national intercourse. Such would be the appraisal to be had at the hands of those who speak for a strenuous national life and for the arbitrament of sportsmanlike contention in human affairs. And the latterday growth of more militant aspirations, together with the more settled and sedulous attention to a development of control and of formidable armaments, such as followed on through the latter half of the nineteenth century, would then be rated as a resumption of those older aims and ideals that had been falling somewhat into abeyance in the slack water days of Liberalism.

There is much to be said for this latter view; and, indeed, much has been said for it, particularly by the spokesmen of imperialist politics. This bias of Natural Liberty has been associated in history with the English-speaking peoples, more intimately and more extensively than with any other. Not that this amiable conceit is in any peculiar degree a race characteristic of this group of peoples; nor even that the history of its rise and decline runs wholly within the linguistic frontiers indicated by this characterisation. The French and the Dutch have borne their share, and at an earlier day Italian sentiment and speculation lent its impulsion to the same genial drift of faith and aspiration. But, by historical accident, its center of gravity and of diffusion has lain with the English-speaking communities during the period when this bias made history and left its impress on the institutional scheme of the Western civilisation. By grace of what may, for the present purpose, be called historical accident, it happens that the interval of history during which the bias of Natural Liberty made visible headway was also a period during which these English-speaking peoples, among whom its effects are chiefly visible, were relatively secure from international disturbance, by force of inaccessibility. Little strain was put upon their sense of national solidarity or national prowess; so little, indeed, that there was some danger of their patriotic animosity falling into decay by disuse; and then they were also busy with other things. Peaceable intercourse, it is true, was relatively easy, active and far-reaching--eighteenth and nineteenth centuries--as compared with what had been the case before that time; but warlike intercourse on such a scale as would constitute a substantial menace to any large nation was nearly out of the question, so far as regards the English-speaking peoples. The available means of aggression, as touches the case of these particular communities, were visibly and consciously inadequate as compared with the means of defense. The means of internal or intra-national control or coercion were also less well provided by the state of the arts current at that time than the means of peaceable intercourse. These means of transport and communication were, at that stage of their development, less well suited for the purposes of far-reaching warlike strategy and the exercise of surveillance and coercion over large spaces than for the purposes of peaceable traffic.

But the continued improvement in the means of communication during the nineteenth century presently upset that situation, and so presently began to neutralise the geographical quarantine which had hedged about these communities that were inclined to let well enough alone. The increasing speed and accuracy of movement in shipping, due to the successful introduction of steam, as well as the concomitant increasing size of the units of equipment, all runs to this effect and presently sets at naught the peace barriers of sea and weather. So also the development of railways and their increasing availability for strategic uses, together with the far-reaching coordination of movement made possible by their means and by the telegraph; all of which is further facilitated by the increasing mass and density of population. Improvements in the technology of arms and armament worked to the like effect, of setting the peace of any community on an increasingly precarious footing, through the advantage which this new technology gave to a ready equipment and a rapid mobilisation. The new state of the industrial arts serviceable for warlike enterprise put an increasingly heavy premium on readiness for offense or defense, but more particularly it all worked increasingly to the advantage of the offensive. It put the Fabian strategy out of date, and led to the doctrine of a defensive offense.

Gradually it came true, with the continued advance in those industrial arts that lend themselves to strategic uses, and it came also to be realised, that no corner of the earth was any longer secure by mere favor of distance and natural difficulty, from eventual aggression at the hands of any provident and adventurous assailant,--even by help of a modicum of defensive precaution. The fear of aggression then came definitively to take the place of international good-will and became the chief motive in public policy, so fast and so far as the state of the industrial arts continued to incline the balance of advantage to the side of the aggressor. All of which served greatly to strengthen the hands of those statesmen who, by interest or temperament, were inclined to imperialistic enterprise. Since that period all armament has conventionally been accounted defensive, and all statesmen have professed that the common defense is their chief concern. Professedly all armament has been designed to keep the peace; so much of a shadow of the peaceable bias there still stands over.

Throughout this latest phase of modern civilisation the avowed fear of aggression has served as apology, possibly as provocation in fact, to national armaments; and throughout the same period any analysis of the situation will finally run the chain of fear back to Prussia as the putative or actual, center of disturbance and apprehension. No doubt, Prussian armament has taken the lead and forced the pace among the nations of Christendom; but the Prussian policy, too, has been diligently covered with the same decorous plea of needful provision for the common defense and an unremitting solicitude for international peace,--to which has been added the canny afterthought of the "defensive offense."

It is characteristic of this era of armed peace that in all these extensive preparations for breaking the peace any formal avowal of other than a defensive purpose has at all times been avoided as an insufferable breach of diplomatic decorum. It is likewise characteristic of the same era that armaments have unremittingly been increased, beyond anything previously known; and that all men have known all the while that the inevitable outcome of this avowedly defensive armament must eventually be war on an unprecedented scale and of unexampled ferocity. It would be neither charitable nor otherwise to the point to call attention to the reflection which this state of the case throws on the collective sagacity or the good faith of the statesmen who have had the management of affairs. It is not practicable to imagine how such an outcome as the present could have been brought about by any degree of stupidity or incapacity alone, nor is it easier to find evidence that the utmost sagacity of the statecraft engaged has had the slightest mitigating effect on the evil consummation to which the whole case has been brought. It has long been a commonplace among observers of public events that these professedly defensive warlike preparations have in effect been preparations for breaking the peace; against which, at least ostensibly, a remedy had been sought in the preparation of still heavier armaments, with full realisation that more armament would unfailingly entail a more unsparing and more disastrous war,--which sums up the statecraft of the past half century.

Prussia, and afterwards Prussianised Germany, has come in for the distinction of taking the lead and forcing the pace in this competitive preparation--or "preparedness"--for war in time of peace. That such has been the case appears in good part to be something of a fortuitous circumstance. The season of enterprising force and fraud to which that country owes its induction into the concert of nations is an episode of recent history; so recent, indeed, that the German nation has not yet had time to live it down and let it be forgotten; and the Imperial State is consequently burdened with an irritably uneasy sense of odium and an established reputation for unduly bad faith. From which it has followed, among other things, that the statesmen of the Empire have lived in the expectation of having their unforgotten derelictions brought home, and so have, on the one hand, found themselves unable to credit any pacific intentions professed by the neighboring Powers, while on the other hand they have been unable to gain credence for their own voluble professions of peace and amity. So it has come about that, by a fortuitous conjuncture of scarcely relevant circumstances, Prussia and the Empire have been thrown into the lead in the race of "preparedness" and have been led assiduously to hasten a breach which they could ill afford. It is, to say the least, extremely doubtful if the event would have been substantially different in the absence of that special provocation to competitive preparedness that has been injected into the situation by this German attitude; but the rate of approach to a warlike climax has doubtless been hastened by the anticipatory policy of preparedness which the Prussian dynasty has seen itself constrained to pursue. Eventually, the peculiar circumstances of its case--embarrassment at home and distaste and discredit abroad--have induced the Imperial State to take the line of a defensive offense, to take war by the forelock and retaliate on presumptive enemies for prospective grievances. But in any case, the progressive improvement in transport and communication, as well as in the special technology of warfare, backed by greatly enhanced facilities for indoctrinating the populace with militant nationalism,--these ways and means, working under the hand of patriotic statesmen must in course of the past century have brought the peace of Europe to so precarious a footing as would have provoked a material increase in the equipment for national defense; which would unavoidably have led to competitive armament and an enhanced international distrust and animosity, eventually culminating in hostilities.

* * * * *

It may well be that the plea of defensive preparation advanced by the statesmen, Prussian and others, in apology for competitive armaments is a diplomatic subterfuge,--there are indications that such has commonly been the case; but even if it commonly is visibly disingenuous, the need of making such a plea to cover more sinister designs is itself an evidence that an avowedly predatory enterprise no longer meets with the requisite popular approval. Even if an exception to this rule be admitted in the recent attitude of the German people, it is to be recalled that the exception was allowed to stand only transiently, and that presently the avowal of a predatory design in this case was urgently disclaimed in the face of adversity. Even those who speak most fluently for the necessity of war, and for its merits as a needed discipline in the manly virtues, are constrained by the prevailing sentiment to deprecate its necessity.

Yet it is equally evident that when once a warlike enterprise has been entered upon so far as to commit the nation to hostilities, it will have the cordial support of popular sentiment even if it is patently an aggressive war. Indeed, it is quite a safe generalisation that when hostilities have once been got fairly under way by the interested statesmen, the patriotic sentiment of the nation may confidently be counted on to back the enterprise irrespective of the merits of the quarrel. But even if the national sentiment is in this way to be counted in as an incidental matter of course, it is also to be kept in mind in this connection that any quarrel so entered upon by any nation will forthwith come to have the moral approval of the community. Dissenters will of course be found, sporadically, who do not readily fall in with the prevailing animus; but as a general proposition it will still hold true that any such quarrel forthwith becomes a just quarrel in the eyes of those who have so been committed to it.

A corollary following from this general theorem may be worth noting in the same connection. Any politician who succeeds in embroiling his country in a war, however nefarious, becomes a popular hero and is reputed a wise and righteous statesman, at least for the time being. Illustrative instances need perhaps not, and indeed can not gracefully, be named; most popular heroes and reputed statesmen belong in this class.

Another corollary, which bears more immediately on the question in hand, follows also from the same general proposition: Since the ethical values involved in any given international contest are substantially of the nature of afterthought or accessory, they may safely be left on one side in any endeavour to understand or account for any given outbreak of hostilities. The moral indignation of both parties to the quarrel is to be taken for granted, as being the statesman's chief and necessary ways and means of bringing any warlike enterprise to a head and floating it to a creditable finish. It is a precipitate of the partisan animosity that inspires both parties and holds them to their duty of self-sacrifice and devastation, and at its best it will chiefly serve as a cloak of self-righteousness to extenuate any exceptionally profligate excursions in the conduct of hostilities.

Any warlike enterprise that is hopefully to be entered on must have the moral sanction of the community, or of an effective majority in the community. It consequently becomes the first concern of the warlike statesman to put this moral force in train for the adventure on which he is bent. And there are two main lines of motivation by which the spiritual forces of any Christian nation may so be mobilised for warlike adventure: (1) The preservation or furtherance of the community's material interests, real or fancied, and (2) vindication of the national honour. To these should perhaps be added as a third, the advancement and perpetuation of the nation's "Culture;" that is to say, of its habitual scheme of use and wont. It is a nice question whether, in practical effect, the aspiration to perpetuate the national Culture is consistently to be distinguished from the vindication of the national honour. There is perhaps the distinction to be made that "the perpetuation of the national Culture" lends a readier countenance to gratuitous aggression and affords a broader cover for incidental atrocities, since the enemies of the national Culture will necessarily be conceived as an inferior and obstructive people, falling beneath the rules of commonplace decorum.

Those material interests for which modern nations are in the habit of taking to arms are commonly of a fanciful character, in that they commonly have none but an imaginary net value to the community at large. Such are, e.g., the national trade or the increase of the national territory. These and the like may serve the warlike or dynastic ambitions of the nation's masters; they may also further the interests of office-holders, and more particularly of certain business houses or businessmen who stand to gain some small advantage by help of the powers in control; but it all signifies nothing more to the common man than an increased bill of governmental expense and a probable increase in the cost of living.

That a nation's trade should be carried in vessels owned by its citizens or registered in its ports will doubtless have some sentimental value to the common run of its citizens, as is shown by the fact that disingenuous politicians always find it worth their while to appeal to this chauvinistic predilection. But it patently is all a completely idle question, in point of material advantage, to anyone but the owners of the vessels; and to these owners it is also of no material consequence under what flag their investments sail, except so far as the government in question may afford them some preferential opportunity for gain,--always at the cost of their fellow citizens. The like is equally true as regards the domicile and the national allegiance of the businessmen who buy and sell the country's imports and exports. The common man plainly has no slightest material interest in the nationality or the place of residence of those who conduct this traffic; though all the facts go to say that in some puzzle-headed way the common man commonly persuades himself that it does make some occult sort of difference to him; so that he is commonly willing to pay something substantial toward subsidising businessmen of his own nationality, in the way of a protective tariff and the like.

The only material advantage to be derived from such a preferential trade policy arises in the case of international hostilities, in which case the home-owned vessels and merchants may on occasion count toward military readiness; although even in that connection their value is contingent and doubtful. But in this way they may contribute in their degree to a readiness to break off peaceable relations with other countries. It is only for warlike purposes, that is to say for the dynastic ambitions of warlike statesmen, that these preferential contrivances in economic policy have any substantial value; and even in that connection their expediency is always doubtful. They are a source of national jealousy, and they may on occasion become a help to military strategy when this national jealousy eventuates in hostilities.

The run of the facts touching this matter of national trade policy is something as follows: At the instance of businessmen who stand to gain by it, and with the cordial support of popular sentiment, the constituted authorities sedulously further the increase of shipping and commerce under protection of the national power. At the same time they spend substance and diplomatic energy in an endeavor to extend the international market facilities open to the country's businessmen, with a view always to a preferential advantage in favor of these businessmen, also with the sentimental support of the common man and at his cost. To safeguard these commercial interests, as well as property-holdings of the nation's citizens in foreign parts, the nation maintains naval, military, consular and diplomatic establishments, at the common expense. The total gains derivable from these commercial and investment interests abroad, under favorable circumstances, will never by any chance equal the cost of the governmental apparatus installed to further and safeguard them. These gains, such as they are, go to the investors and businessmen engaged in these enterprises; while the costs incident to the adventure are borne almost wholly by the common man, who gets no gain from it all. Commonly, as in the case of a protective tariff or a preferential navigation law, the cost to the common man is altogether out of proportion to the gain which accrues to the businessmen for whose benefit he carries the burden. The only other class, besides the preferentially favored businessmen, who derive any material benefit from this arrangement is that of the officeholders who take care of this governmental traffic and draw something in the way of salaries and perquisites; and whose cost is defrayed by the common man, who remains an outsider in all but the payment of the bills. The common man is proud and glad to bear this burden for the benefit of his wealthier neighbors, and he does so with the singular conviction that in some occult manner he profits by it. All this is incredible, but it is everyday fact.

In case it should happen that these business interests of the nation's businessmen interested in trade or investments abroad are jeopardised by a disturbance of any kind in these foreign parts in which these business interests lie, then it immediately becomes the urgent concern of the national authorities to use all means at hand for maintaining the gainful traffic of these businessmen undiminished, and the common man pays the cost. Should such an untoward situation go to such sinister lengths as to involve actual loss to these business interests or otherwise give rise to a tangible grievance, it becomes an affair of the national honour; whereupon no sense of proportion as between the material gains at stake and the cost of remedy or retaliation need longer be observed, since the national honour is beyond price. The motivation in the case shifts from the ground of material interest to the spiritual ground of the moral sentiments.

In this connection "honour" is of course to be taken in the euphemistic sense which the term has under the ***code duello*** governing "affairs of honour." It carries no connotation of honesty, veracity, equity, liberality, or unselfishness. This national honour is of the nature of an intangible or immaterial asset, of course; it is a matter of prestige, a sportsmanlike conception; but that fact must not be taken to mean that it is of any the less substantial effect for purposes of a ***casus belli*** than the material assets of the community. Quite the contrary: "Who steals my purse, steals trash," etc. In point of fact, it will commonly happen that any material grievance must first be converted into terms of this spiritual capital, before it is effectually turned to account as a stimulus to warlike enterprise.

Even among a people with so single an eye to the main chance as the American community it will be found true, on experiment or on review of the historical evidence, that an offense against the national honour commands a profounder and more unreserved resentment than any infraction of the rights of person or property simply. This has latterly been well shown in connection with the manoeuvres of the several European belligerents, designed to bend American neutrality to the service of one side or the other. Both parties have aimed to intimidate and cajole; but while the one party has taken recourse to effrontery and has made much and ostentatious use of threats and acts of violence against person and property, the other has constantly observed a deferential attitude toward American national self-esteem, even while engaged on a persistent infraction of American commercial rights. The first named line of diplomacy has convicted itself of miscarriage and has lost the strategic advantage, as against the none too adroit finesse of the other side. The statesmen of this European war power were so ill advised as to enter on a course of tentatively cumulative intimidation, by threats and experimentally graduated crimes against the property and persons of American citizens, with a view to coerce American cupidity and yet to avoid carrying these manoeuvres of terrorism far enough to arouse an unmanageable sense of outrage. The experiment has served to show that the breaking point in popular indignation will be reached before the terrorism has gone far enough to raise a serious question of pecuniary caution.

This national honour, which so is rated a necessary of life, is an immaterial substance in a peculiarly high-wrought degree, being not only not physically tangible but also not even capable of adequate statement in pecuniary terms,--as would be the case with ordinary immaterial assets. It is true, where the point of grievance out of which a question of the national honour arises is a pecuniary discrepancy, the national honour can not be satisfied without a pecuniary accounting; but it needs no argument to convince all right-minded persons that even at such a juncture the national honour that has been compromised is indefinitely and indefinably more than what can be made to appear on an accountant's page. It is a highly valued asset, or at least a valued possession, but it is of a metaphysical, not of a physical nature, and it is not known to serve any material or otherwise useful end apart from affording a practicable grievance consequent upon its infraction.

This national honour is subject to injury in divers ways, and so may yield a fruitful grievance even apart from offences against the person or property of the nation's businessmen; as, e.g., through neglect or disregard of the conventional punctilios governing diplomatic intercourse, or by disrespect or contumelious speech touching the Flag, or the persons of national officials, particularly of such officials as have only a decorative use, or the costumes worn by such officials, or, again, by failure to observe the ritual prescribed for parading the national honour on stated occasions. When duly violated the national honour may duly be made whole again by similarly immaterial instrumentalities; as, e.g., by recital of an appropriate formula of words, by formal consumption of a stated quantity of ammunition in the way of a salute, by "dipping" an ensign, and the like,--procedure which can, of course, have none but a magical efficacy. The national honour, in short, moves in the realm of magic, and touches the frontiers of religion.

Throughout this range of duties incumbent on the national defense, it will be noted, the offenses or discrepancies to be guarded against or corrected by recourse to arms have much of a ceremonial character. Whatever may be the material accidents that surround any given concrete grievance that comes up for appraisal and redress, in bringing the case into the arena for trial by combat it is the spiritual value of the offense that is played up and made the decisive ground of action, particularly in so far as appeal is made to the sensibilities of the common man, who will have to bear the cost of the adventure. And in such a case it will commonly happen that the common man is unable, without advice, to see that any given hostile act embodies a sacrilegious infraction of the national honour. He will at any such conjuncture scarcely rise to the pitch of moral indignation necessary to float a warlike reprisal, until the expert keepers of the Code come in to expound and certify the nature of the transgression. But when once the lesion to the national honour has been ascertained, appraised and duly exhibited by those persons whose place in the national economy it is to look after all that sort of thing, the common man will be found nowise behindhand about resenting the evil usage of which he so, by force of interpretation, has been a victim.

CHAPTER II
ON THE NATURE AND USES OF PATRIOTISM

Patriotism may be defined as a sense of partisan solidarity in respect of prestige. What the expert psychologists, and perhaps the experts in Political Science, might find it necessary to say in the course of an exhaustive analysis and definition of this human faculty would presumably be something more precise and more extensive. There is no inclination here to forestall definition, but only to identify and describe the concept that loosely underlies the colloquial use of this term, so far as seems necessary to an inquiry into the part played by the patriotic animus in the life of modern peoples, particularly as it bears on questions of war and peace.

On any attempt to divest this concept of all extraneous or adventitious elements it will be found that such a sense of an undivided joint interest in a collective body of prestige will always remain as an irreducible minimum. This is the substantial core about which many and divers subsidiary interests cluster, but without which these other clustering interests and aspirations will not, jointly or severally, make up a working palladium of the patriotic spirit.

It is true, seen in some other light or rated in some other bearing or connection, one and another of these other interests, ideals, aspirations, beatitudes, may well be adjudged nobler, wiser, possibly more urgent than the national prestige; but in the forum of patriotism all these other necessaries of human life--the glory of God and the good of man--rise by comparison only to the rank of subsidiaries, auxiliaries, amenities. He is an indifferent patriot who will let "life, liberty and the pursuit of happiness" cloud the issue and get in the way of the main business in hand.

There once were, we are told, many hardy and enterprising spirits banded together along the Spanish Main for such like ends, just as there are in our day an even greater number of no less single-minded spirits bent on their own "life, liberty and pursuit of happiness," according to their light, in the money-markets of the modern world; but for all their admirable qualities and splendid achievements, their passionate quest of these amenities has not entitled these Gentlemen Adventurers to claim rank as patriots. The poet says:

"Strike for your altars and your fires!
Strike for the green graves of your sires!
God and your native land!"

But, again, a temperate scrutiny of the list of desiderata so enumerated in the poet's flight, will quickly bring out the fact that any or all of them might drop out of the situation without prejudice to the plain call of patriotic duty. In the last resort, when the patriotic spirit falls back on its naked self alone, it is not reflection on the merits of these good and beautiful things in Nature that gives him his cue and enforces the ultimate sacrifice. Indeed it is something infinitely more futile and infinitely more urgent,--provided only that the man is imbued with the due modicum of patriotic devotion; as, indeed, men commonly are. It is not faith, hope or charity that abide as the irreducible minimum of virtue in the patriot's scheme of things; particularly not that charity that has once been highly spoken of as being the greatest of these. It may be that, viewed in the light of reason, as Doctor Katzenberger would say, patriotic devotion is the most futile thing in the world; but, for good or ill, the light of reason has nothing to do with the case,--no more than "The flowers that bloom in the spring."

The patriotic spirit is a spirit of emulation, evidently, at the same time that it is emulation shot through with a sense of solidarity. It belongs under the general caption of sportsmanship, rather than of workmanship. Now, any enterprise in sportsmanship is bent on an invidious success, which must involve as its major purpose the defeat and humiliation of some competitor, whatever else may be comprised in its aim. Its aim is a differential gain, as against a rival; and the emulative spirit that comes under the head of patriotism commonly, if not invariably, seeks this differential advantage by injury of the rival rather than by an increase of home-bred well-being.

Indeed, well-being is altogether out of the perspective, except as underpinning for an edifice of national prestige. It is, at least, a safe generalisation that the patriotic sentiment never has been known to rise to the consummate pitch of enthusiastic abandon except when bent on some work of concerted malevolence. Patriotism is of a contentious complexion, and finds its full expression in no other outlet than warlike enterprise; its highest and final appeal is for the death, damage, discomfort and destruction of the party of the second part.

It is not that the spirit of patriotism will tolerate no other sentiments bearing on matters of public interest, but only that it will tolerate none that traverse the call of the national prestige. Like other men, the patriot may be moved by many and divers other considerations, besides that of the national prestige; and these other considerations may be of the most genial and reasonable kind, or they may also be as foolish and mischievous as any comprised in the range of human infirmities. He may be a humanitarian given over to the kindliest solicitude for the common good, or a religious devotee hedged about in all his motions by the ever present fear of God, or taken up with artistic, scholarly or scientific pursuits; or, again, he may be a spendthrift devotee of profane dissipation, whether in the slums or on the higher levels of gentility, or he may be engaged on a rapacious quest of gain, as a businessman within the law or as a criminal without its benefit, or he may spend his best endeavors in advancing the interests of his class at the cost of the nation at large. All that is understood as a matter of course and is beside the point. In so far as he is a complete patriot these other interests will fall away from him when the one clear call of patriotic duty comes to enlist him in the cause of the national prestige. There is, indeed, nothing to hinder a bad citizen being a good patriot; nor does it follow that a good citizen--in other respects--may not be a very indifferent patriot.

Many and various other preferences and considerations may coincide with the promptings of the patriotic spirit, and so may come in to coalesce with and fortify its driving force; and it is usual for patriotic men to seek support for their patriotic impulses in some reasoned purpose of this extraneous kind that is believed to be served by following the call of the national prestige,--it may be a presumptive increase and diffusion of culture at large, or the spread and enhancement of a presumptively estimable religious faith, or a prospective liberation of mankind from servitude to obnoxious masters and outworn institutions; or, again, it may be the increase of peace and material well-being among men, within the national frontiers or impartially throughout the civilised world. There are, substantially, none of the desirable things in this world that are not so counted on by some considerable body of patriots to be accomplished by the success of their own particular patriotic aspirations. What they will not come to an understanding about is the particular national ascendency with which the attainment of these admirable ends is conceived to be bound up.

The ideals, needs and aims that so are brought into the patriotic argument to lend a color of rationality to the patriotic aspiration in any given case will of course be such ideals, needs and aims as are currently accepted and felt to be authentic and self-legitimating among the people in whose eyes the given patriotic enterprise is to find favor. So one finds that, e.g., among the followers of Islam, devout and resolute, the patriotic statesman (that is to say the politician who designs to make use of the popular patriotic fervor) will in the last resort appeal to the claims and injunctions of the faith. In a similar way the Prussian statesman bent on dynastic enterprise will conjure in the name of the dynasty and of culture and efficiency; or, if worse comes to worst, an outbreak will be decently covered with a plea of mortal peril and self-defense. Among English-speaking peoples much is to be gained by showing that the path of patriotic glory is at the same time the way of equal-handed justice under the rule of free institutions; at the same time, in a fully commercialised community, such as the English-speaking commonly are, material benefits in the way of trade will go far to sketch in a background of decency for any enterprise that looks to the enhancement of the national prestige.

But any promise of gain, whether in the nation's material or immaterial assets, will not of itself carry full conviction to the commonplace modern citizen; or even to such modern citizens as are best endowed with a national spirit. By and large, and overlooking that appreciable contingent of morally defective citizens that is to be counted on in any hybrid population, it will hold true that no contemplated enterprise or line of policy will fully commend itself to the popular sense of merit and expediency until it is given a moral turn, so as to bring it to square with the dictates of right and honest dealing. On no terms short of this will it effectually coalesce with the patriotic aspiration. To give the fullest practical effect to the patriotic fervor that animates any modern nation, and so turn it to use in the most effective way, it is necessary to show that the demands of equity are involved in the case. Any cursory survey of modern historical events bearing on this point, among the civilised peoples, will bring out the fact that no concerted and sustained movement of the national spirit can be had without enlisting the community's moral convictions. The common man must be persuaded that right is on his side. "Thrice is he armed who knows his quarrel just." The grounds of this conviction may often be tawdry enough, but the conviction is a necessary factor in the case.

The requisite moral sanction may be had on various grounds, and, on the whole, it is not an extremely difficult matter to arrange. In the simplest and not infrequent case it may turn on a question of equity in respect of trade or investment as between the citizens or subjects of the several rival nations; the Chinese "Open Door" affords as sordid an example as may be desired. Or it may be only an envious demand for a share in the world's material resources--"A Place in the Sun," as a picturesque phrase describes it; or "The Freedom of the Seas," as another equally vague and equally invidious demand for international equity phrases it. These demands are put forward with a color of demanding something in the way of equitable opportunity for the commonplace peaceable citizen; but quite plainly they have none but a fanciful bearing on the fortunes of the common man in time of peace, and they have a meaning to the nation only as a fighting unit; apart from their prestige value, these things are worth fighting for only as prospective means of fighting. The like appeal to the moral sensibilities may, again, be made in the way of a call to self-defense, under the rule of Live and let live; or it may also rest on the more tenuous obligation to safeguard the national integrity of a weaker neighbor, under a broader interpretation of the same equitable rule of Live and let live. But in one way or another it is necessary to set up the conviction that the promptings of patriotic ambition have the sanction of moral necessity.

It is not that the line of national policy or patriotic enterprise so entered upon with the support of popular sentiment need be right and equitable as seen in dispassionate perspective from the outside, but only that it should be capable of being made to seem right and equitable to the biased populace whose moral convictions are requisite to its prosecution; which is quite another matter. Nor is it that any such patriotic enterprise is, in fact, entered on simply or mainly on these moral grounds that so are alleged in its justification, but only that some such colorable ground of justification or extenuation is necessary to be alleged, and to be credited by popular belief.

It is not that the common man is not sufficiently patriotic, but only that he is a patriot hampered with a plodding and uneasy sense of right and honest dealing, and that one must make up one's account with this moral bias in looking to any sustained and concerted action that draws on the sentiment of the common man for its carrying on. But the moral sense in the case may be somewhat easily satisfied with a modicum of equity, in case the patriotic bias of the people is well pronounced, or in case it is reenforced with a sufficient appeal to self-interest. In those cases where the national fervor rises to an excited pitch, even very attenuated considerations of right and justice, such as would under ordinary conditions doubtfully bear scrutiny as extenuating circumstances, may come to serve as moral authentication for any extravagant course of action to which the craving for national prestige may incite. The higher the pitch of patriotic fervor, the more tenuous and more thread-bare may be the requisite moral sanction. By cumulative excitation some very remarkable results have latterly been attained along this line.

*   *   *   *   *

Patriotism is evidently a spirit of particularism, of aliency and animosity between contrasted groups of persons; it lives on invidious comparison, and works out in mutual hindrance and jealousy between nations. It commonly goes the length of hindering intercourse and obstructing traffic that would patently serve the material and cultural well-being of both nationalities; and not infrequently, indeed normally, it eventuates in competitive damage to both.

All this holds true in the world of modern civilisation, at the same time that the modern civilised scheme of life is, notoriously, of a cosmopolitan character, both in its cultural requirements and in its economic structure. Modern culture is drawn on too large a scale, is of too complex and multiform a character, requires the cooperation of too many and various lines of inquiry, experience and insight, to admit of its being confined within national frontiers, except at the cost of insufferable crippling and retardation. The science and scholarship that is the peculiar pride of civilised Christendom is not only international, but rather it is homogeneously cosmopolitan; so that in this bearing there are, in effect, no national frontiers; with the exception, of course, that in a season of patriotic intoxication, such as the current war has induced, even the scholars and scientists will be temporarily overset by their patriotic fervour. Indeed, with the best efforts of obscurantism and national jealousy to the contrary, it remains patently true that modern culture is the culture of Christendom at large, not the culture of one and another nation in severalty within the confines of Christendom. It is only as and in so far as they partake in and contribute to the general run of Western civilisation at large that the people of any one of these nations of Christendom can claim standing as a cultured nation; and even any distinctive variation from this general run of civilised life, such as may give a "local colour" of ideals, tastes and conventions, will, in point of cultural value, have to be rated as an idle detail, a species of lost motion, that serves no better purpose than a transient estrangement.

So also, the modern state of the industrial arts is of a like cosmopolitan character, in point of scale, specialisation, and the necessary use of diversified resources, of climate and raw materials. None of the countries of Europe, e.g., is competent to carry on its industry by modern technological methods without constantly drawing on resources outside of its national boundaries. Isolation in this industrial respect, exclusion from the world market, would mean intolerable loss of efficiency, more pronounced the more fully the given country has taken over this modern state of the industrial arts. Exclusion from the general body of outlying resources would seriously cripple any one or all of them, and effectually deprive them of the usufruct of this technology; and partial exclusion, by prohibitive or protective tariffs and the like, unavoidably results in a partial lowering of the efficiency of each, and therefore a reduction of the current well-being among them all together.

Into this cultural and technological system of the modern world the patriotic spirit fits like dust in the eyes and sand in the bearings. Its net contribution to the outcome is obscuration, distrust, and retardation at every point where it touches the fortunes of modern mankind. Yet it is forever present in the counsels of the statesmen and in the affections of the common man, and it never ceases to command the regard of all men as the prime attribute of manhood and the final test of the desirable citizen. It is scarcely an exaggeration to say that no other consideration is allowed in abatement of the claims of patriotic loyalty, and that such loyalty will be allowed to cover any multitude of sins. When the ancient philosopher described Man as a "political animal," this, in effect, was what he affirmed; and today the ancient maxim is as good as new. The patriotic spirit is at cross purposes with modern life, but in any test case it is found that the claims of life yield before those of patriotism; and any voice that dissents from this order of things is as a voice crying in the wilderness.

* * * * *

To anyone who is inclined to moralise on the singular discrepancies of human life this state of the case will be fruitful of much profound speculation. The patriotic animus appears to be an enduring trait of human nature, an ancient heritage that has stood over unshorn from time immemorial, under the Mendelian rule of the stability of racial types. It is archaic, not amenable to elimination or enduring suppression, and apparently not appreciably to be mitigated by reflection, education, experience or selective breeding.

Throughout the historical period, and presumably through an incalculable period of the unrecorded past, patriotic manslaughter has consistently been weeding out of each successive generation of men the most patriotic among them; with the net result that the level of patriotic ardor today appears to be no lower than it ever was. At the same time, with the advance of population, of culture and of the industrial arts, patriotism has grown increasingly disserviceable; and it is to all appearance as ubiquitous and as powerful as ever, and is held in as high esteem.

The continued prevalence of this archaic animus among the modern peoples, as well as the fact that it is universally placed high among the virtues, must be taken to argue that it is, in its elements, an hereditary trait, of the nature of an inborn impulsive propensity, rather than a product of habituation. It is, in substance, not something that can be learned and unlearned. From one generation to another, the allegiance may shift from one nationality to another, but the fact of unreflecting allegiance at large remains. And it all argues also that no sensible change has taken effect in the hereditary endowment of the race, at least in this respect, during the period known by record or by secure inference,--say, since the early Neolithic in Europe; and this in spite of the fact that there has all this while been opportunity for radical changes in the European population by cross-breeding, infiltration and displacement of the several racial stocks that go to make up this population. Hence, on slight reflection the inference has suggested itself and has gained acceptance that this trait of human nature must presumably have been serviceable to the peoples of the earlier time, on those levels of savagery or of the lower barbarism on which the ancestral stocks of the European population first made good their survival and proved their fitness to people that quarter of the earth. Such, indeed, is the common view; so common as to pass for matter-of-course, and therefore habitually to escape scrutiny.

Still it need not follow, as more patient reflection will show. All the European peoples show much the same animus in this respect; whatever their past history may have been, and whatever the difference in past experience that might be conceived to have shaped their temperament. Any difference in the pitch of patriotic conceit and animosity, between the several nationalities or the several localities, is by no means wide, even in cases where the racial composition of the population is held to be very different, as, e.g., between the peoples on the Baltic seaboard and those on the Mediterranean. In point of fact, in this matter of patriotic animus there appears to be a wider divergence, temperamentally, between individuals within any one of these communities than between the common run in any one community and the corresponding common run in any other. But even such divergence of individual temper in respect of patriotism as is to be met with, first and last, is after all surprisingly small in view of the scope for individual variation which this European population would seem to offer.

* * * * *

These peoples of Europe, all and several, are hybrids compounded out of the same run of racial elements, but mixed in varying proportions. On any parallel of latitude--taken in the climatic rather than in the geometric sense--the racial composition of the west-European population will be much the same, virtually identical in effect, although always of a hybrid complexion; whereas on any parallel of longitude--also in the climatic sense--the racial composition will vary progressively, but always within the limits of the same general scheme of hybridisation,--the variation being a variation in the proportion in which the several racial elements are present in any given case. But in no case does a notable difference in racial composition coincide with a linguistic or national frontier. But in point of patriotic animus these European peoples are one as good as another, whether the comparison be traced on parallels of latitude or of longitude. And the inhabitants of each national territory, or of each detail locality, appear also to run surprisingly uniform in respect of their patriotic spirit.

Heredity in any such community of hybrids will, superficially, appear to run somewhat haphazard. There will, of course, be no traceable difference between social or economic classes, in point of heredity,--as is visibly the case in Christendom. But variation--of an apparently haphazard description--will be large and ubiquitous among the individuals of such a populace. Indeed, it is a matter of course and of easy verification that individual variation within such a hybrid stock will greatly exceed the extreme differences that may subsist between the several racial types that have gone to produce the hybrid stock. Such is the case of the European peoples. The inhabitants vary greatly among themselves, both in physical and in mental traits, as would be expected; and the variation between individuals in point of patriotic animus should accordingly also be expected to be extremely wide,--should, in effect, greatly exceed the difference, if any, in this respect between the several racial elements engaged in the European population. Some appreciable difference in this respect there appears to be, between individuals; but individual divergence from the normal or average appears always to be of a sporadic sort,--it does not run on class lines, whether of occupation, status or property, nor does it run at all consistently from parent to child. When all is told the argument returns to the safe ground that these variations in point of patriotic animus are sporadic and inconsequential, and do not touch the general proposition that, one with another, the inhabitants of Europe and the European Colonies are sufficiently patriotic, and that the average endowment in this respect runs with consistent uniformity across all differences of time, place and circumstance. It would, in fact, be extremely hazardous to affirm that there is a sensible difference in the ordinary pitch of patriotic sentiment as between any two widely diverse samples of these hybrid populations, in spite of the fact that the diversity in visible physical traits may be quite pronounced.

In short, the conclusion seems safe, on the whole, that in this respect the several racial stocks that have gone to produce the existing populations of Christendom have all been endowed about as richly one as another. Patriotism appears to be a ubiquitous trait, at least among the races and peoples of Christendom. From which it should follow, that since there is, and has from the beginning been, no differential advantage favoring one racial stock or one fashion of hybrid as against another, in this matter of patriotic animus, there should also be no ground of selective survival or selective elimination on this account as between these several races and peoples. So that the undisturbed and undiminished prevalence of this trait among the European population, early or late, argues nothing as to its net serviceability or disserviceability under any of the varying conditions of culture and technology to which these Europeans have been subjected, first and last; except that it has, in any case, not proved so disserviceable under the conditions prevailing hitherto as to result in the extinction of these Europeans, one with another.[4]

The patriotic frame of mind has been spoken of above as if it were an hereditary trait, something after the fashion of a Mendelian unit character. Doubtless this is not a competent account of the matter; but the present argument scarcely needs a closer analysis. Still, in a measure to quiet title and avoid annoyance, it may be noted that this patriotic animus is of the nature of a "frame of mind" rather than a Mendelian unit character; that it so involves a concatenation of several impulsive propensities (presumably hereditary); and that both the concatenation and the special mode and amplitude of the response are a product of habituation, very largely of the nature of conventionalised use and wont. What is said above, therefore, goes little farther than saying that the underlying aptitudes requisite to this patriotic frame of mind are heritable, and that use and wont as bearing on this point run with sufficient uniformity to bring a passably uniform result. It may be added that in this concatenation spoken of there seems to be comprised, ordinarily, that sentimental attachment to habitat and custom that is called love of home, or in its accentuated expression, home-sickness; so also an invidious self-complacency, coupled with a gregarious bent which gives the invidious comparison a group content; and further, commonly if not invariably, a bent of abnegation, self-abasement, subservience, or whatever it may best be called, that inclines the bearer unreasoningly and unquestioningly to accept and serve a prescriptive ideal given by custom or by customary

---

4 For a more extended discussion of this matter, cf. ***Imperial Germany and the Industrial Revolution***, ch. i. and Supplementary Notes i. and ii.

authority.

*   *   *   *   *

The conclusion would therefore provisionally run to the effect that under modern conditions the patriotic animus is wholly a disserviceable trait in the spiritual endowment of these peoples,--in so far as bears on the material conditions of life unequivocally, and as regards the cultural interests more at large presumptively; whereas there is no assured ground for a discriminating opinion as touches its possible utility or disutility at any remote period in the past. There is, of course, always room for the conservative estimate that, as the possession of this spiritual trait has not hitherto resulted in the extinction of the race, so it may also in the calculable future continue to bring no more grievous results than a degree of mischief, without even stopping or greatly retarding the increase of population.

All this, of course, is intended to apply only so far as it goes. It must not be taken as intending to say any least word in derogation of those high qualities that inspire the patriotic citizen. In its economic, biological and cultural incidence patriotism appears to be an untoward trait of human nature; which has, of course, nothing to say as to its moral excellence, its aesthetic value, or its indispensability to a worthy life. No doubt, it is in all these respects deserving of all the esteem and encomiums that fall to its share. Indeed, its well-known moral and aesthetic value, as well as the reprobation that is visited on any shortcomings in this respect, signify, for the purposes of the present argument, nothing more than that the patriotic animus meets the unqualified approval of men because they are, all and several, infected with it. It is evidence of the ubiquitous, intimate and ineradicable presence of this quality in human nature; all the more since it continues untiringly to be held in the highest esteem in spite of the fact that a modicum of reflection should make its disserviceability plain to the meanest understanding. No higher praise of moral excellence, and no profounder test of loyalty, can be asked than this current unreserved commendation of a virtue that makes invariably for damage and discomfort. The virtuous impulse must be deep-seated and indefeasible that drives men incontinently to do good that evil may come of it. "Though He slay me, yet will I trust in Him."

In the light--and it is a dim and wavering light--of the archaeological evidence, helped out by circumstantial evidence from such parallel or analogous instances as are afforded by existing communities on a comparable level of culture, one may venture more or less confidently on a reconstruction of the manner of life among the early Europeans, of early neolithic times and later.[5] And so one may form some conception of the part played by this patriotic animus among those beginnings, when, if not the race, at least its institutions were young; and when the native temperament of these peoples was tried out and found fit to survive through the age-long and slow-moving eras of stone and bronze. In this connection, it appears safe to assume that since early neolithic times no sensible change has taken effect in the racial complexion of the European peoples; and therefore no sensible change in their spiritual and mental make-up. So that in respect of the spiritual elements that go to make up this patriotic animus the Europeans of today will be substantially identical with the Europeans of that early time. The like is true as regards those other traits of temperament that come in question here, as being included among the stable characteristics that still condition the life of these peoples under the altered circumstances of the modern age.

The difference between prehistoric Europe and the present state of these peoples resolves itself on analysis into a difference in the state of the industrial arts, together with such institutional changes as have come on in the course of working out this advance in the industrial arts. The habits and the exigencies of life among these peoples have greatly changed; whereas in temperament and capacities the peoples that now live by and under the rule of this altered state of the industrial arts are the same as they were. It is to be noted, therefore, that the fact of their having successfully come through the long ages of prehistory by the use of this mental and spiritual endowment can not be taken to argue that these peoples are thereby fit to meet the exigencies of this later and gravely altered age; nor will it do to assume that because these peoples have themselves worked out this modern culture and its technology, therefore it must all be suitable for their use and conducive to their biological success. The single object lesson of the modern urban community, with its endless requirements in the way of sanitation, police, compulsory education, charities,--all this and many other discrepancies in modern life should enjoin caution on anyone who is inclined off-hand to hold that because modern men have

---

5   Cf. *Imperial Germany and the Industrial Revolution*, as above.

created these conditions, therefore these must be the most suitable conditions of life for modern mankind.

In the beginning, that is to say in the European beginning, men lived in small and close groups. Control was close within the group, and the necessity of subordinating individual gains and preferences to the common good was enjoined on the group by the exigencies of the case, on pain of common extinction. The situation and usages of existing Eskimo villages may serve to illustrate and enforce the argument on this head. The solidarity of sentiment necessary to support the requisite solidarity of action in the case would be a prime condition of survival in any racial stock exposed to the conditions which surrounded these early Europeans. This needful sense of solidarity would touch not simply or most imperatively the joint prestige of the group, but rather the joint material interests; and would enforce a spirit of mutual support and dependence. Which would be rather helped than hindered by a jealous attitude of joint prestige; so long as no divergent interests of members within the group were in a position to turn this state of the common sentiment to their own particular advantage.

This state of the case will have lasted for a relatively long time; long enough to have tested the fitness of these peoples for that manner of life,--longer, no doubt, than the interval that has elapsed since history began. Special interests--e.g., personal and family interests--will have been present and active in these days of the beginning; but so long as the group at large was small enough to admit of a close neighborly contact throughout its extent and throughout the workday routine of life, at the same time that it was too small and feeble to allow any appreciable dissipation of its joint energies in such pursuit of selfish gains as would run counter to the paramount business of the common livelihood, so long the sense of a common livelihood and a joint fortune would continue to hold any particularist ambitions effectually in check. Had it fallen out otherwise, the story of the group in question would have been ended, and another and more suitably endowed type of men would have taken the place vacated by its extinction.

With a sensible advance in the industrial arts the scale of operations would grow larger, and the group more numerous and extensive. The margin between production and subsistence would also widen and admit additional scope for individual ambitions and personal gains. And as this process of growth and increasing productive efficiency went on, the control exercised by neighborly surveillance, through the sentiment of the common good as against the self-seeking pursuits of individuals and sub-groups, would gradually slacken; until by progressive disuse it would fall into a degree of abeyance; to be called into exercise and incite to concerted action only in the face of unusual exigencies touching the common fortunes of the group at large, or on persuasion that the collective interest of the group at large was placed in jeopardy in the molestation of one and another of its members from without. The group's prestige at least would be felt to suffer in the defeat or discourtesy suffered by any of its members at the hands of any alien; and, under compulsion of the ancient sense of group solidarity, whatever material hardship or material gain might so fall to individual members in their dealings with the alien would pass easy scrutiny as material detriment or gain inuring to the group at large,--in the apprehension of men whose sense of community interest is inflamed with a jealous disposition to safeguard their joint prestige.

With continued advance in the industrial arts the circumstances conditioning life will undergo a progressive change of such a character that the joint interest of the group at large, in the material respect, will progressively be less closely bound up with the material fortunes of any particular member or members; until in the course of time and change there will, in effect, in ordinary times be no general and inclusive community of material interest binding the members together in a common fortune and working for a common livelihood. As the rights of ownership begin to take effect, so that the ownership of property and the pursuit of a livelihood under the rules of ownership come to govern men's economic relations, these material concerns will cease to be a matter of undivided joint interest, and will fall into the shape of interest in severalty. So soon and so far as this institution of ownership or property takes effect, men's material interests cease to run on lines of group solidarity. Solely, or almost solely, in the exceptional case of defense against a predatory incursion from outside, do the members of the group have a common interest of a material kind. Progressively as the state of the arts advances, the industrial organisation advances to a larger scale and a more extensive specialisation, with increasing divergence among individual interests and individual fortunes; and intercourse over larger distances grows easier and makes a larger grouping practicable; which enables a larger, prompter and more effective mobilisation of forces with which to defend or assert any joint claims. But by the same move it also follows, or at least it appears uniformly to have followed in the European case, that the accumulation of property and the rights of ownership have progressively come into the first place among the material interests of these peoples; while anything like a community of usufruct has imperceptibly fallen into the background, and has presently gone virtually into abeyance, except as an eventual recourse *in extremis* for the common defense. Property rights have displaced community of usufruct; and invidious distinctions as between persons, sub-groups, and classes have displaced community of prestige in the workday routine of these peoples; and the distinctions between contrasted persons or classes have come to rest, in an ever increasing degree, directly or indirectly, on invidious comparisons in respect of pecuniary standing rather than on personal affiliation with the group at large.

So, with the advance of the industrial arts a differentiation of a new character sets in and presently grows progressively more pronounced and more effectual, giving rise to a regrouping on lines that run regardless of those frontiers that divide one community from another for purposes of patriotic emulation. So far as it comes chiefly and typically in question here, this regrouping takes place on two distinct but somewhat related principles of contrast: that of wealth and poverty, and that of master and servant, or authority and obedience. The material interests of the population in this way come to be divided between the group of those who own and those who command, on the one hand, and of those who work and who obey, on the other hand.

Neither of these two contrasted categories of persons have any direct material interest in the maintenance of the patriotic community; or at any rate no such interest as should reasonably induce them to spend their own time and substance in support of the political (patriotic) organisation within which they live. It is only in so far as one or another of these interests looks for a more than proportionate share in any prospective gain from the joint enterprise, that the group or class in question can reasonably be counted on to bear its share in the joint venture. And it is only when and in so far as their particular material or self-regarding interest is reenforced by patriotic conceit, that they can be counted on to spend themselves in furtherance of the patriotic enterprise, without the assurance of a more than proportionate share in any gains that may be held in prospect from any such joint enterprise; and it is only in its patriotic bearing that the political community continues to be a joint venture. That is to say, in more generalised terms, through the development of the rights of property, and of such like prescriptive claims of privilege and prerogative, it has come about that other community interests have fallen away, until the collective prestige remains as virtually the sole community interest which can hold the sentiment of the group in a bond of solidarity.

To one or another of these several interested groups or classes within the community the political organisation may work a benefit; but only to one or another, not to each and several, jointly or collectively. Since by no chance will the benefit derived from such joint enterprise on the part of the community at large equal the joint cost; in as much as all joint enterprise of the kind that looks to material advantage works by one or another method of inhibition and takes effect, if at all, by lowering the aggregate efficiency of the several countries concerned, with a view to the differential gain of one at the cost of another. So, e.g., a protective tariff is plainly a conspiracy in restraint of trade, with a view to benefit the conspirators by hindering their competitors. The aggregate cost to the community at large of such an enterprise in retardation is always more than the gains it brings to those who may benefit by it.

In so speaking of the uses to which the common man's patriotic devotion may be turned, there is no intention to underrate its intrinsic value as a genial and generous trait of human nature. Doubtless it is best and chiefly to be appreciated as a spiritual quality that beautifies and ennobles its bearer, and that endows him with the full stature of manhood, quite irrespective of ulterior considerations. So it is to be conceded without argument that this patriotic animus is a highly meritorious frame of mind, and that it has an aesthetic value scarcely to be overstated in the farthest stretch of poetic license. But the question of its serviceability to the modern community, in any other than this decorative respect, and particularly its serviceability to the current needs of the common man in such a modern community, is not touched by such an admission; nor does this recognition of its generous spiritual nature afford any help toward answering a further question as to how and with what effect this animus may be turned to account by anyone who is in position to make use of the forces which it sets free.

Among Christian nations there still is, on the whole, a decided predilection for that ancient and authentic line of national repute that springs from warlike prowess. This repute for warlike prowess is what first comes to mind among civilised peoples when speaking of national greatness. And among those who have best preserved this warlike ideal of worth, the patriotic ambition is likely to converge on the prestige of their sovereign; so that it takes the concrete form of personal loyalty to a master, and so combines or coalesces with a servile habit of mind.

But peace hath its victories no less renowned than war, it is said; and peaceable folk of a patriotic temper have learned to make the best of their meager case and have found self-complacency in these victories of the peaceable order. So it may broadly be affirmed that all nations look with complacency on their own peculiar Culture--the organised complex of habits of thought and of conduct by which their own routine of life is regulated--as being in some way worthier than the corresponding habits of their neighbors. The case of the German Culture has latterly come under a strong light in this way. But while it may be that no other nation has been so naive as to make a concerted profession of faith to the effect that their own particular way of life is altogether commendable and is the only fashion of civilisation that is fit to survive; yet it will scarcely be an extravagance to assert that in their own secret mind these others, too, are blest with much the same consciousness of unique worth. Conscious virtue of this kind is a good and sufficient ground for patriotic inflation, so far as it goes. It commonly does not go beyond a defensive attitude, however. Now and again, as in the latterday German animation on this head, these phenomena of national use and wont may come to command such a degree of popular admiration as will incite to an aggressive or proselyting campaign.

In all this there is nothing of a self-seeking or covetous kind. The common man who so lends himself to the aggressive enhancement of the national Culture and its prestige has nothing of a material kind to gain from the increase of renown that so comes to his sovereign, his language, his countrymen's art or science, his dietary, or his God. There are no sordid motives in all this. These spiritual assets of self-complacency are, indeed, to be rated as grounds of high-minded patriotism without afterthought. These aspirations and enthusiasms would perhaps be rated as Quixotic by men whose horizon is bounded by the main chance; but they make up that substance of things hoped for that inflates those headlong patriotic animosities that stir universal admiration.

So also, men find an invidious distinction in such matters of physical magnitude as their country's area, the number of its population, the size of its cities, the extent of its natural resources, its aggregate wealth and its wealth per capita, its merchant marine and its foreign trade. As a ground of invidious complacency these phenomena of physical magnitude and pecuniary traffic are no better and no worse than such immaterial assets as the majesty of the sovereign or the perfections of the language. They are matters in which the common man is concerned only by the accident of domicile, and his only connection with these things is an imaginary joint interest in their impressiveness. To these things he has contributed substantially nothing, and from them he derives no other merit or advantage than a patriotic inflation. He takes pride in these things in an invidious way, and there is no good reason why he should not; just as there is also no good reason why he should, apart from the fact that the common man is so constituted that he, mysteriously, takes pride in these things that concern him not.

* * * * *

Of the several groups or classes of persons within the political frontiers, whose particular interests run systematically at cross purposes with those of the community at large under modern conditions, the class of masters, rulers, authorities,--or whatever term may seem most suitable to designate that category of persons whose characteristic occupation is to give orders and command deference,--of the several orders and conditions of men these are, in point of substantial motive and interest, most patently at variance with all the rest, or with the fortunes of the common man. The class will include civil and military authorities and whatever nobility there is of a prescriptive and privileged kind. The substantial interest of these classes in the common welfare is of the same kind as the interest which a parasite has in the well-being of his host; a sufficiently substantial interest, no doubt, but there is in this relation nothing like a community of interest. Any gain on the part of the community at large will materially serve the needs of this group of personages, only in so far as it may afford them a larger volume or a wider scope for what has in latterday colloquial phrase been called "graft." These personages are, of course, not to be spoken of with disrespect or with the slightest inflection of discourtesy.

They are all honorable men. Indeed they afford the conventional pattern of human dignity and meritorious achievement, and the "Fountain of Honor" is found among them. The point of the argument is only that their material or other self-regarding interests are of such a nature as to be furthered by the material wealth of the community, and more particularly by the increasing volume of the body politic; but only with the proviso that this material wealth and this increment of power must accrue without anything like a corresponding cost to this class. At the same time, since this class of the superiors is in some degree a specialised organ of prestige, so that their value, and therefore their tenure, both in the eyes of the community and in their own eyes, is in the main a "prestige value" and a tenure by prestige; and since the prestige that invests their persons is a shadow cast by the putative worth of the community at large, it follows that their particular interest in the joint prestige is peculiarly alert and insistent. But it follows also that these personages cannot of their own substance or of their own motion contribute to this collective prestige in the same proportion in which it is necessary for them to draw on it in support of their own prestige value. It would, in other words, be a patent absurdity to call on any of the current ruling classes, dynasties, nobility, military and diplomatic corps, in any of the nations of Europe, e.g., to preserve their current dignity and command the deference that is currently accorded them, by recourse to their own powers and expenditure of their own substance, without the usufruct of the commonalty whose organ of dignity they are. The current prestige value which they enjoy is beyond their unaided powers to create or maintain, without the usufruct of the community. Such an enterprise does not lie within the premises of the case.

In this bearing, therefore, the first concern with which these personages are necessarily occupied is the procurement and retention of a suitable usufruct in the material resources and good-will of a sufficiently large and industrious population. The requisite good-will in these premises is called loyalty, and its retention by the line of personages that so trade on prestige rests on a superinduced association of ideas, whereby the national honour comes to be confounded in popular apprehension with the prestige of these personages who have the keeping of it. But the potentates and the establishments, civil and military, on whom this prestige value rests will unavoidably come into invidious comparison with others of their kind; and, as invariably happens in matters of invidious comparison, the emulative needs of all the competitors for prestige are "indefinitely extensible," as the phrase of the economists has it. Each and several of them incontinently needs a further increment of prestige, and therefore also a further increment of the material assets in men and resources that are needful as ways and means to assert and augment the national honor.

It is true, the notion that their prestige value is in any degree conditioned by the material circumstances and the popular imagination of the underlying nation is distasteful to many of these vicars of the national honour. They will incline rather to the persuasion that this prestige value is a distinctive attribute, of a unique order, intrinsic to their own persons. But, plainly, any such detached line of magnates, notables, kings and mandarins, resting their notability on nothing more substantial than a slightly sub-normal intelligence and a moderately scrofulous habit of body could not long continue to command that eager deference that is accounted their due. Such a picture of majesty would be sadly out of drawing. There is little conviction and no great dignity to be drawn from the unaided pronouncement:

"We're here because,
We're here because,
We're here because
We're here,"

even when the doggerel is duly given the rhetorical benefit of a "Tenure by the Grace of God." The personages that carry this dignity require the backing of a determined and patriotic populace in support of their prestige value, and they commonly have no great difficulty in procuring it. And their prestige value is, in effect, proportioned to the volume of material resources and patriotic credulity that can be drawn on for its assertion. It is true, their draught on the requisite sentimental and pecuniary support is fortified with large claims of serviceability to the common good, and these claims are somewhat easily, indeed eagerly, conceded and acted upon; although the alleged benefit to the common good will scarcely be visible except in the light of glory shed by the blazing torch of patriotism.

In so far as it is of a material nature the benefit which the constituted authorities so engage to contribute to the common good, or in other words to confer on the common man, falls under two heads: defense against aggression from without; and promotion of the community's material gain. It is to be presumed that the constituted authorities commonly believe more or less implicitly in their own professions in so professing to serve the needs of the common man in these respects. The common defense is a sufficiently grave matter, and doubtless it claims the best affections and endeavour of the citizen; but it is not a matter that should claim much attention at this point in the argument, as bearing on the service rendered the common man by the constituted authorities, taken one with another. Any given governmental establishment at home is useful in this respect only as against another governmental establishment elsewhere. So that on the slightest examination it resolves itself into a matter of competitive patriotic enterprise, as between the patriotic aspirations of different nationalities led by different governmental establishments; and the service so rendered by the constituted authorities in the aggregate takes on the character of a remedy for evils of their own creation. It is invariably a defense against the concerted aggressions of other patriots. Taken in the large, the common defense of any given nation becomes a detail of the competitive struggle between rival nationalities animated with a common spirit of patriotic enterprise and led by authorities constituted for this competitive purpose.

Except on a broad basis of patriotic devotion, and except under the direction of an ambitious governmental establishment, no serious international aggression is to be had. The common defense, therefore, is to be taken as a remedy for evils arising out of the working of the patriotic spirit that animates mankind, as brought to bear under a discretionary authority; and in any balance to be struck between the utility and disutility of this patriotic spirit and of its service in the hands of the constituted authorities, it will have to be cancelled out as being at the best a mitigation of some of the disorders brought on by the presence of national governments resting on patriotic loyalty at large.

But this common defense is by no means a vacant rubric in any attempted account of modern national enterprise. It is the commonplace and conclusive plea of the dynastic statesmen and the aspiring warlords, and it is the usual blind behind which events are put in train for eventual hostilities. Preparation for the common defense also appears unfailingly to eventuate in hostilities. With more or less ***bona fides*** the statesmen and warriors plead the cause of the common defense, and with patriotic alacrity the common man lends himself to the enterprise aimed at under that cover. In proportion as the resulting equipment for defense grows great and becomes formidable, the range of items which a patriotically biased nation are ready to include among the claims to be defended grows incontinently larger, until by the overlapping of defensive claims between rival nationalities the distinction between defense and aggression disappears, except in the biased fancy of the rival patriots.

Of course, no reflections are called for here on the current American campaign of "Preparedness." Except for the degree of hysteria it appears to differ in no substantial respect from the analogous course of auto-intoxication among the nationalities of Europe, which came to a head in the current European situation. It should conclusively serve the turn for any self-possessed observer to call to mind that all the civilised nations of warring Europe are, each and several, convinced that they are fighting a defensive war.

The aspiration of all right-minded citizens is presumed to be "Peace with Honour." So that first, as well as last, among those national interests that are to be defended, and in the service of which the substance and affections of the common man are enlisted under the aegis of the national prowess, comes the national prestige, as a matter of course. And the constituted authorities are doubtless sincere and single-minded in their endeavors to advance and defend the national honour, particularly those constituted authorities that hold their place of authority on grounds of fealty; since the national prestige in such a case coalesces with the prestige of the nation's ruler in much the same degree in which the national sovereignty devolves upon the person of its ruler. In so defending or advancing the national prestige, such a dynastic or autocratic overlord, together with the other privileged elements assisting and dependent on him, is occupied with his own interest; his own tenure is a tenure by prestige, and the security of his tenure lies in the continued maintenance of that popular fancy that invests his person with this national prestige and so constitutes him and his retinue of notables and personages its keeper.

But it is uniformly insisted by the statesmen--potentates, notables, kings and mandarins--that this aegis of the national prowess in their hands covers also many interests of a more substantial and more tangible kind. These other, more tangible interests of the community have also a value of a direct and personal sort to the dynasty and its hierarchy of privileged subalterns, in that it is only by use of the material forces of the nation that the dynastic prestige can be advanced and maintained. The interest of such constituted authorities in the material welfare of the nation is consequently grave and insistent; but it is evidently an interest of a special kind and is subject to strict and peculiar limitations. The common good, in the material respect, interests the dynastic statesman only as a means to dynastic ends; that is to say, only in so far as it can be turned to account in the achievement of dynastic aims. These aims are "The Kingdom, the Power and the Glory," as the sacred formula phrases the same conception in another bearing.

That is to say, the material welfare of the nation is a means to the unfolding of the dynastic power; provided always that this material welfare is not allowed to run into such ramifications as will make the commonwealth an unwieldy instrument in the hands of the dynastic statesmen. National welfare is to the purpose only in so far as it conduces to political success, which is always a question of warlike success in the last resort. The limitation which this consideration imposes on the government's economic policy are such as will make the nation a self sufficient or self-balanced economic commonwealth. It must be a self-balanced commonwealth at least in such measure as will make it self-sustaining in case of need, in all those matters that bear directly on warlike efficiency.

Of course, no community can become fully self-sustaining under modern conditions, by use of the modern state of the industrial arts, except by recourse to such drastic measures of repression as would reduce its total efficiency in an altogether intolerable degree. This will hold true even of those nations who, like Russia or the United States, are possessed of extremely extensive territories and extremely large and varied resources; but it applies with greatly accentuated force to smaller and more scantily furnished territorial units. Peoples living under modern conditions and by use of the modern state of the industrial arts necessarily draw on all quarters of the habitable globe for materials and products which they can procure to the best advantage from outside their own special field so long as they are allowed access to these outlying sources of supply; and any arbitrary limitation on this freedom of traffic makes the conditions of life that much harder, and lowers the aggregate efficiency of the community by that much. National self-sufficiency is to be achieved only by a degree of economic isolation; and such a policy of economic isolation involves a degree of impoverishment and lowered efficiency, but it will also leave the nation readier for warlike enterprise on such a scale as its reduced efficiency will compass.

So that the best that can be accomplished along this line by the dynastic statesmen is a shrewd compromise, embodying such a degree of isolation and inhibition as will leave the country passably self-sufficient in case of need, without lowering the national efficiency to such a point as to cripple its productive forces beyond what will be offset by the greater warlike readiness that is so attained. The point to which such a policy of isolation and sufficiency will necessarily be directed is that measure of inhibition that will yield the most facile and effective ways and means of warlike enterprise, the largest product of warlike effectiveness to be had on multiplying the nation's net efficiency into its readiness to take the field.

Into any consideration of this tactical problem a certain subsidiary factor enters, in that the patriotic temper of the nation is always more or less affected by such an economic policy. The greater the degree of effectual isolation and discrimination embodied in the national policy, the greater will commonly be its effect on popular sentiment in the way of national animosity and spiritual self-sufficiency; which may be an asset of great value for the purposes of warlike enterprise.

Plainly, any dynastic statesman who should undertake to further the common welfare regardless of its serviceability for warlike enterprise would be defeating his own purpose. He would, in effect, go near to living up to his habitual professions touching international peace, instead of professing to live up to them, as the exigencies of his national enterprise now conventionally require him to do. In effect, he would be *functus officio*.

There are two great administrative instruments available for this work of repression and national self-sufficiency at the hands of the imperialistic statesman: the protective tariff, and commercial subvention. The two are not consistently to be distinguished from one another at all points, and each runs out into a multifarious convolution of variegated details; but the principles involved are, after all, fairly neat and consistent. The former is of the nature of a conspiracy in restraint of trade by repression; the latter, a conspiracy to the like effect by subsidised monopoly; both alike act to check the pursuit of industry in given lines by artificially increasing the cost of production for given individuals or classes of producers, and both alike impose a more than proportionate cost on the community within which they take effect. Incidentally, both of these methods of inhibition bring a degree, though a less degree, of hardship, to the rest of the industrial world.

All this is matter of course to all economic students, and it should, reasonably, be plain to all intelligent persons; but its voluble denial by interested parties, as well as the easy credulity with which patriotic citizens allow themselves to accept the sophistries offered in defense of these measures of inhibition, has made it seem worth while here to recall these commonplaces of economic science.

The ground of this easy credulity is not so much infirmity of intellect as it is an exuberance of sentiment, although it may reasonably be believed that its more pronounced manifestations--as, e.g., the high protective tariff--can be had only by force of a formidable cooperation of the two. The patriotic animus is an invidious sentiment of joint prestige; and it needs no argument or documentation to bear out the affirmation that its bias will lend a color of merit and expediency to any proposed measure that can, however speciously, promise an increase of national power or prestige. So that when the statesmen propose a policy of inhibition and mitigated isolation on the professed ground that such a policy will strengthen the nation economically by making it economically self-supporting, as well as ready for any warlike adventure, the patriotic citizen views the proposed measures through the rosy haze of national aspirations and lets the will to believe persuade him that whatever conduces to a formidable national battle-front will also contribute to the common good. At the same time all these national conspiracies in restraint of trade are claimed, with more or less reason, to inflict more or less harm on rival nationalities with whom economic relations are curtailed; and patriotism being an invidious sentiment, the patriotic citizen finds comfort in the promise of mischief to these others, and is all the more prone to find all kinds of merit in proposals that look to such an invidious outcome. In any community imbued with an alert patriotic spirit, the fact that any given circumstance, occurrence or transaction can be turned to account as a means of invidious distinction or invidious discrimination against humanity beyond the national pale, will always go far to procure acceptance of it as being also an article of substantial profit to the community at large, even though the slightest unbiased scrutiny would find it of no ascertainable use in any other bearing than that of invidious mischief. And whatever will bear interpretation as an increment of the nation's power or prowess, in comparison with rival nationalities, will always be securely counted as an item of joint credit, and will be made to serve the collective conceit as an invidious distinction; and patriotic credulity will find it meritorious also in other respects.

So, e.g., it is past conception that such a patent imbecility as a protective tariff should enlist the support of any ordinarily intelligent community except by the help of some such chauvinistic sophistry. So also, the various royal establishments of Europe, e.g., afford an extreme but therefore all the more convincing illustration of the same logical fallacy. These establishments and personages are great and authentic repositories of national prestige, and they are therefore unreflectingly presumed by their several aggregations of subjects to be of some substantial use also in some other bearing; but it would be a highly diverting exhibition of credulity for any outsider to fall into that amazing misconception. But the like is manifestly true of commercial turnover and export trade among modern peoples; although on this head the infatuation is so ingrained and dogmatic that even a rank outsider is expected to accept the fallacy without reflection, on pain of being rated as unsafe or unsound. Such matters again, as the dimensions of the national territory, or the number of the population and the magnitude of the national resources, are still and have perhaps always been material for patriotic exultation, and are fatuously believed to have some great significance for the material fortunes of the common man; although it should be plain on slight reflection that under modern conditions of ownership, these things, one and all, are of no consequence to the common man except as articles of prestige to stimulate his civic pride. The only conjuncture under which these and the like national holdings can come to have a meaning as joint or collective assets would arise in case of a warlike adventure carried to such extremities as would summarily cancel vested rights of ownership and turn them to warlike uses. While the rights of ownership hold, the common man, who does not own these things, draws no profit from their inclusion in the national domain; indeed, he is at some cost to guarantee their safe tenure by their rightful owners.

In so pursuing their quest of the Kingdom, the Power and the Glory, by use of the national resources and by sanction of the national spirit, the constituted authorities also assume the guardianship of sundry material interests that are presumed to touch the common good; such as security of person and property in dealings with aliens, whether at home or abroad; security of investment and trade, and vindication of their citizens before the law in foreign parts; and, chiefly and ubiquitously, furtherance and extension of the national trade into foreign parts, particularly of the export trade, on terms advantageous to the traders of the nation.

The last named of these advantages is the one on which stress is apt to fall in the argument of all those who advocate an unfolding of national power, as being a matter of vital material benefit to the common man. The other items indicated above, it is plain on the least reflection, are matters of slight if any material consequence to him. The common man--that is ninety-nine and a fraction in one hundred of the nation's common men--has no dealings with aliens in foreign parts, as capitalist, trader, missionary or wayfaring man, and has no occasion for security of person or property under circumstances that raise any remotest question of the national prowess or the national prestige; nor does he seek or aspire to trade to foreign parts on any terms, equitable or otherwise, or to invest capital among aliens under foreign rule, or to exploit concessions or take orders, for acceptance or delivery; nor, indeed, does he at all commonly come into even that degree of contact with abroad that is implied in the purchase of foreign securities. Virtually the sole occasion on which he comes in touch with the world beyond the frontier is when, and if, he goes away from home as an emigrant, and so ceases to enjoy the tutelage of the nation's constituted authorities. But the common man, in point of fact, is a home-keeping body, who touches foreign parts and aliens outside the national frontiers only at the second or third remove, if at all, in the occasional purchase of foreign products, or in the sale of goods that may find their way abroad after he has lost sight of them. The exception to this general rule would be found in the case of those under-sized nations that are too small to contain the traffic in which their commonplace population are engaged, and that have neither national prowess nor national prestige to fall back on in a conceivable case of need,--and whose citizens, individually, appear to be as fortunately placed in their workday foreign relations, without a background of prowess and prestige, as the citizens of the great powers who are most abundantly provided in these respects.

With wholly negligible exceptions, these matters touch the needs or the sensibilities of the common man only through the channel of the national honour, which may be injured in the hardships suffered by his compatriots in foreign parts, or which may, again, be repaired or enhanced by the meritorious achievements of the same compatriots; of whose existence he will commonly have no other or more substantial evidence, and in whose traffic he has no share other than this vicarious suffering of vague and remote indignity or vainglory by force of the wholly fortuitous circumstance that they are (inscrutably) his compatriots. These immaterial goods of vicarious prestige are, of course, not to be undervalued, nor is the fact to be overlooked or minimised that they enter into the sum total of the common citizen's "psychic income," for whatever they may foot up to; but evidently their consideration takes us back to the immaterial category of prestige value, from which the argument just now was hopefully departing with a view to consideration of the common man's material interest in that national enterprise about which patriotic aspirations turn.

These things, then, are matters in which the common man has an interest only as they have a prestige value. But there need be no question as to their touching his sensibilities and stirring him to action, and even to acts of bravery and self-sacrifice. Indignity or ill treatment of his compatriots in foreign parts, even when well deserved, as is not infrequently the case, are resented with a vehemence that is greatly to the common man's credit, and greatly also to the gain of those patriotic statesmen who find in such grievances their safest and most reliable raw materials for the production of international difficulty. That he will so respond to the stimulus of these, materially speaking irrelevant, vicissitudes of good or ill that touch the fortunes of his compatriots, as known to him by hearsay, bears witness, of course, to the high quality of his manhood; but it falls very far short of arguing that these promptings of his patriotic spirit have any value as traits that count toward his livelihood or his economic serviceability in the community in which he lives. It is all to his credit, and it goes to constitute him a desirable citizen, in the sense that he is properly amenable to the incitements of patriotic emulation; but it is none the less to be admitted, however reluctantly, that this trait of impulsively vicarious indignation or vainglory is neither materially profitable to himself nor an asset of the slightest economic value to the community in which he lives. Quite the contrary, in fact. So also is it true that the common man derives no material advantage from the national success along this line, though he commonly believes that it all somehow inures to his benefit. It would seem that an ingrown bias of community interest, blurred and driven by a jealously sensitive patriotic pride, bends his faith uncritically to match his inclination. His persuasion is a work of preconception rather than of perception.

But the most substantial and most unqualified material benefit currently believed to be derivable from a large unfolding of national prowess and a wide extension of the national domain is an increased volume of the nation's foreign trade, particularly of the export trade. "Trade follows the Flag." And this larger trade and enhanced profit is presumed to inure to the joint benefit of the citizens. Such is the profession of faith of the sagacious statesmen and such is also the unreflecting belief of the common man.

It may be left an open question if an unfolding of national prowess and prestige increases the nation's trade, whether in imports or in exports. There is no available evidence that it has any effect of the kind. What is not an open question is the patent fact that such an extension of trade confers no benefit on the common man, who is not engaged in the import or export business. More particularly does it yield him no advantage at all commensurate with the cost involved in any endeavour so to increase the volume of trade by increasing the nation's power and extending its dominion. The profits of trade go not to the common man at large but to the traders whose capital is invested; and it is a completely idle matter to the common citizen whether the traders who profit by the nation's trade are his compatriots or not.[6]

The pacifist argument on the economic futility of national ambitions will commonly rest its case at this point; having shown as unreservedly as need be that national ambition and all its works belong of right under that rubric of the litany that speaks of Fire, Flood and Pestilence. But an hereditary bent of human nature is not to be put out of the way with an argument showing that it has its disutilities. So with the patriotic animus; it is a factor to be counted with, rather than to be exorcised.

As has been remarked above, in the course of time and change the advance of the industrial arts and of the institutions of ownership have taken such a turn that the working system of industry and business no longer runs on national lines and, indeed, no longer takes account of national frontiers,--except in so far as the national policies and legislation, arbitrarily and partially, impose these frontiers on the workings of trade and industry. The effect of such regulation for political ends

---

6 All this, which should be plain without demonstration, has been repeatedly shown in the expositions of various peace advocates, typically by Mr. Angell.

is, with wholly negligible exceptions, detrimental to the efficient working of the industrial system under modern conditions; and it is therefore detrimental to the material interests of the common citizen. But the case is not the same as regards the interests of the traders. Trade is a competitive affair, and it is to the advantage of the traders engaged in any given line of business to extend their own markets and to exclude competing traders. Competition may be the soul of trade, but monopoly is necessarily the aim of every trader. And the national organisation is of service to its traders in so far as it shelters them, wholly or partly, from the competition of traders of other nationalities, or in so far as it furthers their enterprise by subvention or similar privileges as against their competitors, whether at home or abroad. The gain that so comes to the nation's traders from any preferential advantage afforded them by national regulations, or from any discrimination against traders of foreign nationality, goes to the traders as private gain. It is of no benefit to any of their compatriots; since there is no community of usufruct that touches these gains of the traders. So far as concerns his material advantage, it is an idle matter to the common citizen whether he deals with traders of his own nationality or with aliens; both alike will aim to buy cheap and sell dear, and will charge him "what the traffic will bear." Nor does it matter to him whether the gains of this trade go to aliens or to his compatriots; in either case equally they immediately pass beyond his reach, and are equally removed from any touch of joint interest on his part. Being private property, under modern law and custom he has no use of them, whether a national frontier does or does not intervene between his domicile and that of their owner.

These are facts that every man of sound mind knows and acts on without doubt or hesitation in his own workday affairs. He would scarcely even find amusement in so futile a proposal as that his neighbor should share his business profits with him for no better reason than that he is a compatriot. But when the matter is presented as a proposition in national policy and embroidered with an invocation of his patriotic loyalty the common citizen will commonly be found credulous enough to accept the sophistry without abatement. His archaic sense of group solidarity will still lead him at his own cost to favor his trading compatriots by the imposition of onerous trade regulations for their private advantage, and to interpose obstacles in the way of alien traders. All this ingenious policy of self-defeat is greatly helped out by the patriotic conceit of the citizens; who persuade themselves to see in it an accession to the power and prestige of their own nation and a disadvantage to rival nationalities. It is, indeed, more than doubtful if such a policy of self-defeat as is embodied in current international trade discriminations could be insinuated into the legislation of any civilized nation if the popular intelligence were not so clouded with patriotic animosity as to let a prospective detriment to their foreign neighbors count as a gain to themselves.

So that the chief material use of the patriotic bent in modern populations, therefore, appears to be its use to a limited class of persons engaged in foreign trade, or in business that comes in competition with foreign industry. It serves their private gain by lending effectual countenance to such restraint of international trade as would not be tolerated within the national domain. In so doing it has also the secondary and more sinister effect of dividing the nations on lines of rivalry and setting up irreconcilable claims and ambitions, of no material value but of far-reaching effect in the way of provocation to further international estrangement and eventual breach of the peace.

How all this falls in with the schemes of militant statesmen, and further reacts on the freedom and personal fortunes of the common man, is an extensive and intricate topic, though not an obscure one; and it has already been spoken of above, perhaps as fully as need be.

CHAPTER III
ON THE CONDITIONS OF A LASTING PEACE

The considerations set out in earlier chapters have made it appear that the patriotic spirit of modern peoples is the abiding source of contention among nations. Except for their patriotism a breach of the peace among modern peoples could not well be had. So much will doubtless be assented to as a matter of course. It is also a commonplace of current aphoristic wisdom that both parties to a warlike adventure in modern times stand to lose, materially; whatever nominal--that is to say political--gains may be made by one or the other. It has also appeared from these considerations recited in earlier passages that this patriotic spirit prevails throughout, among all civilised peoples, and that it pervades one nation about as ubiquitously as another. Nor is there much evidence of a weakening of this sinister proclivity with the passage of time or the continued advance in the arts of life. The only civilized nations that can be counted on as habitually peaceable are those who are so feeble or are so placed as to be cut off from hope of gain through contention. Vainglorious arrogance may run at a higher tension among the more backward and boorish nations; but it is not evident that the advance guard among the civilised peoples are imbued with a less complete national self-complacency. If the peace is to be kept, therefore, it will have to be kept by and between peoples made up, in effect, of complete patriots; which comes near being a contradiction in terms. Patriotism is useful for breaking the peace, not for keeping it. It makes for national pretensions and international jealously and distrust, with warlike enterprise always in perspective; as a way to national gain or a recourse in case of need. And there is commonly no settled demarkation between these two contrasted needs that urge a patriotic people forever to keep one eye on the chance of a recourse to arms.

Therefore any calculus of the Chances of Peace appears to become a reckoning of the forces which may be counted on to keep a patriotic nation in an unstable equilibrium of peace for the time being. As has just been remarked above, among civilised peoples only those nations can be counted on consistently to keep the peace who are so feeble or otherwise so placed as to be cut off from hope of national gain. And these can apparently be so counted on only as regards aggression, not as regards the national defense, and only in so far as they are not drawn into warlike enterprise, collectively, by their more competent neighbors. Even the feeblest and most futile of them feels in honour bound to take up arms in defense of such national pretensions as they still may harbour; and all of them harbour such pretensions. In certain extreme cases, which it might seem invidious to specify more explicitly, it is not easy to discover any specific reasons for the maintenance of a national establishment, apart from the vindication of certain national pretensions which would quietly lapse in the absence of a national establishment on whom their vindication is incumbent.

Of the rest, the greater nations that are spoken of as Powers no such general statement will hold. These are the peoples who stand, in matters of national concern, on their own initiative; and the question of peace and war at large is in effect, a question of peace and war among these Powers. They are not so numerous that they can be sifted into distinct classes, and yet they differ among themselves in such a way that they may, for the purpose in hand, fairly be ranged under two distinguishable if not contrasted heads: those which may safely be counted on spontaneously to take the offensive, and those which will fight on provocation. Typically of the former description are Germany and Japan. Of the latter are the French and British, and less confidently the American republic. In any summary statement of this kind Russia will have to be left on one side as a doubtful case, for reasons to which the argument may return at a later point; the prospective course of things in Russia is scarcely to be appraised on the ground of its past. Spain and Italy, being dubious Powers at the best, need not detain the argument; they are, in the nature of things, subsidiaries who wait on the main chance. And Austria, with whatever the name may cover, is for the immediate purpose to be counted under the head of Germany.

There is no invidious comparison intended in so setting off these two classes of nations in contrast to one another. It is not a contrast of merit and demerit or of prestige. Imperial Germany and Imperial Japan are, in the nature of things as things go, bent in effect on a disturbance of the peace,--with a view to advance the cause of their own dominion. On a large view of the case, such as many German statesmen were in the habit of professing in the years preceding the great war, it may perhaps appear reasonable to say--as they were in the habit of saying--that these Imperial Powers are as well within the lines of fair and honest dealing in their campaign of aggression as the other Powers are in taking a defensive attitude against their aggression. Some sort of international equity has been pleaded in justification of their demand for an increased share of dominion. At least it has appeared that these Imperial statesmen have so persuaded themselves after very mature deliberation; and they have showed great concern to persuade others of the equity of their Imperial claim to something more than the law would allow. These sagacious, not to say astute, persons have not only reached a conviction to this effect, but they have become possessed of this conviction in such plenary fashion that, in the German case, they have come to admit exceptions or abatement of the claim only when and in so far as the campaign of equitable aggression on which they had entered has been proved impracticable by the fortunes of war.

With some gift for casuistry one may, at least conceivably, hold that the felt need of Imperial self-aggrandisement may become so urgent as to justify, or at least to condone, forcible dispossession of weaker nationalities. This might, indeed it has, become a sufficiently perplexing question of casuistry, both as touches the punctilios of national honour and as regards an equitable division between rival Powers in respect of the material means of mastery. So in private life it may become a moot question--in point of equity--whether the craving of a kleptomaniac may not on occasion rise to such an intolerable pitch of avidity as to justify him in seizing whatever valuables he can safely lay hands on, to ease the discomfort of ungratified desire. In private life any such endeavour to better oneself at one's neighbors' cost is not commonly reprobated if it takes effect on a decently large scale and shrewdly within the flexibilities of the law or with the connivance of its officers. Governing international endeavours of this class there is no law so inflexible that it can not be conveniently made over to fit particular circumstances. And in the absence of law the felt need of a formal justification will necessarily appeal to the unformulated equities of the case, with some such outcome as alluded to above. All that, of course, is for the diplomatists to take care of.

But any speculation on the equities involved in the projected course of empire to which these two enterprising nations are committing themselves must run within the lines of diplomatic parable, and will have none but a speculative interest. It is not a matter of equity. Accepting the situation as it stands, it is evident that any peace can only have a qualified meaning, in the sense of armistice, so long as there is opportunity for national enterprise of the character on which these two enterprising national establishments are bent, and so long as these and the like national establishments remain. So, taking the peaceable professions of their spokesmen at a discount of one hundred percent, as one necessarily must, and looking to the circumstantial evidence of the case, it is abundantly plain that at least these two imperial Powers may be counted on consistently to manoeuvre for warlike advantage so long as any peace compact holds, and to break the peace so soon as the strategy of Imperial enterprise appears to require it.

There has been much courteous make-believe of amiable and upright solicitude on this head the past few years, both in diplomatic intercourse and among men out of doors; and since make-believe is a matter of course in diplomatic intercourse it is right and seemly, of course, that no overt recognition of unavowed facts should be allowed to traverse this run of make-believe within the precincts of diplomatic intercourse. But in any ingenuous inquiry into the nature of peace and the conditions of its maintenance there can be no harm in conveniently leaving the diplomatic make-believe on one side and looking to the circumstances that condition the case, rather than to the formal professions designed to mask the circumstances.

*   *   *   *   *

Chief among the relevant circumstances in the current situation are the imperial designs of Germany and Japan. These two national establishments are very much alike. So much so that for the present purpose a single line of analysis will passably cover both cases. The same line of analysis will also apply, with slight adaptation, to more than one of the other Powers, or near-Powers, of the modern world; but in so far as such is held to be the case, that is not a consideration that weakens the argument as applied to these two, which are to be taken as the consummate type-form of a species of national establishments. They are, between them, the best instance there is of what may be called a Dynastic State.

Except as a possible corrective of internal disorders and discontent, neither of the two States "desires" war; but both are bent on dominion, and as the dominion aimed at is not to be had except by fighting for it, both in effect are incorrigibly bent on warlike enterprise. And in neither case will considerations of equity, humanity, decency, veracity, or the common good be allowed to trouble the quest of dominion. As lies in the nature of the dynastic State, imperial dominion, in the ambitions of both, is beyond price; so that no cost is too high so long as ultimate success attends the imperial enterprise. So much is commonplace knowledge among all men who are at all conversant with the facts.

To anyone who harbors a lively sentimental prejudice for or against either or both of the two nations so spoken of, or for or against the manner of imperial enterprise to which both are committed, it may seem that what has just been said of them and their relation to the world's peace runs on something of a bias and conveys something of dispraise and reprobation. Such is not the intention, however, though the appearance is scarcely to be avoided. It is necessary for the purposes of the argument unambiguously to recognise the nature of these facts with which the inquiry is concerned; and any plain characterisation of the facts will unavoidably carry a fringe of suggestions of this character, because current speech is adapted for their reprobation. The point aimed at is not this inflection of approval or disapproval. The facts are to be taken impersonally for what they are worth in their causal bearing on the chance of peace or war; not at their sentimental value as traits of conduct to be appraised in point of their goodness or expediency.

So seen without prejudice, then, if that may be, this Imperial enterprise of these two Powers is to be rated as the chief circumstance bearing on the chances of peace and conditioning the terms on which any peace plan must be drawn. Evidently, in the presence of these two Imperial Powers any peace compact will be in a precarious case; equally so whether either or both of them are parties to such compact or not. No engagement binds a dynastic statesman in case it turns out not to further the dynastic enterprise. The question then recurs: How may peace be maintained within the horizon of German or Japanese ambitions? There are two obvious alternatives, neither of which promises an easy way out of the quandary in which the world's peace is placed by their presence: Submission to their dominion, or Elimination of these two Powers. Either alternative would offer a sufficiently deterrent outlook, and yet any project for devising some middle course of conciliation and amicable settlement, which shall be practicable and yet serve the turn, scarcely has anything better to promise. The several nations now engaged on a war with the greater of these Imperial Powers hold to a design of elimination, as being the only measure that merits hopeful consideration. The Imperial Power in distress bespeaks peace and good-will.

Those advocates, whatever their nationality, who speak for negotiation with a view to a peace compact which is to embrace these States intact, are aiming, in effect, to put things in train for ultimate submission to the mastery of these Imperial Powers. In these premises an amicable settlement and a compact of perpetual peace will necessarily be equivalent to arranging a period of recuperation and recruiting for a new onset of dynastic enterprise. For, in the nature of the case, no compact binds the dynastic statesman, and no consideration other than the pursuit of Imperial dominion commands his attention.

There is, of course, no intention to decry this single-mindedness that is habitually put in evidence by the dynastic statesmen. Nor should it be taken as evidence of moral obliquity in them. It is rather the result of a peculiar moral attitude or bent, habitual to such statesmen, and in its degree also habitual to their compatriots, and is indispensably involved in the Imperial frame of mind. The consummation of Imperial mastery being the highest and ubiquitously ulterior end of all endeavour, its pursuit not only relieves its votaries from the observance of any minor obligations that run counter to its needs, but it also imposes a moral obligation to make the most of any opportunity for profitable deceit and chicanery that may offer. In short, the dynastic statesman is under the governance of a higher morality, binding him to the service of his nation's ambition--or in point of fact, to the personal service of his dynastic master--to which it is his dutiful privilege loyally to devote all his powers of force and fraud.

Democratically-minded persons, who are not moved by the call of loyalty to a gratuitous personal master, may have some difficulty in appreciating the force and the moral austerity of this spirit of devotion to an ideal of dynastic aggrandisement, and in seeing how its paramount exigence will set aside all meticulous scruples of personal rectitude and veracity, as being a shabby with-holding of service due.

To such of these doubters as still have retained some remnants of their religious faith this attitude of loyalty may perhaps be made intelligible by calling to mind the analogous self-surrender of the religious devotee. And in this connection it may also be to the purpose to recall that in point of its genesis and derivation that unreserved self-abasement and surrender to the divine ends and guidance, which is the chief grace and glory of the true believer, is held by secular students of these matters to be only a sublimated analogue or counterfeit of this other dutiful abasement that constitutes loyalty to a temporal master. The deity is currently spoken of as The Heavenly King, under whose dominion no sinner has a right that He is bound to respect; very much after the fashion in which no subject of a dynastic state has a right which the State is bound to respect. Indeed, all these dynastic establishments that so seek the Kingdom, the Power and the Glory are surrounded with a penumbra of divinity, and it is commonly a bootless question where the dynastic powers end and the claims of divinity begin. There is something of a coalescence.[7]

The Kaiser holds dominion by divine grace and is accountable to none but God, if to Him. The whole case is in a still better state of repair as touches the Japanese establishment, where the Emperor is a lineal descendant of the supreme deity, Amaterazu (o mi Kami), and where, by consequence, there is no line of cleavage between a divine and a secular mastery. Pursuant to this more unqualified authenticity of autocratic rule, there is also to be found in this case a correspondingly unqualified devotion in the subjects and an unqualified subservience to dynastic ends on the part of the officers of the crown. The coalescence of dynastic rule with the divine order is less complete in the German case, but all observers bear witness that it all goes far enough also in the German case. This state of things is recalled here as a means of making plain that the statesmen of these Imperial Powers must in the nature of

---

7 "To us the state is the most indispensable as well as the highest requisite to our earthly existence.... All individualistic endeavor ... must be unreservedly subordinated to this lofty claim.... The state ... eventually is of infinitely more value than the sum of all the individuals within its jurisdiction." "This conception of the state, which is as much a part of our life as is the blood in our veins, is nowhere to be found in the English Constitution, and is quite foreign to English thought, and to that of America as well."--Eduard Meyer, *England, its Political Organisation and Development and the War against Germany*, translated by H.S. White. Boston 1916. pp. 30-31

the case, and without blame, be drawn out from under the customary restraint of those principles of vulgar morality that are embodied in the decalogue. It is not that the subject, or--what comes to the same thing--the servant of such a dynastic State may not be upright, veracious and humane in private life, but only that he must not be addicted to that sort of thing in such manner or degree as might hinder his usefulness for dynastic purposes. These matters of selfishly individual integrity and humanity have no weight as against the exigencies of the dynastic enterprise.

These considerations may not satisfy all doubters as to the moral sufficiency of these motives that so suffice to decide the dynastic statesmen on their enterprise of aggression by force and fraud; but it should be evident that so long as these statesmen continue in the frame of mind spoken of, and so long as popular sentiment in these countries continues, as hitherto, to lend them effectual support in the pursuit of such Imperial enterprise, so long it must also remain true that no enduring peace can be maintained within the sweep of their Imperial ambition. Any peace compact would necessarily be, in effect, an armistice terminable at will and serving as a season of preparation to meet a deferred opportunity. For the peaceable nations it would, in effect, be a respite and a season of preparation for eventual submission to the Imperial rule.

By advocates of such a negotiated compact of perpetual peace it has been argued that the populace underlying these Imperial Powers will readily be brought to realise the futility and inexpediency of such dynastic enterprise, if only the relevant facts are brought to their knowledge, and that so these Powers will be constrained to keep the peace by default of popular support for their warlike projects. What is required, it is believed by these sanguine persons, is that information be competently conveyed to the common people of these warlike nations, showing them that they have nothing to apprehend in the way of aggression or oppressive measures from the side of their more peaceable neighbours; whereupon their warlike animus will give place to a reasonable and enlightened frame of mind. This argument runs tacitly or explicitly, on the premise that these peoples who have so enthusiastically lent themselves to the current warlike enterprise are fundamentally of the same racial complexion and endowed with the same human nature as their peaceable neighbours, who would be only too glad to keep the peace on any terms of tolerable security from aggression. If only a fair opportunity is offered for the interested peoples to come to an understanding, it is held, a good understanding will readily be reached; at least so far as to result in a reasonable willingness to submit questions in dispute to an intelligent canvass and an equitable arbitration.

Projects for a negotiated peace compact, to include the dynastic States, can hold any prospect of a happy issue only if this line of argument, or its equivalent, is pertinent and conclusive; and the argument is to the point only in so far as its premises are sound and will carry as far as the desired conclusion. Therefore a more detailed attention to the premises on which it runs will be in place, before any project of the kind is allowed to pass inspection.

As to homogeneity of race and endowment among the several nations in question, the ethnologists, who are competent to speak of that matter, are ready to assert that this homogeneity goes much farther among the nations of Europe than any considerable number of peace advocates would be ready to claim. In point of race, and broadly speaking, there is substantially no difference between these warring nations, along any east-and-west line; while the progressive difference in racial complexion that is always met with along any north-and-south line, nowhere coincides with a national or linguistic frontier. In no case does a political division between these nations mark or depend on a difference of race or of hereditary endowment. And, to give full measure, it may be added that also in no case does a division of classes within any one of these nations, into noble and base, patrician and plebeian, lay and learned, innocent and vicious, mark or rest on any slightest traceable degree of difference in race or in heritable endowment. On the point of racial homogeneity there is no fault to find with the position taken.

If the second postulate in this groundwork of premises on which the advocates of negotiable peace base their hopes were as well taken there need be no serious misgiving as to the practicability of such a plan. The plan counts on information, persuasion and reflection to subdue national animosities and jealousies, at least in such measure as would make them amenable to reason. The question of immediate interest on this head, therefore, would be as to how far this populace may be accessible to the contemplated line of persuasion. At present they are, notoriously, in a state of obsequious loyalty to the dynasty, single-minded devotion to the fortunes of the Fatherland, and uncompromising hatred of its enemies. In this frame of mind there is nothing that is new, except the degree of excitement. The animus, it will be recalled, was all there and on the alert when the call came, so that the excitement came on with the sweep of a conflagration on the first touch of a suitable stimulus. The German people at large was evidently in a highly unstable equilibrium, so that an unexampled enthusiasm of patriotic self-sacrifice followed immediately on the first incitement to manslaughter, very much as if the nation had been held under an hypnotic spell. One need only recall the volume of overbearing magniloquence that broke out all over the place in that beginning, when The Day was believed to be dawning.

Such a popular frame of mind is not a transient episode, to be created at short notice and put aside for a parcel of salutary advice. The nation that will make such a massive concerted move with the alacrity shown in this instance must be living in a state of alert readiness for just such an onset. Yet this is not to be set down as anything in the way of a racial trait specifically distinguishing the German people from those other adjacent nationalities that are incapable of a similarly swift and massive response to the appeal of patriotism. These adjacent nationalities are racially identical with the German people, but they do not show the same warlike abandon in nearly the same degree.

But for all that, it is a national trait, not to be acquired or put away by taking thought. It is just here that the line of definition runs: it is a national trait, not a racial one. It is not Nature, but it is Second Nature. But a national trait, while it is not heritable in the simple sense of that term, has the same semblance, or the same degree, of hereditary persistence that belongs to the national institutions, usages, conventionalities, beliefs, which distinguish the given nation from its neighbors. In this instance it may be said more specifically that this eager loyalty is a heritage of the German people at large in the same sense and with the same degree of permanence as the institution of an autocratic royalty has among them, or a privileged nobility. Indeed, it is the institutional counterfoil of these establishments. It is of an institutional character, just as the corresponding sense of national solidarity and patriotic devotion is among the neighboring peoples with whom the German nation comes in comparison. And an institution is an historical growth, with just so much of a character of permanence and continuity of transmission as is given it by the circumstances out of which it has grown. Any institution is a product of habit, or perhaps more accurately it is a body of habits of thought bearing on a given line of conduct, which prevails with such generality and uniformity throughout the group as to have become a matter of common sense.

Such an article of institutional furniture is an outcome of usage, not of reflection or deliberate choice; and it has consequently a character of self-legitimation, so that it stands in the accredited scheme of things as intrinsically right and good, and not merely as a shrewdly chosen expedient ***ad interim***. It affords a norm of life, inosculating with a multiplicity of other norms, with which it goes to make up a balanced scheme of ends, ways and means governing human conduct; and no one such institutional item, therefore, is materially to be disturbed, discarded or abated except at the cost of serious derangement to the balanced scheme of things in which it belongs as an integral constituent. Nor can such a detail norm of conduct and habitual propensity come into bearing and hold its place, except by force of habituation which is at the same time consonant with the common run of habituation to which the given community is subject. It follows that the more rigorous, comprehensive, unremitting and long-continued the habituation to which a given institutional principle owes its vogue, the more intimately and definitively will it be embedded in the common sense of the community, the less chance is there of its intrinsic necessity being effectually questioned or doubted, and the less chance is there of correcting it or abating its force in case circumstances should so change as to make its continued rule visibly inexpedient. Its abatement will be a work not of deliberation and design, but of defection through disuse.

Not that reflection and sane counsel will count for nothing in these premises, but only that these exertions of intelligence will count for relatively very little by comparison with the run of habituation as enforced by the circumstances conditioning any given case; and further, that wise counsel and good resolutions can take effect in the way of amending any untoward institutional bent only by way of suitable habituation, and only at such a rate of change as the circumstances governing habituation will allow. It is, at the best, slow work to shift the settled lines of any community's scheme of common sense. Now, national solidarity, and more particularly an unquestioning loyalty to the sovereign and the dynasty, is a matter of course and of commonsense necessity with the German people. It is not necessary to call to mind that the Japanese nation, which has here been coupled with the German, are in the same case, only more so.

Doubtless it would be exceeding the premises to claim that it should necessarily take the German people as long-continued and as harsh a schooling to unlearn their excess of chauvinism, their servile stooping to gratuitous authority, and their eager subservience to the dynastic ambitions of their masters, as that which has in the course of history induced these habits in them. But it would seem reasonable to expect that there should have to be some measure of proportion between what it has cost them in time and experience to achieve their current frame of mind in this bearing and what it would cost to divest themselves of it. It is a question of how long a time and how exacting a discipline would be required so far to displace the current scheme of commonsense values and convictions in force in the Fatherland as to neutralise their current high-wrought principles of servility, loyalty and national animosity; and on the solution of this difficulty appear to depend the chances of success for any proposed peace compact to which the German nation shall be made a party, on terms of what is called an "honorable peace."

The national, or rather the dynastic and warlike, animus of this people is of the essence of their social and political institutions. Without such a groundwork of popular sentiment neither the national establishment, nor the social order on which it rests and through which it works, could endure. And with this underlying national sentiment intact nothing but a dynastic establishment of a somewhat ruthless order, and no enduring system of law and order not based on universal submission to personal rule, could be installed. Both the popular animus and the correlative coercive scheme of law and order are of historical growth. Both have been learned, acquired, and are in no cogent sense original with the German people. But both alike and conjointly have come out of a very protracted, exacting and consistent discipline of mastery and subjection, running virtually unbroken over the centuries that have passed since the region that is now the Fatherland first passed under the predaceous rule of its Teutonic invaders,--for no part of the "Fatherland" is held on other tenure than that of forcible seizure in ancient times by bands of invaders, with the negligible exception of Holstein and a slight extent of territory adjoining that province to the south and south-west. Since the time when such peoples as were overtaken in this region by the Germanic barbarian invasions, and were reduced to subjection and presently merged with their alien masters, the same general fashion of law and order that presently grew out of that barbarian conquest has continued to govern the life of those peoples, with relatively slight and intermittent relaxation of its rigors. Contrasted with its beginnings, in the shameful atrocities of the Dark Ages and the prehistoric phases of this German occupation, the later stages of this system of coercive law and order in the Fatherland will appear humane, not to say genial; but as compared with the degree of mitigation which the like order of things presently underwent elsewhere in western Europe, it has throughout the historical period preserved a remarkable degree of that character of arrogance and servility which it owes to its barbarian and predatory beginnings.

* * * * *

The initial stages of this Germanic occupation of the Fatherland are sufficiently obscure under the cloud of unrecorded antiquity that covers them; and then, an abundance of obscurantism has also been added by the vapours of misguided vanity that have surrounded so nearly all historical inquiry on the part of patriotic German scholars. Yet there are certain outstanding features in the case, in history and prehistory, that are too large or too notorious to be set aside or to be covered over, and these may suffice to show the run of circumstances which have surrounded the German peoples and shaped their civil and political institutions, and whose discipline has guided German habits of thought and preserved the German spirit of loyalty in the shape in which it underlies the dynastic State of the present day.

Among the most engaging of those fables that make the conventional background of German history is the academic legend of a free agricultural village community made up of ungraded and masterless men. It is not necessary here to claim that such a village community never played a part in the remoter prehistoric experiences out of which the German people, or their ruling classes, came into the territory of the Fatherland; such a claim might divert the argument. But it is sufficiently patent to students of those matters today that no such community of free and ungraded men had any part in the Germanic beginnings; that is to say, in the early experiences of the Fatherland under German rule. The meager and ambiguous remarks of Tacitus on the state of domestic and civil economy among the inhabitants of Germany need no longer detain anyone, in the presence of the available archaeological and historical evidence. The circumstantial evidence of the prehistoric antiquities which touch this matter, as well as the slight allusions of historical records in antiquity, indicate unambiguously enough that when the Germanic immigrants moved into the territories of the Fatherland they moved in as invaders, or rather as marauders, and made themselves masters of the people already living on the land. And history quite as unambiguously declares that when the Fatherland first comes under its light it presents a dark and bloody ground of tumultuous contention and intrigue; where princes and princelings, captains of war and of rapine as well as the captains of superstition, spend the substance of an ignominiously sordid and servile populace in an endless round of mutual raiding, treachery, assassinations and supersession.

Taken at their face value, the recorded stories of that early time would leave one to infer that the common people, whose industry supported this superstructure of sordid mastery, could have survived only by oversight. But touched as it is with poetic license and devoted to the admirable life of the master class--admirable in their own eyes and in those of their chroniclers, as undoubtedly also in the eyes of the subject populace--the history of that time doubtless plays up the notable exploits and fortunes of its conspicuous personages, somewhat to the neglect of the obscure vicissitudes of life and fortune among that human raw material by use of which the admirable feats of the master class were achieved, and about the use of which the dreary traffic of greed and crime went on among the masters.

Of the later history, what covers, say, the last one thousand years, there is no need to speak at length. With transient, episodic, interruptions it is for the Fatherland a continuation out of these beginnings, leading out into a more settled system of subjection and mastery and a progressively increased scale of princely enterprise, resting on an increasingly useful and increasingly loyal populace. In all this later history the posture of things in the Fatherland is by no means unique, nor is it even strikingly peculiar, by contrast with the rest of western Europe, except in degree. It is of the same general kind as the rest of what has gone to make the historical advance of medieval and modern times; but it differs from the generality in a more sluggish movement and a more tenacious adherence to what would be rated as the untoward features of mediaevalism. The approach to a modern scheme of institutions and modern conceptions of life and of human values has been slow, and hitherto incomplete, as compared with those communities that have, for good or ill, gone farthest along the ways of modernity. Habituation to personal subjection and subservience under the rigorous and protracted discipline of standardised service and fealty has continued later, and with later and slighter mitigation, in the Fatherland; so as better to have conserved the spiritual attitude of the feudal order. Law and order in the Fatherland has in a higher degree continued to mean unquestioning obedience to a personal master and unquestioning subservience to the personal ambitions of the master. And since freedom, in the sense of discretionary initiative on the part of the common man, does not fit into the framework of such a system of dependence on personal authority and surveillance, any degree of such free initiative will be "licence" in the eyes of men bred into the framework of this system; whereas "liberty," as distinct from "licence," is not a matter of initiative and self-direction, but of latitude in the service of a master. Hence no degree of curtailment in this delegated "liberty" will be resented or repudiated by popular indignation, so long as the master to whom service is due can give assurance that it is expedient for his purposes.

The age-long course of experience and institutional discipline out of which the current German situation has come may be drawn schematically to the following effect: In the beginning a turmoil of conquest, rapine, servitude, and contention between rival bands of marauders and their captains, gradually, indeed imperceptibly, fell into lines of settled and conventionalised exploitation; with repeated interruptions due to new incursions and new combinations of rapacious chieftains. Out of it all in the course of time came a feudal regime, under which personal allegiance and service to petty chiefs was the sole and universal accredited bond of solidarity. As the outcome of further unremitting intrigue and contention among feudal chiefs, of high and low degree, the populace fell into larger parcels, under the hands of feudal lords of larger dominion, and the bias of allegiance and service came to hold with some degree of permanence and uniformity, or at least of consistency, over a considerable reach of country, including its inhabitants. With the rise of States came allegiance to a dynasty, as distinguished from the narrower and more ephemeral allegiance to the semi-detached person of a victorious prince; and the relative permanence of territorial frontiers under this rule gave room for an effectual recrudescence of the ancient propensity to a sentimental group solidarity; in which the accredited territorial limits of the dynastic dominion served to outline the group that so was felt to belong together under a joint dispensation and with something of a joint interest in matters of fame and fortune. As the same notion is more commonly and more suggestively expressed, a sense of nationality arose within the sweep of the dynastic rule. This sense of community interest that is called nationality so came in to reenforce the sense of allegiance to the dynastic establishment and so has coalesced with it to produce that high-wrought loyalty to the State, that draws equally on the sentiment of community interest in the nation and on the prescriptive docility to the dynastic head. The sense of national solidarity and of feudal loyalty and service have coalesced, to bring this people to that climax of patriotic devotion beyond which there lies no greater height along this way. But this is also as far as the German people have gone; and it is scarcely to be claimed that the Japanese have yet reached this stage; they would rather appear to be, essentially, subjects of the emperor, and only inchoately a Japanese nation. Of the German people it seems safe to say that they have achieved such a coalescence of unimpaired feudal fealty to a personal master and a full-blown sense of national solidarity, without any perceptible slackening in either strand of the double tie which so binds them in the service of the dynastic State.

Germany, in other words, is somewhat in arrears, as compared with those Europeans that have gone farthest along this course of institutional growth, or perhaps rather institutional permutation. It is not that this retardation of the German people in this matter of national spirit is to be counted as an infirmity, assuredly not as a handicap in the pursuit of that national prestige on which all patriotic endeavour finally converges. For this purpose the failure to distinguish between the ambitions of the dynastic statesmen and the interests of the commonwealth is really a prodigious advantage, which their rivals, of more mature growth politically, have lost by atrophy of this same dynastic axiom of subservience. These others, of whom the French and the English-speaking peoples make up the greater part and may be taken as the typical instance, have had a different history, in part. The discipline of experience has left a somewhat different residue of habits of thought embedded in their institutional equipment and effective as axiomatic premises in their further apprehension of what is worth while, and why.

It is not that the difference between these two contrasted strains of the Western civilisation is either profound or very pronounced; it is perhaps rather to be stated as a difference of degree than of kind; a retardation of spiritual growth, in respect of the prevalent and controlling habits of thought on certain heads, in the one case as against the other. Therefore any attempt to speak with sufficient definition, so as to bring out this national difference of animus in any convincing way, will unavoidably have an appearance of overstatement, if not also of bias. And in any case, of course, it is not to be expected that the national difference here spoken for can be brought home to the apprehension of any unspoiled son of the Fatherland, since it does not lie within that perspective.

It is not of the nature of a divergence, but rather a differential in point of cultural maturity, due to a differential in the rate of progression through that sequence of institutional phases through which the civilised peoples of Europe, jointly and severally, have been led by force of circumstance. In this movement out of the Dark Ages and onward, circumstances have fallen out differently for those Europeans that chanced to live within the confines of the Fatherland, different with such effect as to have in the present placed these others at a farther remove from the point of departure, leaving them furnished with less of that archaic frame of mind that is here in question. Possessed of less, but by no means shorn of all--perhaps not of the major part--of that barbaric heritage.

Circumstances have so fallen out that these--typically the French and the English-speaking peoples--have left behind and partly forgotten that institutional phase in which the people of Imperial Germany now live and move and have their being. The French partly because they--that is the common people of the French lands--entered the procession with a very substantial lead, having never been put back to a point abreast of their neighbors across the Rhine, in that phase of European civilisation from which the peoples of the Fatherland tardily emerged into the feudal age. So, any student who shall set out to account for the visible lead which the French people still so obstinately maintain in the advance of European culture, will have to make up his account with this notable fact among the premises of his inquiry, that they have had a shorter course to cover and have therefore, in the sporting phrase, had the inside track. They measure from a higher datum line. Among the advantages which so have come, in a sense unearned, to the French people, is their uninterrupted retention, out of Roman--and perhaps pre-Roman--times, of the conception of a commonwealth, a community of men with joint and mutual interests apart from any superimposed dependence on a joint feudal superior. The French people therefore became a nation, with unobtrusive facility, so soon as circumstances permitted, and they are today the oldest "nation" in Europe. They therefore were prepared from long beforehand, with an adequate principle (habit of thought) of national cohesion and patriotic sentiment, to make the shift from a dynastic State to a national commonwealth whenever the occasion for such a move should arise; that is to say, whenever the dynastic State, by a suitable conjunction of infirmity and irksomeness, should pass the margin of tolerance in this people's outraged sense of national shame. The case of the German people in their latterday attitude toward dynastic vagaries may afford a term of comparison. These appear yet incapable of distinguishing between national shame and dynastic ambition.

By a different course and on lines more nearly parallel with the life-history of the German peoples, the English-speaking peoples have reached what is for the present purpose much the same ground as the French, in that they too have made the shift from the dynastic State to the national commonwealth. The British started late, but the discipline of servitude and unmitigated personal rule in their case was relatively brief and relatively ineffectual; that is to say, as compared with what their German cousins had to endure and to learn in the like connection. So that the British never learned the lesson of dynastic loyalty fully by heart; at least not the populace; whatever may be true for the privileged classes, the gentlemen, whose interests were on the side of privilege and irresponsible mastery. Here as in the French case it was the habits of thought of the common man, not of the class of gentlemen, that made the obsolescence of the dynastic State a foregone conclusion and an easy matter--as one speaks of easy achievement in respect of matters of that magnitude. It is now some two and a half centuries since this shift in the national point of view overtook the English-speaking community. Perhaps it would be unfair to say that that period, or that period plus what further time may yet have to be added, marks the interval by which German habits of thought in these premises are in arrears, but it is not easy to find secure ground for a different and more moderate appraisal.

The future, of course, is not to be measured in terms of the past, and the tempo of the present and of the calculable future is in many bearings very different from that which has ruled even in the recent historical past. But then, on the other hand, habituation always requires time; more particularly such habituation as is to take effect throughout a populous nation and is counted on to work a displacement of a comprehensive institutional system and of a people's outlook on life.

Germany is still a dynastic State. That is to say, its national establishment is, in effect, a self-appointed and irresponsible autocracy which holds the nation in usufruct, working through an appropriate bureaucratic organisation, and the people is imbued with that spirit of abnegation and devotion that is involved in their enthusiastically supporting a government of that character. Now, it is in the nature of a dynastic State to seek dominion, that being the whole of its nature. And a dynastic establishment which enjoys the unqualified usufruct of such resources as are placed at its disposal by the feudalistic loyalty of the German people runs no chance of keeping the peace, except on terms of the unconditional surrender of all those whom it may concern. No solemn engagement and no pious resolution has any weight in the balance against a cultural fatality of this magnitude.

*   *   *   *   *

This account of the derivation and current state of German nationalism will of course appear biased to anyone who has been in the habit of rating German Culture high in all its bearings, and to whom at the same time the ideals of peace and liberty appeal. Indeed, such a critic, gifted with the due modicum of asperity, might well be provoked to call it all a more or less ingenious diatribe of partisan malice. But it can be so construed only by those who see the question at issue as a point of invidious distinction between this German animus on the one hand and the corresponding frame of mind of the neighboring peoples on the other hand. There may also appear to the captious to be some air of deprecation about the characterisation here offered of the past history of political traffic within the confines of the Fatherland. All of which, of course, touches neither the veracity of the characterisation nor the purpose with which so ungrateful a line of analysis and exposition has been entered upon. It is to be regretted if facts that may flutter the emotions of one and another among the sensitive and unreflecting can not be drawn into such an inquiry without having their cogency discounted beforehand on account of the sentimental value imputed to them. Of course no offense is intended and no invidious comparison is aimed at.

Even if the point of it all were an invidious comparison it would immediately have to be admitted that the net showing in favor of these others, e.g., the French or the English-speaking peoples, is by no means so unreservedly to their credit as such a summary statement of the German case might seem to imply. As bearing on the chances of a peace contingent upon the temper of the contracting nationalities, it is by no means a foregone conclusion that such a peace compact would hold indefinitely even if it depended solely on the pacific animus of these others that have left the dynastic State behind. These others, in fact, are also not yet out of the woods. They may not have the same gift of gratuitous and irresponsible truculence as their German cousins, in the same alarming degree; but as was said in an earlier passage, they too are ready to fight on provocation. They are patriotic to a degree; indeed to such a degree that anything which visibly touches the national prestige will readily afford a *casus belli*. But it remains true that the popular temper among them is of the defensive order; perhaps of an unnecessarily enthusiastic defensive order, but after all in such a frame of mind as leaves them willing to let well enough alone, to live and let live.

And herein appears to lie the decisive difference between those peoples whose patriotic affections center about the fortunes of an impersonal commonwealth and those in whom is superadded a fervent aspiration for dynastic ascendency. The latter may be counted on to break the peace when a promising opportunity offers.

The contrast may be illustrated, though not so sharply as might be desirable, in the different temper shown by the British people in the Boer war on the one hand, as compared with the popularity of the French-Prussian war among the German people on the other hand. Both were aggressive wars, and both were substantially unprovoked. Diplomatically speaking, of course, sufficient provocation was found in either case, as how should it not? But in point of substantial provocation and of material inducement, both were about equally gratuitous. In either case the war could readily have been avoided without material detriment to the community and without perceptible lesion to the national honour. Both were "engineered" on grounds shamelessly manufactured *ad hoc* by interested parties; in the one case by a coterie of dynastic statesmen, in the other by a junta of commercial adventurers and imperialistic politicians. In neither case had the people any interest of gain or loss in the quarrel, except as it became a question of national prestige. But both the

German and the British community bore the burden and fought the campaign to a successful issue for those interested parties who had precipitated the quarrel. The British people at large, it is true, bore the burden; which comes near being all that can be said in the way of popular approval of this war, which political statesmen have since then rated as one of the most profitable enterprises in which the forces of the realm have been engaged. On the subject of this successful war the common man is still inclined to cover his uneasy sense of decency with a recital of extenuating circumstances. What parallels all this in the German case is an outbreak of patriotic abandon and an admirable spirit of unselfish sacrifice in furtherance of the dynastic prestige, an intoxication of patriotic blare culminating in the triumphant coronation at Versailles. Nor has the sober afterthought of the past forty-six years cast a perceptible shadow of doubt across the glorious memory of that patriotic debauch.

Such is the difference of animus between a body of patriotic citizens in a modern commonwealth on the one hand and the loyal subjects of a dynastic State on the other hand. There need be no reflections on the intrinsic merits of either. Seen in dispassionate perspective from outside the turmoil, there is not much to choose, in point of sane and self-respecting manhood, between the sluggish and shamefaced abettor of a sordid national crime, and a ranting patriot who glories in serving as cat's-paw to a syndicate of unscrupulous politicians bent on dominion for dominion's sake. But the question here is not as to the relative merits or the relative manhood contents of the two contrasted types of patriot. Doubtless both and either have manhood enough and to spare; at least, so they say. But the point in question is the simpler and nowise invidious one, as to the availability of both or either for the perpetuation of the world's peace under a compact of vigilant neutrality. Plainly the German frame of mind admits of no neutrality; the quest of dominion is not compatible with neutrality, and the substantial core of German national life is still the quest of dominion under dynastic tutelage. How it stands with the spirit that has repeatedly come in sight in the international relations of the British community is a question harder to answer.

It may be practicable to establish a peace of neutrals on the basis of such national spirit as prevails among these others--the French and English-speaking peoples, together with the minor nationalities that cluster about the North Sea--because their habitual attitude is that of neutrality, on the whole and with allowance for a bellicose minority in all these countries. By and large, these peoples have come to the tolerant attitude that finds expression in the maxim, Live and let live. But they are all and several sufficiently patriotic. It may, indeed, prove that they are more than sufficiently patriotic for the purposes of a neutral peace. They stand for peace, but it is "peace with honour;" which means, in more explicit terms, peace with undiminished national prestige. Now, national prestige is a very particular commodity, as has been set out in earlier passages of this inquiry; and a peace which is to be kept only on terms of a jealous maintenance of the national honour is likely to be in a somewhat precarious case. If, and when, the national honour is felt to require an enhanced national ascendancy, the case for a neutral peace immediately becomes critical. And the greater the number and diversity of pretensions and interests that are conceived to be bound up with the national honour, the more unstable will the resulting situation necessarily be.

The upshot of all this recital of considerations appears to be that a neutral peace compact may, or it may not, be practicable in the absence of such dynastic States as Germany and Japan; whereas it has no chance in the presence of these enterprising national establishments.

No one will be readier or more voluble in exclaiming against the falsity of such a discrimination as is here attempted, between the democratic and the dynastic nations of the modern world, than the spokesmen of these dynastic Powers. No one is more outspoken in professions of universal peace and catholic amity than these same spokesmen of the dynastic Powers; and nowhere is there more urgent need of such professions. Official and "inspired" professions are, of course, to be overlooked; at least, so charity would dictate. But there have, in the historic present, been many professions of this character made also by credible spokesmen of the German, and perhaps of the Japanese, people, and in all sincerity. By way of parenthesis it should be said that this is not intended to apply to expressions of conviction and intention that have come out of Germany these two years past (December 1916). Without questioning the credibility of these witnesses that have borne witness to the pacific and genial quality of national sentiment in the German people, it will yet be in place to recall the run of facts in the national life of Germany in this historical present and the position of these spokesmen in the German community.

* * * * *

The German nation is of a peculiar composition in respect of its social structure. So far as bears on the question in hand, it is made up of three distinctive constituent factors, or perhaps rather categories or conditions of men. The populace is of course the main category, and in the last resort always the main and decisive factor. Next in point of consequence as well as of numbers and initiative is the personnel of the control,--the ruling class, the administration, the official community, the hierarchy of civil and political servants, or whatever designation may best suit; the category comprises that pyramidal superstructure of privilege and control whereof the sovereign is the apex, and in whom, under any dynastic rule, is in effect vested the usufruct of the populace. These two classes or conditions of men, the one of which orders and the other obeys, make up the working structure of the nation, and they also between them embody the national life and carry forward the national work and aim. Intermediate between them, or rather beside them and overlapping the commissure, is a third category whose life articulates loosely with both the others at the same time that it still runs along in a semi-detached way. This slighter but more visible, and particularly more audible, category is made up of the "Intellectuals," as a late, and perhaps vulgar, designation would name them.

These are they who chiefly communicate with the world outside, and at the same time they do what is academically called thinking. They are in intellectual contact and communication with the world at large, in a contact of give and take, and they think and talk in and about those concepts that go in under the caption of the humanities in the world at large. The category is large enough to constitute an intellectual community, indeed a community of somewhat formidable magnitude, taken in absolute terms, although in percentages of the population at large their numbers will foot up to only an inconsiderable figure. Their contact with the superior class spoken of above is fairly close, being a contact, in the main, of service on the one side and of control on the other. With the populace their contact and communion is relatively slight, the give and take in the case being neither intimate nor far-reaching. More particularly is there a well-kept limit of moderation on any work of indoctrination or intellectual guidance which this class may carry down among the people at large, dictated and enforced by dynastic expediency. This category, of the Intellectuals, is sufficiently large to live its own life within itself, without drawing on the spiritual life of the community at large, and of sufficiently substantial quality to carry its own peculiar scheme of intellectual conventions and verities. Of the great and highly meritorious place and work of these Intellectuals in the scheme of German culture it is needless to speak. What is to the point is that they are the accredited spokesmen of the German nation in all its commonplace communication with the rest of civilised Europe.

The Intellectuals have spoken with conviction and sincerity of the spiritual state of the German people, but in so doing, and in so far as bears on the character of German nationalism, they have been in closer contact, intellectually and sympathetically, with the intellectual and spiritual life of civilised Europe at large than with the movements of the spirit among the German populace. And their canvassing of the concepts which so have come under their attention from over the national frontiers has been carried forward--so far, again, as bears on the questions that are here in point--with the German-dynastic principles, logic and mechanism of execution under their immediate observation and supplying the concrete materials for inquiry. Indeed, it holds true, by and large, that nothing else than this German-dynastic complement of ways and means has, or can effectually, come under their observation in such a degree of intimacy as to give body and definition to the somewhat abstract theorems on cultural aims and national preconceptions that have come to them from outside. In short, they have borrowed these theoretical formulations from abroad, without the concrete apparatus of ways and means in which these theorems are embodied in their foreign habitat, and have so found themselves construing these theoretical borrowings in the only concrete terms of which they have had first-hand and convincing knowledge. Such an outcome would be fairly unavoidable, inasmuch as these Intellectuals, however much they are, in the spirit, citizens of the cosmopolitan republic of knowledge and intelligence, they are after all, *in propria persona*, immediately and unremittingly subjects of the German-dynastic State; so that all their detail thinking on the aims, ways and means of life, in all its civil and political bearings, is unavoidably shaped by the unremitting discipline of their workday experience under this dynastic scheme. The outcome has been that while they have taken up, as they have understood them, the concepts that rule the civic life of these other, maturer nations, they have apprehended and developed these theorems of civic life in the terms and by the logic enforced in that system of control and surveillance known to them by workday experience,--the only empirical terms at hand.

The apex of growth and the center of diffusion as regards the modern culture in respect of the ideals and logic of civic life--other phases of this culture than this its civil aspect do not concern the point here in question--this apex of growth and center of diffusion lie outside the Fatherland, in an environment alien to the German institutional scheme. Yet so intrinsic to the cultural drift of modern mankind are these aims and this logic, that in taking over and further enriching the intellectual heritage of this modern world the Intellectuals of the Fatherland have unavoidably also taken over those conceptions of civil initiative and masterless self-direction that rule the logic of life in a commonwealth of ungraded men. They have taken these over and assimilated them as best their experience would permit. But workday experience and its exigencies are stubborn things; and in this process of assimilation of these alien conceptions of right and honest living, it is the borrowed theorems concerning civic rights and duties that have undergone adaptation and revision, not the concrete system of ways and means in which these principles, so accepted, are to be put in practice. Necessarily so, since in the German scheme of law and order the major premise is the dynastic State, whereas the major premise of the modern civilised scheme of civic life is the absence of such an organ. So, the development and elaboration of these modern principles of civic liberty--and this elaboration has taken on formidable dimensions--under the hand of the German Intellectuals has uniformly run out into Pickwickian convolutions, greatly suggestive of a lost soul seeking a place to rest. With unquestionably serious purpose and untiring endeavour, they have sought to embody these modern civilised preconceptions in terms afforded by, or in terms compatible with, the institutions of the Fatherland; and they have been much concerned and magniloquently elated about the German spirit of freedom that so was to be brought to final and consummate realisation in the life of a free people. But at no point and in no case have either the proposals or their carrying out taken shape as a concrete application of the familiar principle of popular self-direction. It has always come to something in the way of a concessive or expedient mitigation of the antagonistic principle of personal authority. Where the forms of self-government or of individual self-direction have concessively been installed, under the Imperial rule, they have turned out to be an imitative structure with some shrewd provision for their coercion or inhibition at the discretion of an irresponsible authority.

Neither the sound intelligence nor the good faith of these Intellectuals of the Fatherland is to be impugned. That the--necessarily vague and circumlocutory-- expositions of civic institutions and popular liberty which they have so often and so largely promulgated should have been used as a serviceable blind of dynastic statecraft is not to be set down to their discredit. Circumstances over which they could have no control, since they were circumstances that shaped their own habits of thought, have placed it beyond their competence to apprehend or to formulate these alien principles (habits of thought) concretely in those alien institutional details and by the alien logic with which they could have no working acquaintance.

To one and another this conception of cultural solidarity within the nation, and consequent cultural aliency between nations, due to the different habits of life and of thought enforced by the two diverse institutional systems, may be so far unfamiliar as to carry no conviction. It may accordingly not seem out of place to recall that the institutional system of any given community, particularly for any community living under a home-bred and time-tried system of its own, will necessarily be a balanced system of interdependent and mutually concordant parts working together in one comprehensive plan of law and order. Through such an institutional system, as, e.g., the German Imperial organisation, there will run a degree of logical consistency, consonant with itself throughout, and exerting a consistent discipline throughout the community; whereby there is enforced a consistent drift or bent in the prevalent habits of life, and a correlative bent in the resulting habits of thought prevalent in the community. It is, in fact, this possession of a common scheme of use and wont, and a consequent common outlook and manner of thinking, that constitutes the most intrinsic bond of solidarity in any nationality, and that finally marks it off from any other.

It is equally a matter of course that any other given community, living under the rule of a substantially different, or divergent, system of institutions, will be exposed to a course of workday discipline running to a different, perhaps divergent, effect; and that this other community will accordingly come in for a characteristically different discipline and fall under the rule of a different commonsense outlook. Where an institutional difference of this kind is somewhat large and consistent, so as to amount in effect to a discrepancy, as may fairly be said of the difference between Imperial Germany and its like on the one hand, and the English-speaking nations on the other hand, there the difference in everyday conceptions may readily make the two peoples mutually unintelligible to one another, on those points of institutional principle that are involved in the discrepancy. This is the state of the case as between the German people, including the Intellectuals, and the peoples against whom their preconceptions of national destiny have arrayed them. And the many vivid expressions of consternation, abhorrence and incredulity that have come out of this community of Intellectuals in the course of the past two years of trial and error, bear sufficient testimony to the rigorous constraint which these German preconceptions and their logic exercise over the Intellectuals, no less than over the populace.

Conversely, of course, it is nearly as impracticable for those who have grown up under the discipline of democratic institutions to comprehend the habitual outlook of the commonplace German patriot on national interests and aims; not quite, perhaps, because the discipline of use and wont and indoctrination is neither so rigorous nor so consistent in their case. But there is, after all, prevalent among them a sufficiently evident logical inability to understand and appreciate the paramount need of national, that is to say dynastic, ascendancy that actuates all German patriots; just as these same patriots are similarly unable to consider national interests in any other light than that of dynastic ascendancy.

Going simply on the face value of the available evidence, any outsider might easily fall into the error of believing that when the great adventure of the war opened up before them, as well as when presently the shock of baffled endeavour brought home its exasperating futility, the Intellectuals of the Fatherland distinguished themselves above all other classes and conditions of men in the exuberance of their patriotic abandon. Such a view would doubtless be almost wholly erroneous. It is not that the Intellectuals reached a substantially superior pitch of exaltation, but only that, being trained in the use of language, they were able to express their emotions with great facility. There seems no reason to believe that the populace fell short of the same measure in respect of their prevalent frame of mind.

To return to the workings of the Imperial dynastic State and the forces engaged. It plainly appears that the Intellectuals are to be counted as supernumeraries, except so far as they serve as an instrument of publicity and indoctrination in the hands of the discretionary authorities. The working factors in the case are the dynastic organisation of control, direction and emolument, and the populace at large by use of whose substance the traffic in dynastic ascendancy and emolument is carried on. These two are in fairly good accord, on the ancient basis of feudal loyalty. Hitherto there is no evident ground for believing that this archaic tie that binds the populace to the dynastic ambitions has at all perceptibly weakened. And the possibility of dynastic Germany living at peace with the world under any compact, therefore translates itself into the possibility of the German people's unlearning its habitual deference and loyalty to the dynasty.

As its acquirement has been a work of protracted habituation, so can its obsolescence also come about only through more or less protracted habituation under a system of use and wont of a different or divergent order. The elements of such a systematic discipline running to an effect at cross purposes with this patriotic animus are not absent from the current situation in the Fatherland; the discipline of the modern industrial system, for instance, runs to such a divergent effect; but this, and other conceivable forces which may reenforce it, will after all take time, if they are to work a decisive change in the current frame of mind of the patriotic German community. During the interval required for such a change in the national temper, the peace of the world would be conditioned on the inability of the dynastic State to break it. So that the chances of success for any neutral peace league will vary inversely as the available force of Imperial Germany, and it could be accounted secure only in the virtual elimination of the Imperial State as a national Power.

If the gradual obsolescence of the spirit of militant loyalty in the German people, through disuse under a regime of peace, industry, self government and free trade, is to be the agency by force of which dynastic imperialism is to cease, the chance of a neutral peace will depend on the thoroughness with which such a regime of self-direction can be installed in this case, and on the space of time required for such obsolescence through disuse. Obviously, the installation of a workable regime of self-government on peaceable lines would in any case be a matter of great difficulty among a people whose past experience has so singularly incapacitated them for self-government; and obviously, too, the interval of time required to reach secure ground along this line of approach would be very considerable. Also, in view of these conditions, obviously, this scheme for maintaining the peace of nations by a compact of neutrals based on a compromise with an aspiring dynastic State resolves itself into the second of the two alternatives spoken of at the outset, viz., a neutral peace based on the elimination of Germany as a war power, together with the elimination of any materials suitable for the formation of a formidable coalition. And then, with Imperial Germany supposedly eliminated or pacified, there would still remain the Japanese establishment, to which all the arguments pertinent in the case of Germany will apply without abatement; except that, at least hitherto, the dynastic statesmen of Japan have not had the disposal of so massive a body of resources, in population, industry, or raw materials.

CHAPTER IV
PEACE WITHOUT HONOUR

The argument therefore turns back to a choice between the two alternatives alluded to: peace in submission to the rule of the German dynastic establishment (and to Japan), or peace through elimination of these enterprising Powers. The former alternative, no doubt, is sufficiently unattractive, but it is not therefore to be put aside without a hearing. As goes without saying, it is repugnant to the patriotic sentiments of those peoples whom the Imperial German establishment have elected for submission. But if this unreflecting patriotic revulsion can once be made amenable to reason, there is always something to be said in favor of such a plan of peaceable submission, or at least in extenuation of it; and if it is kept in mind that the ulterior necessity of such submission must always remain in perspective as a condition precedent to a peaceful settlement, so long as one or both of these enterprising Powers remains intact, it will be seen that a sane appraisal of the merits of such a regime of peace is by no means uncalled for. For neither of these two Powers is there a conclusive issue of endeavour short of paramount dominion.

*   *   *   *   *

There should also be some gain of insight and sobriety in recalling that the Intellectuals of the Fatherland, who have doubtless pondered this matter longer and more dispassionately than all other men, have spoken very highly of the merits of such a plan of universal submission to the rule of this German dynastic establishment. They had, no doubt, been considering the question both long and earnestly, as to what would, in the light of reason, eventually be to the best interest of those peoples whose manifest destiny was eventual tutelage under the Imperial crown; and there need also be no doubt that in that time (two years past) they therefore spoke advisedly and out of the fulness of the heart on this head. The pronouncements that came out of the community of Intellectuals in that season of unembarrassed elation and artless avowal are doubtless to be taken as an outcome of much thoughtful canvassing of what had best be done, not as an enforced compromise with untoward necessities but as the salutary course freely to be pursued with an eye single to the best good of all concerned.

It is true, the captious have been led to speak slightingly of the many utterances of this tenure coming out of the community of Intellectuals, as, e.g., the lay sermons of Professor Ostwald dating back to that season; but no unprejudiced reader can well escape the persuasion that these, as well as the very considerable volume of similar pronouncements by many other men of eminent scholarship and notable for benevolent sentiments, are faithfully to be accepted as the expressions of a profound conviction and a consciously generous spirit. In so speaking of the advantages to be derived by any subject people from submission to the German Imperial rule, these Intellectuals are not to be construed as formulating the drift of vulgar patriotic sentiment among their compatriots at large, but rather as giving out the deliverances of their own more sensitive spirit and maturer deliberation, as men who are in a position to see human affairs and interests in a larger perspective. Such, no doubt, would be their own sense of the matter.

Reflection on the analogous case of the tutelage exercised by the American government over the subject Philippinos may contribute to a just and temperate view of what is intended in the regime of tutelage and submission so spoken for by the German Intellectuals,--and, it may be added, found good by the Imperial statesmen. There would, of course, be the difference, as against the case of the Philippinos, that whereas the American government is after all answerable, in the last resort and in a somewhat random fashion, to a popular opinion that runs on democratic preconceptions, the German Imperial establishment on the other hand is answerable to no one, except it be to God, who is conceived to stand in somewhat the relation of a silent partner, or a minority stockholder in this dynastic enterprise.

Yet it should not be overlooked that any presumptive hard usage which the vassal peoples might look for at the hands of the German dynasty would necessarily be tempered with considerations of expediency as dictated by the exigencies of usufruct. The Imperial establishment has shown itself to be wise, indeed more wise than amiable, but wise at least in its intentions, in the use which it has made of subject peoples hitherto. It is true, a somewhat accentuated eagerness on the part of the Imperial establishment to get the maximum service in a minimum of time and at a minimum cost from these subject populations,--as, e.g., in Silesia and Poland, in Schleswig-Holstein, in Alsace-Lorraine, or in its African and Oceanic possessions,--has at times led to practices altogether dubious on humanitarian grounds, at the same time that in point of thrifty management they have gone beyond "what the traffic will bear." Yet it is not to be overlooked--and in this connection it is a point of some weight--that, so far as the predatory traditions of its statecraft will permit, the Imperial establishment has in all these matters been guided by a singularly unreserved attention to its own material advantage. Where its management in these premises has yielded a less profitable usufruct than the circumstances would reasonably admit, the failure has been due to an excess of cupidity rather than the reverse.

The circumstantial evidence converges to the effect that the Imperial establishment may confidently be counted on to manage the affairs of its subject peoples with an eye single to its own material gain, and it may with equal confidence be counted on that in the long run no unadvised excesses will be practised. Of course, an excessive adventure in atrocity and predation, due to such human infirmity in its agents or in its directorate as has been shown in various recent episodes, is to be looked for now and again; but these phenomena would come in by way of fluctuating variations from the authentic routine, rather than as systematic features of it.

That superfluity of naughtiness that has given character to the current German Imperial policy in Belgium, e.g., or that similarly has characterised the dealings of Imperial Japan in Korea during the late "benevolent assimilation" of that people into Japanese-Imperial usufruct, is not fairly to be taken to indicate what such an Imperial establishment may be expected to do with a subject people on a footing of settled and long-term exploitation. At the outset, in both instances, the policy of frightfulness was dictated by a well-advised view to economy of effort in reducing the subject people to an abject state of intimidation, according to the art of war as set forth in the manuals; whereas latterly the somewhat profligate excesses of the government of occupation--decently covered with diplomatic parables on benevolence and legality--have been dictated by military convenience, particularly by the need of forced labor and the desirability of a reduced population in the acquired territory. So also the "personally conducted" dealings with the Armenians by use of the Turks should probably also best be explained as an endeavour to reduce the numbers of an undesirable population beforehand, without incurring unnecessary blame. All these things are, at the most, misleading indications of what the Imperial policy would be like under settled conditions and in the absence of insubordination.

By way of contrast, such as may serve to bring the specific traits of this prospective Imperial tutelage of nations into a better light, the Ottoman usufruct of the peoples of the Turkish dominions offers an instructive instance. The Ottoman tutelage is today spoken of by its apologists in terms substantially identical with the sketches of the future presented by hopeful German patriots in the early months of the current war. But as is so frequently the case in such circumstances, these expressions of the officers have to be understood in a diplomatic sense; not as touching the facts in any other than a formal way. It is sufficiently evident that the Ottoman management of its usufruct has throughout been ill-advised enough persistently to charge more than the traffic would bear, probably due in great part to lack of control over its agents or ramifications, by the central office. The Ottoman establishment has not observed, or enforced, the plain rules of economy in its utilisation of the subject peoples, and finds itself today bankrupt in consequence. What may afford more of a parallel to the prospective German tutelage of the nations is the procedure of the Japanese establishment in Korea, Manchuria, or China; which is also duly covered with an ostensibly decent screen of diplomatic parables, but the nature and purpose of which is overt enough in all respects but the nomenclature. It is not unlikely that even this Japanese usufruct and tutelage runs on somewhat less humane and complaisant lines than a well-advised economy of resources would dictate for the prospective German usufruct of the Western nations.

There is the essential difference between the two cases that while Japan is overpopulated, so that it becomes the part of a wise government to find additional lands for occupancy, and that so it is constrained by its imperial ambitions to displace much of the population in its subject territories, the Fatherland on the other hand is under-populated-- notoriously, though not according to the letter of the diplomatic parables on this head--and for the calculable future must continue to be under-populated; provided that the state of the industrial arts continues subject to change in the same general direction as hitherto, and provided that no radical change affects the German birth-rate. So, since the Imperial government has no need of new lands for occupancy by its home population, it will presumably be under no inducement to take measures looking to the partial depopulation of its subject territories.

The case of Belgium and the measures looking to a reduction of its population may raise a doubt, but probably not a well taken doubt. It is rather that since it has become evident that the territory can not be held, it is thought desirable to enrich the Fatherland with whatever property can be removed, and to consume the accumulated man-power of the Belgian people in the service of the war. It would appear that it is a war-measure, designed to make use of the enemy's resources for his defeat. Indeed, under conditions of settled occupation or subjection, any degree of such depopulation would entail an economic loss, and any well-considered administrative policy would therefore look to the maintenance of the inhabitants of the acquired territories in undiminished numbers and unimpaired serviceability.

The resulting scheme of Imperial usufruct should accordingly be of a considerate, not to say in effect humane, character,--always provided that the requisite degree of submission and subservience ("law and order") can be enforced by a system of coercion so humane as not to reduce the number of the inhabitants or materially to lower their physical powers. Such would, by reasonable expectation, be the character of this projected Imperial tutelage and usufruct of the nations of Christendom. In its working-out this German project should accordingly differ very appreciably from the policy which its imperial ambitions have constrained the Japanese establishment to pursue in its dealings with the life and fortunes of its recently, and currently, acquired subject peoples.

The better to appreciate in some concrete fashion what should, by reasonable expectation, be the terms on which life might so be carried on ***sub pace germanica***, attention may be invited to certain typical instances of such peace by abnegation among contemporary peoples. Perhaps at the top of the list stands India, with its many and varied native peoples, subject to British tutelage, but, the British apologists say, not subject to British usufruct. The margin of tolerance in this instance is fairly wide, but its limits are sharply drawn. India is wanted and held, not for tribute or revenue to be paid into the Imperial treasury, nor even for exclusive trade privileges or preferences, but mainly as a preserve to provide official occupation and emoluments for British gentlemen not otherwise occupied or provided for; and secondarily as a means of safeguarding lucrative British investments, that is to say, investments by British capitalists of high and low degree. The current British professions on the subject of this occupation of India, and at times the shamefaced apology for it, is that the people of India suffer no hardship by this means; the resulting governmental establishment being no more onerous and no more expensive to them than any equally, or even any less, competent government of their own would necessarily be. The fact, however, remains, that India affords a much needed and very considerable net revenue to the class of British gentlemen, in the shape of official salaries and pensions, which the British gentry at large can on no account forego. Narrowed to these proportions it is readily conceivable that the British usufruct of India should rest with no extraordinary weight on the Indian people at large, however burdensome it may at times become to those classes who aspire to take over the usufruct in case the British establishment can be dislodged. This case evidently differs very appreciably from the projected German usufruct of neighboring countries in Europe.

A case that may be more nearly in point would be that of any one of the countries subject to the Turkish rule in recent times; although these instances scarcely show just what to expect under the projected German regime. The Turkish rule has been notably inefficient, considered as a working system of dynastic usufruct; whereas it is confidently expected that the corresponding German system would show quite an exceptional degree of efficiency for the purpose. This Turkish inefficiency has had a two-fold effect, which should not appear in the German case. Through administrative abuses intended to serve the personal advantage of the irresponsible officials, the underlying peoples have suffered a progressive exhaustion and dilapidation; whereby the central authority, the dynastic establishment, has also grown progressively, cumulatively weaker and therefore less able to control its agents; and, in the second place, on the same grounds, in the pursuit of personal gain, and prompted by personal animosities, these irresponsible agents have persistently carried their measures of extortion beyond reasonable bounds,--that is to say beyond the bounds which a well considered plan of permanent usufruct would countenance. All this would be otherwise and more sensibly arranged under German Imperial auspices.

One of the nations that have fallen under Turkish rule--and Turkish peace--affords a valuable illustration of a secondary point that is to be considered in connection with any plan of peace by submission. The Armenian people have in later time come partly under Russian dominion, and so have been exposed to the Russian system of bureaucratic exploitation; and the difference between Russian and Turkish Armenia is instructive. According to all credible--that is unofficial--accounts, conditions are perceptibly more tolerable in Russian Armenia. Well informed persons relate that the cause for this more lenient, or less extreme, administration of affairs under Russian officials is a selective death rate among them, such that a local official who persistently exceeds a certain ill-defined limit of tolerance is removed by what would under other circumstances be called an untimely death. No adequate remedy has been found, within the large limits which Russian bureaucratic administration habitually allows itself in questions of coercion. The Turk, on the other hand, less deterred by considerations of long-term expediency, and, it may be, less easily influenced by outside opinion on any point of humanity, has found a remedy in the systematic extirpation of any village in which an illicit death occurs. One will incline to presume that on this head the German Imperial procedure would be more after the Russian than after the Turkish pattern; although latterday circumstantial evidence will throw some sinister doubt on the reasonableness of such an expectation.

It is plain, however, that the Turkish remedy for this form of insubordination is a wasteful means of keeping the peace. Plainly, to the home office, the High Command, the extinction of a village with its population is a more substantial loss than the unseasonable decease of one of its administrative agents; particularly when it is called to mind that such a decease will presumably follow only on such profligate excesses of naughtiness as are bound to be inexcusably unprofitable to the central authority. It may be left an open question how far a corrective of this nature can hopefully be looked to as applicable, in case of need, under the projected German Imperial usufruct.

It may, I apprehend, be said without offense that there is no depth of depravity below the ordinary reach of the Russian bureaucracy; but this organisation finds itself constrained, after all, to use circumspection and set some limits on individual excursions beyond the bounds of decency and humanity, so soon as these excesses touch the common or joint interest of the organisation. Any excess of atrocity, beyond a certain margin of tolerance, on the part of any one of its members is likely to work pecuniary mischief to the rest; and then, the bureaucratic conduct of affairs is also, after all, in an uncertain degree subject to some surveillance by popular sentiment at home or abroad. The like appears not to hold true of the Turkish official organisation. The difference may be due to a less provident spirit among the latter, as already indicated. But a different tradition, perhaps an outgrowth of this lack of providence and of the consequent growth of a policy of "frightfulness," may also come in for a share in the outcome; and there is also a characteristic difference in point of religious convictions, which may go some way in the same direction. The followers of Islam appear on the whole to take the tenets of their faith at their face value--servile, intolerant and fanatic--whereas the Russian official class may perhaps without undue reproach be considered to have on the whole outlived the superstitious conceits to which they yield an expedient ***pro forma*** observance. So that when worse comes to worst, and the Turk finds himself at length with his back against the last consolations of the faith that makes all things straight, he has the assured knowledge that he is in the right as against the unbelievers; whereas the Russian bureaucrat in a like case only knows that he is in the wrong. The last extremity is a less conclusive argument to the man in whose apprehension it is not the last extremity. Again, there is some shadow of doubt falls on the question as to which of these is more nearly in the German Imperial spirit.

On the whole, the case of China is more to the point. By and large, the people of China, more particularly the people of the coastal-plains region, have for long habitually lived under a regime of peace by non-resistance. The peace has been broken transiently from time to time, and local disturbances have not been infrequent; but, taken by and large, the situation has habitually been of the peaceful order, on a ground of non-resisting submission. But this submission has not commonly been of a whole-hearted kind, and it has also commonly been associated with a degree of persistent sabotage; which has clogged and retarded the administration of governmental law and order, and has also been conducive to a large measure of irresponsible official corruption. The habitual scheme of things Chinese in this bearing may fairly be described as a peace of non-resistance tempered with sabotage and assassination. Such was the late Manchu regime, and there is no reason in China for expecting a substantially different outcome from the Japanese invasion that is now under way. The nature of this Japanese incursion should be sufficiently plain. It is an enterprise in statecraft after the order of Macchiavelli, Metternich, and Bismarck. Of course, the conciliatory fables given out by the diplomatic service, and by the other apologists, are to be taken at the normal discount of one-hundred percent. The relatively large current output of such fables may afford a hint as to the magnitude of the designs which the fables are intended to cover.

The Chinese people have had a more extended experience in peace of this order than all others, and their case should accordingly be instructive beyond all others. Not that a European peace by non-resistance need be expected to run very closely on the Chinese lines, but there should be a reasonable expectation that the large course of things would be somewhat on the same order in both cases. Neither the European traditions and habitual temperament nor the modern state of the industrial arts will permit one to look for anything like a close parallel in detail; but it remains true, when all is said, that the Chinese experience of peace under submission to alien masters affords the most instructive illustration of such a regime, as touches its practicability, its methods, its cultural value, and its effect on the fortunes of the subject peoples and of their masters.

Now, it may be said by way of preliminary generalisation that the life-history of the Chinese people and their culture is altogether the most imposing achievement which the records of mankind have to show; whereas the history of their successive alien establishments of mastery and usufruct is an unbroken sequence of incredibly shameful episodes,--always beginning in unbounded power and vainglory, running by way of misrule, waste and debauchery, to an inglorious finish in abject corruption and imbecility. Always have the gains in civilisation, industry and in the arts, been made by the subject Chinese, and always have their alien masters contributed nothing to the outcome but misrule, waste, corruption and decay. And yet in the long run, with all this handicap and misrule, the Chinese people have held their place and made headway in those things to which men look with affection and esteem when they come to take stock of what things are worth while. It would be a hopeless task to count up how many dynasties of masterful barbarians, here and there, have meanwhile come up and played their ephemeral role of vainglorious nuisance and gone under in shame and confusion, and dismissed with the invariable verdict of "Good Riddance!"

It may at first sight seem a singular conjuncture of circumstances, but it is doubtless a consequence of the same conjuncture, that the Chinese people have also kept their hold through all history on the Chinese lands. They have lived and multiplied and continued to occupy the land, while their successive alien masters have come and gone. So that today, as the outcome of conquest, and of what would be rated as defeat, the people continue to be Chinese, with an unbroken pedigree as well as an unbroken line of home-bred culture running through all the ages of history. In the biological respect the Chinese plan of non-resistance has proved eminently successful.

And, by the way, much the same, though not in the same degree, is true for the Armenian people; who have continued to hold their hill country through good days and evil, apparently without serious or enduring reduction of their numbers and without visible lapse into barbarism, while the successive disconnected dynasties of their conquering rulers have come and gone, leaving nothing but an ill name. "This fable teaches" that a diligent attention to the growing of crops and children is the sure and appointed way to the maintenance of a people and its culture even under the most adverse conditions, and that eventual death and shameful destruction inexorably wait on any "ruling race." Hitherto the rule has not failed. The rule, indeed, is grounded in the heritable traits of human nature, from which there is no escape.

For its long-term biological success, as well as for the continued integrity of a people's culture, a peace of non-resistance, under good or evil auspices, is more to be desired than imperial dominion. But these things are not all that modern peoples live for, perhaps it is safe to say that in no case are these chief among the things for which civilised Europeans are willing to live. They urgently need also freedom to live their own life in their own way, or rather to live within the bonds of convention which they have come in for by use and wont, or at least they believe that such freedom is essential to any life that shall be quite worth while. So also they have a felt need of security from arbitrary interference in their pursuit of a livelihood and in the free control of their own pecuniary concerns. And they want a discretionary voice in the management of their joint interests, whether as a nation or in a minor civil group. In short, they want personal, pecuniary and political liberty, free from all direction or inhibition from without. They are also much concerned to maintain favorable economic conditions for themselves and their children. And last, but chiefly rather than least, they commonly are hide-bound patriots inspired with an intractable felt need of national prestige.

It is an assemblage of peoples in such a frame of mind to whom the pacifists are proposing, in effect, a plan for eventual submission to an alien dynasty, under the form of a neutral peace compact to include the warlike Powers. There is little likelihood of such a scheme being found acceptable, with popular sentiment running as it now does in the countries concerned. And yet, if the brittle temper in which any such proposal is rejected by popular opinion in these countries today could be made to yield sufficiently to reflection and deliberate appraisal, it is by no means a foregone conclusion that its acceptance would not be the best way out of a critical situation. The cost of disabling and eliminating the warlike Power whose dominion is feared, or even of staving off the day of surrender, is evidently serious enough. The merits of the alternative should be open to argument, and should, indeed, be allowed due consideration. And any endeavour to present them without heat should presumably find a hearing. It appears to have been much of the fault of the pacifists who speak for the Peace League that they have failed or refused to recognise these ulterior consequences of the plan which they advocate; so that they appear either not to know what they are talking about, or to avoid talking about what they know.

It will be evident from beforehand that the grave difficulty to be met in any advocacy of peace on terms of non-resistant subjection to an alien dynastic rule--"peace at any price"--is a difficulty of the psychological order. Whatever may be conceived to hold true for the Chinese people, such submission is repugnant to the sentiments of the Western peoples. Which in turn evidently is due to the prevalence of certain habitual preconceptions among modern civilised men,--certain acquired traits of temper and bias, of the nature of fixed ideas. That something in the way of a reasonably contented and useful life is possible under such a regime as is held in prospect, and even some tolerable degree of well-being, is made evident in the Chinese case. But the Chinese tolerance of such a regime goes to argue that they are charged with fewer preconceptions at variance with the exigencies of life under these conditions. So, it is commonly accepted, and presumably to be accepted, that the Chinese people at large have little if any effectual sense of nationality; their patriotism appears to be nearly a negligible quantity. This would appear to an outsider to have been their besetting weakness, to which their successful subjection by various and sundry ambitious aliens has been due. But it appears also to have been the infirmity by grace of which this people have been obliged to learn the ways of submission, and so have had the fortune to outlive their alien masters, all and sundry, and to occupy the land and save the uncontaminated integrity of their long-lived civilisation.

* * * * *

Some account of the nature and uses of this spirit of patriotism that is held of so great account among Western nations has already been set out in an earlier passage. One or two points in the case, that bear on the argument here, may profitably be recalled. The patriotic spirit, or the tie of nationalism, is evidently of the nature of habit, whatever proclivity to the formation of such a habit may be native to mankind. More particularly is it a matter of habit--it might even be called a matter of fortuitous habit--what particular national establishment a given human subject will become attached to on reaching what is called "years of discretion" and so becoming a patriotic citizen.

The analogy of the clam may not be convincing, but it may at least serve to suggest what may be the share played by habituation in the matter of national attachment. The young clam, after having passed the free-swimming phase of his life, as well as the period of attachment to the person of a carp or similar fish, drops to the bottom and attaches himself loosely in the place and station in life to which he has been led; and he loyally sticks to his particular patch of ooze and sand through good fortune and evil. It is, under Providence, something of a fortuitous matter where the given clam shall find a resting place for the sole of his foot, but it is also, after all, "his own, his native land" etc. It lies in the nature of a clam to attach himself after this fashion, loosely, to the bottom where he finds a living, and he would not be a "good clam and true" if he failed to do so; but the particular spot for which he forms this attachment is not of the essence of the case. At least, so they say.

It may be, as good men appear to believe or know, that all men of sound, or at least those of average, mind will necessarily be of a patriotic temper and be attached by ties of loyalty to some particular national establishment, ordinarily the particular establishment which is formally identified with the land in which they live; although it is always possible that a given individual may be an alien in the land, and so may owe allegiance to and be ruled by a patriotic attachment to another national establishment, to which the conventionalities governing his special case have assigned him as his own proper nation. The analogy of the clam evidently does not cover the case. The patriotic citizen is attached to his own proper nationality not altogether by the accident of domicile, but rather by the conventions, legal or customary, which assign him to this or that national establishment according to certain principles of use and wont.

Mere legal citizenship or allegiance does not decide the matter either; at least not by any means unavoidably; as appears in the case of the Chinese subject under Manchu or Japanese rule; and as appears perhaps more perspicuously in the case of the "hyphenate" American citizen, whose formal allegiance is to the nation in whose land he prefers to live, all the while that his patriotic affection centers on his spiritual Fatherland in whose fortunes he has none but a non-resident interest. Indeed, the particular national tie that will bind the affections--that is to say the effectual patriotic attachment--of any given individual may turn out on closer scrutiny to be neither that of domicile or of formal legal allegiance, nor that of putative origin or pedigree, but only a reflex of certain national animosities; which may also turn out on examination to rest on putative grounds--as illustrated by a subsidiary class of hyphenate American citizens whose affections have come to be bound up in the national fortunes of one foreign Power for the simple, but sufficient, reason that, on conventional grounds, they bear malice against another equally foreign Power.

Evidently there is much sophistication, not to say conventionalised affectation, in all this national attachment and allegiance. It will perhaps not do to say that it is altogether a matter of sophistication. Yet it may not exceed the premises to say that the particular choice, the concrete incidence, of this national attachment is in any given case a matter of sophistication, largely tempered with fortuity. One is born into a given nationality--or, in case of dynastic allegiance, into service and devotion to a (fortuitously) given sovereign--or at least so it is commonly believed. Still one can without blame, and without excessive shame, shift one's allegiance on occasion. What is not countenanced among civilised men is to shift out of allegiance to any given nationality or dynasty without shifting into the like complication of gainless obligations somewhere else. Such a shifting of national or dynastic base is not quite reputable, though it is also not precisely disreputable. The difficulty in the case appears to be a moral difficulty, not a mental or a pecuniary one, and assuredly not a physical difficulty, since the relation in question is not a physical relation. It would appear to be of the moral order of things, in that sense of the term in which conventional proprieties are spoken of as moral. That is to say, it is a question of conforming to current expectations under a code of conventional proprieties. Like much of the conventional code of behavior this patriotic attachment has the benefit of standardised decorum, and its outward manifestations are enjoined by law. All of which goes to show how very seriously the whole matter is regarded.

And yet it is also a matter of common notoriety that large aggregates of men, not to speak of sporadic individuals, will on occasion shift their allegiance with the most felicitous effect and with no sensible loss of self-respect or of their good name. Such a shift is to be seen in multiple in the German nation within the past half-century, when, for instance, the Hanoverians, the Saxons, and even the Holsteiners in very appreciable numbers, not to mention the subjects of minuscular principalities whose names have been forgotten in the shuffle, all became good and loyal subjects of the Empire and of the Imperial dynasty,--good and loyal without reservation, as has abundantly appeared. So likewise within a similar period the inhabitants of the Southern States repudiated their allegiance to the Union, putting in its place an equivalent loyalty to their new-made country; and then, when the new national establishment slipped out from under their feet they returned as whole-heartedly as need be to their earlier allegiance. In each of these moves, taken with deliberation, it is not to be doubted that this body of citizens have been moved by an unimpeachable spirit of patriotic honour. No one who is in any degree conversant with the facts is likely to question the declaration that it would be a perversion, not to say an inversion, of fact to rate their patriotic devotion to the Union today lower than that of any other section of the country or any other class or condition of men.

But there is more, and in a sense worse, to be found along the same general line of evidence touching this sublimated sentiment of group solidarity that is called nationalism. The nation, of course, is large; the larger the better, it is believed. It is so large, indeed, that considered as a group or community of men living together it has no sensible degree of homogeneity in any of their material circumstances or interests; nor is anything more than an inconsiderable fraction of the aggregate population, territory, industry, or daily life known to any one of these patriotic citizens except by remote and highly dubious hearsay. The one secure point on which there is a (constructive) uniformity is the matter of national allegiance; which grows stronger and more confident with every increase in aggregate mass and volume. It is also not doubtful, e.g., that if the people of the British Dominions in North America should choose to throw in their national lot with the Union, all sections and classes, except those whose pecuniary interest in a protective tariff might be conceived to suffer, would presently welcome them; nor is it doubtful that American nationality would cover the new and larger aggregate as readily as the old. Much the same will hold true with respect to the other countries colonised under British auspices. And there is no conclusive reason for drawing the limit of admissible national extension at that point.

So much, however, is fairly within the possibilities of the calculable future; its realisation would turn in great measure on the discontinuance of certain outworn or disserviceable institutional arrangements; as, e.g., the remnants of a decayed monarchy, and the legally protected vested interests of certain business enterprises and of certain office-holding classes. What more and farther might practically be undertaken in this way, in the absence of marplot office-holders, office-seekers, sovereigns, priests and monopolistic business concerns sheltered under national animosities and restraints of trade, would be something not easy to assign a limit to. All the minor neutrals, that cluster about the North Sea, could unquestionably be drawn into such a composite nationality, in the absence, or with due disregard, of those classes, families and individuals whose pecuniary or invidious gain is dependent on or furthered by the existing division of these peoples.

The projected defensive league of neutrals is, in effect, an inchoate coalescence of the kind. Its purpose is the safeguarding of the common peace and freedom, which is also the avowed purpose and justification of all those modern nations that have outlived the regime of dynastic ambition and so of enterprise in dominion for dominion's sake, and have passed into the neutral phase of nationality; or it should perhaps rather be said that such is the end of endeavour and the warrant of existence and power for these modern national establishments in so far as they have outlived and repudiated such ambitions of a dynastic or a quasi-dynastic order, and so have taken their place as intrinsically neutral commonwealths.

It is only in the common defense (or in the defense of the like conditions of life for their fellowmen elsewhere) that the citizens of such a commonwealth can without shame entertain or put in evidence a spirit of patriotic solidarity; and it is only by specious and sophistical appeal to the national honour--a conceit surviving out of the dynastic past--that the populace of such a commonwealth can be stirred to anything beyond a defense of their own proper liberties or the liberties of likeminded men elsewhere, in so far as they are not still imbued with something of the dynastic animus and the chauvinistic animosities which they have formally repudiated in repudiating the feudalistic principles of the dynastic State.

The "nation," without the bond of dynastic loyalty, is after all a make-shift idea, an episodic half-way station in the sequence, and loyalty, in any proper sense, to the nation as such is so much of a make-believe, that in the absence of a common defense to be safeguarded any such patriotic conceit must lose popular assurance and, with the passing of generations, fall insensibly into abeyance as an archaic affection. The pressure of danger from without is necessary to keep the national spirit alert and stubborn, in case the pressure from within, that comes of dynastic usufruct working for dominion, has been withdrawn. With further extension of the national boundaries, such that the danger of gratuitous infraction from without grows constantly less menacing, while the traditional regime of international animosities falls more and more remotely into the background, the spirit of nationalism is fairly on the way to obsolescence through disuse. In other words, the nation, as a commonwealth, being a partisan organisation for a defensive purpose, becomes *functa officio* in respect of its nationalism and its patriotic ties in somewhat the same measure as the national coalition grows to such a size that partisanship is displaced by a cosmopolitan security.

Doubtless the falling into abeyance through disuse of so pleasing a virtue as patriotic devotion will seem an impossibly distasteful consummation; and about tastes there is no disputing, but tastes are mainly creations of habit. Except for the disquieting name of the thing, there is today little stands in the way of a cosmopolitan order of human intercourse unobtrusively displacing national allegiance; except for vested interests in national offices and international discriminations, and except for those peoples among whom national life still is sufficiently bound up with dynastic ambition.

In an earlier passage the patriotic spirit has been defined as a sense of partisan solidarity in point of prestige, and sufficient argument has been spent in confirming the definition and showing its implications. With the passing of all occasion for a partisan spirit as touches the common good, through coalescence of the parts between which partisan discrepancies have hitherto been kept up, there would also have passed all legitimate occasion for or provocation to an intoxication of invidious prestige on national lines,--and there is no prestige that is not of an invidious nature, that being, indeed, the whole of its nature. He would have to be a person of praeternatural patriotic sensibilities who could fall into an emotional state by reason of the national prestige of such a coalition commonwealth as would be made up, e.g., of the French and English-speaking peoples, together with those other neutrally and peaceably inclined European communities that are of a sufficiently mature order to have abjured dynastic ambitions of dominion, and perhaps including the Chinese people as well. Such a coalition may now fairly be said to be within speaking distance, and with its consummation, even in the inchoate shape of a defensive league of neutrals, the eventual abeyance of that national allegiance and national honour that bulks so large in the repertory of current eloquence would also come in prospect.

All this is by no means saying that love of country, and of use and wont as it runs in one's home area and among one's own people, would suffer decay, or even abatement. The provocation to nostalgia would presumably be as good as ever. It is even conceivable that under such a (contemplated) regime of unconditional security, attachment to one's own habitat and social circumstances might grow to something more than is commonly seen in the precarious situation in which the chances of a quiet life are placed today. But nostalgia is not a bellicose distemper, nor does it make for gratuitous disturbance of peaceable alien peoples; neither is it the spirit in which men lend themselves to warlike enterprise looking to profitless dominion abroad. Men make patriotic sacrifices of life and substance in spite of home-sickness rather than by virtue of it.

* * * * *

The aim of this long digression has been to show that patriotism, of that bellicose kind that seeks satisfaction in inflicting damage and discomfort on the people of other nations, is not of the essence of human life; that it is of the nature of habit, induced by circumstances in the past and handed on by tradition and institutional arrangements into the present; and that men can, without mutilation, divest themselves of it, or perhaps rather be divested of it by force of circumstances which will set the current of habituation the contrary way.

The change of habituation necessary to bring about such a decay of the bellicose national spirit would appear to be of a negative order, at least in the main. It would be an habituation to unconditional peace and security; in other words, to the absence of provocation, rather than a coercive training away from the bellicose temper. This bellicose temper, as it affects men collectively, appears to be an acquired trait; and it should logically disappear in time in the absence of those conditions by impact of which it has been acquired. Such obsolescence of patriotism, however, would not therefore come about abruptly or swiftly, since the patriotic spirit has by past use and wont, and by past indoctrination, been so thoroughly worked into the texture of the institutional fabric and into the commonsense taste and morality, that its effectual obsolescence will involve a somewhat comprehensive displacement and mutation throughout the range of institutions and popular conceits that have been handed down. And institutional changes take time, being creations of habit. Yet, again, there is the qualification to this last, that since the change in question appears to be a matter, not of acquiring a habit and confirming it in the shape of an article of general use and wont, but of forgetting what once was learned, the time and experience to be allowed for its decay need logically not equal that required for its acquirement, either in point of duration or in point of the strictness of discipline necessary to inculcate it.

While the spirit of nationalism is such an acquired trait, and while it should therefore follow that the chief agency in divesting men of it must be disuse of the discipline out of which it has arisen, yet a positive, and even something of a drastic discipline to the contrary effect need not be altogether ineffectual in bringing about its obsolescence. The case of the Chinese people seems to argue something of the sort. Not that the Chinese are simply and neutrally unpatriotic; they appear also to be well charged with disloyalty to their alien rulers. But along with a sense of being on the defensive in their common concerns, there is also the fact that they appear not to be appreciably patriotic in the proper sense; they are not greatly moved by a spirit of nationality. And this failure of the national spirit among them can scarcely be set down to a neutral disuse of that discipline which has on the other hand induced a militant nationalism in the peoples of Christendom; it should seem more probable, at least, that this relative absence of a national ambition is traceable in good part to its having been positively bred out of them by the stern repression of all such aspirations under the autocratic rule of their alien masters.

* * * * *

Peace on terms of submission and non-resistance to the ordinary exactions and rulings of those Imperial authorities to whom such submission may become necessary, then, will be contingent on the virtual abeyance of the spirit of national pride in the peoples who so are to come under Imperial rule. A sufficient, by no means necessarily a total, elimination or decadence of this proclivity will be the condition precedent of any practicable scheme for a general peace on this footing. How large an allowance of such animus these prospectively subject peoples might still carry, without thereby assuring the defeat of any such plan, would in great measure depend on the degree of clemency or rigor with which the superior authority might enforce its rule. It is not that a peace plan of this nature need precisely be considered to fall outside the limits of possibility, on account of this necessary condition, but it is at the best a manifestly doubtful matter. Advocates of a negotiated peace should not fail to keep in mind and make public that the plan which they advocate carries with it, as a sequel or secondary phase, such an unconditional surrender and a consequent regime of non-resistance, and that there still is grave doubt whether the peoples of these Western nations are at present in a sufficiently tolerant frame of mind, or can in the calculable future come in for such a tolerantly neutral attitude in point of national pride, as to submit in any passable fashion to any alien Imperial rule.

If the spiritual difficulty presented by this prevalent spirit of national pride--sufficiently stubborn still, however inane a conceit it may seem on sober reflection--if this animus of factional insubordination could be overcome or in some passable measure be conciliated or abated, there is much to be said in favor of such a plan of peaceable submission to an extraneous and arbitrary authority, and therefore also for that plan of negotiated peace by means of which events would be put in train for its realisation.

Any passably dispassionate consideration of the projected regime will come unavoidably to the conclusion that the prospectively subject peoples should have no legitimate apprehension of loss or disadvantage in the material respect. It is, of course, easy for an unreflecting person to jump to the conclusion that subjection to an alien power must bring grievous burdens, in the way of taxes and similar impositions. But reflection will immediately show that no appreciable increase, over the economic burdens already carried by the populace under their several national establishments, could come of such a move.

As bearing on this question it is well to call to mind that the contemplated imperial dominion is designed to be very wide-reaching and with very ample powers. Its nearest historical analogue, of course, is the Roman imperial dominion--in the days of the Antonines--and that the nearest analogue to the projected German peace is the Roman peace, in the days of its best security. There is every warrant for the presumption that the contemplated Imperial dominion is to be substantially all-inclusive. Indeed there is no stopping place for the projected enterprise short of an all-inclusive dominion. And there will consequently be no really menacing outside power to be provided against. Consequently there will be but little provision necessary for the common defense, as compared, e.g., with the aggregate of such provision found necessary for self-defense on the part of the existing nations acting in severalty and each jealously guarding its own national integrity. Indeed, compared with the burden of competitive armament to which the peoples of Europe have been accustomed, the need of any armed force under the new regime should be an inconsiderable matter, even when there is added to the necessary modicum of defensive preparation the more imperative and weightier provision of force with which to keep the peace at home.

Into the composition of this necessary modicum of armed force slight if any contingents of men would be drawn from the subject peoples, for the reason that no great numbers would be needed; as also because no devoted loyalty to the dynasty could reasonably be looked for among them, even if no positive insecurity were felt to be involved in their employment. On this head the projected scheme unambiguously commends itself as a measure of economy, both in respect of the pecuniary burdens demanded and as regards the personal annoyance of military service.

As a further count, it is to be presumed that the burden of the Imperial government and its bureaucratic administration--what would be called the cost of maintenance and repairs of the dynastic establishment and its apparatus of control--would be borne by the subject peoples. Here again one is warranted in looking for a substantial economy to be effected by such a centralised authority, and a consequent lighter aggregate burden on the subjects. Doubtless, the "overhead charges" would not be reduced to their practicable minimum. Such a governmental establishment, with its bureaucratic personnel, its "civil list" and its privileged classes, would not be conducted on anything like a parsimonious footing. There is no reason to apprehend any touch of modesty in the exactions of such a dynastic establishment for itself or in behalf of its underlying hierarchy of gentlefolk.

There is also to be counted in, in the concrete instance on which the argument here turns, a more or less considerable burden of contributions toward the maintenance and augmentation of that culture that has been the topic of so many encomiums. At this point it should be recalled that it is the pattern of Periclean Athens that is continually in mind in these encomiums. Which brings up, in this immediate connection, the dealings of Periclean Athens with the funds of the League, and the source as well as the destination of these surplus funds. Out of it all came the works on the Acropolis, together with much else of intellectual and artistic life that converged upon and radiated from this Athenian center of culture. The vista of ***Denkmaeler*** that so opens to the vision of a courageous fancy is in itself such a substance of things hoped for as should stir the heart of all humane persons.[8] The

---

8 *Denk 'mall*

cost of this subvention of Culture would doubtless be appreciable, but those grave men who have spent most thought on this prospective cultural gain to be had from the projected Imperial rule appear to entertain no doubt as to its being worth all that it would cost.

Any one who is inclined to rate the prospective pecuniary costs and losses high would doubtless be able to find various and sundry items of minor importance to add to this short list of general categories on the side of cost; but such additional items, not fairly to be included under these general captions, would after all be of minor importance, in the aggregate or in detail, and would not appreciably affect the grand balance of pecuniary profit and loss to be taken account of in any appraisal of the projected Imperial regime. There should evidently be little ground to apprehend that its installation would entail a net loss or a net increase of pecuniary burdens. There is, of course, the ill-defined and scarcely definable item of expenditure under the general head of Gentility, Dignity, Distinction, Magnificence, or whatever term may seem suitable to designate that consumption of goods and services that goes to maintain the high repute of the Court and to keep the underlying gentlefolk in countenance. In its pecuniary incidence this line of (necessary) expenditure belongs under the rubric of Conspicuous Waste; and one will always have to face the disquieting flexibility of this item of expenditure. The consumptive demand of this kind is in an eminent degree "indefinitely extensible," as the phrasing of the economists would have it, and as various historical instances of courtly splendor and fashionable magnificence will abundantly substantiate. There is a constant proclivity to advance this conventional "standard of living" to the limit set by the available means; and yet these conventional necessities will ordinarily not, in the aggregate, take up all the available means; although now and again, as under the ***Ancien Regime***, and perhaps in Imperial Rome, the standard of splendid living may also exceed the current means in hand and lead to impoverishment of the underlying community.

An analysis of the circumstances governing this flexibility of the conventional standard of living and of pecuniary magnificence can not be gone into here. In the case under consideration it will have to be left as an indeterminate but considerable item in the burden of cost which the projected Imperial rule may be counted on to impose on the underlying peoples. The cost of the Imperial court, nobility, and civil service, therefore, would be a matter of estimate, on which no close agreement would be expected; and yet, here as in an earlier connection, it seems a reasonable expectation that sufficient dignity and magnificence could be put in evidence by such a large-scale establishment at a lower aggregate cost than the aggregate of expenditures previously incurred for the like ends by various nations working in severalty and at cross purposes.

Doubtless it would be altogether a mistaken view of this production of dignity by means of a lavish expenditure on superfluities, to believe that the same principle of economy should apply here as was found applicable in the matter of armament for defense. With the installation of a collective national establishment, to include substantially all the previously competing nations, the need of defensive armament should in all reason decline to something very inconsiderable indeed. But it would be hasty to conclude that with the coalescence of these nations under one paramount control the need of creating notoriety and prestige for this resulting central establishment by the consumption of decorative superfluities would likewise decline. The need of such dignity and magnificence is only in part, perhaps a minor part, of a defensive character. For the greater part, no doubt, the motive to this conspicuously wasteful consumption is personal vanity, in Imperial policy as well as in the private life of fashion,--or perhaps one should more deferentially say that it is a certain range of considerations which would be identified as personal vanity in case they were met with among men beneath the Imperial level. And so far as the creation of this form of "good-will" by this manner of advertising is traceable to such, or equivalent, motives of a personal incidence, the provocation to economy along this line would presumably not be a notable factor in the case. And one returns perforce to the principle already spoken of above, that the consumptive need of superfluities is indefinitely extensible, with the resulting inference that nothing conclusive is to be said as to the prospective magnitude of this item in the Imperial bill of expense, or of the consequent pecuniary burdens which it would impose on the underlying peoples.

* * * * *

So far the argument has run on the pecuniary incidence of this projected Imperial dominion as it falls on the underlying community as a whole, with no attempt to discriminate between the divergent interests of the different classes and conditions of men that go to make up any modern community. The question in hand is a question of pecuniary burdens, and therefore of the pecuniary interests of these several distinguishable classes or conditions of men. In all these modern nations that now stand in the article of decision between peace by submission or a doubtful and melancholy alternative,--in all of them men are by statute and custom inviolably equal before the law, of course; they are ungraded and masterless men before the law. But these same peoples are also alike in the respect that pecuniary duties and obligations among them are similarly sacred and inviolable under the dispassionate findings of the law. This pecuniary equality is, in effect, an impersonal equality between pecuniary magnitudes; from which it follows that these citizens of the advanced nations are not ungraded men in the pecuniary respect; nor are they masterless, in so far as a greater pecuniary force will always, under this impersonal equality of the law, stand in a relation of mastery toward a lesser one.

Class distinctions, except pecuniary distinctions, have fallen away. But all these modern nations are made up of pecuniary classes, differing from one another by minute gradations in the marginal cases, but falling, after all, and in the large, into two broadly and securely distinguishable pecuniary categories: those who have more and those who have less. Statisticians have been at pains to ascertain that a relatively very small numerical minority of the citizens in these modern nations own all but a relatively very small proportion of the aggregate wealth in the country. So that it appears quite safe to say that in such a country as America, e.g., something less than ten percent of the inhabitants own something more than ninety percent of the country's wealth. It would scarcely be a wild overstraining of its practical meaning to say that this population is made up of two classes: those who own the country's wealth, and those who do not. In strict accuracy, as before the law, this characterisation will not hold; whereas in practical effect, it is a sufficiently close approximation. This latter class, who have substantially no other than a fancied pecuniary interest in the nation's material fortunes, are the category often spoken of as The Common Man. It is not necessary, nor is it desired, to find a corresponding designation for the other category, those who own.

The articulate recognition of this division into contrasted pecuniary classes or conditions, with correspondingly (at least potentially) divergent pecuniary interests, need imply no degree of approval or disapproval of the arrangement which is so recognised. The recognition of it is necessary to a perspicuous control of the argument, as bears on the possible systematic and inherent discrepancy among these men in respect of their material interests under the projected Imperial rule. Substantially, it is a distinction between those who have and those who have not, and in a question of prospective pecuniary loss the man who has nothing to lose is differently placed from the one who has. It would perhaps seem flippant, and possibly lacking in the courtesy due one's prospective lord paramount, to say with the poet, *Cantabit vacuus coram latrone viator*.

But the whole case is not so simple. It is only so long as the projected pecuniary inroad is conceived as a simple sequestration of wealth in hand, that such a characterisation can be made to serve. The Imperial aim is not a passing act of pillage, but a perpetual usufruct; and the whole question takes on a different and more complex shape when it so touches the enduring conditions of life and livelihood. The citizen who has nothing, or who has no capitalisable source of unearned income, yet has a pecuniary interest in a livelihood to be gained from day to day, and he is yet vulnerable in the pecuniary respect in that his livelihood may with the utmost facility be laid under contribution by various and sundry well-tried contrivances. Indeed, the common man who depends for his livelihood on his daily earnings is in a more immediately precarious position than those who have something appreciable laid up against a rainy day, in the shape of a capitalised source of income. Only that it is still doubtful if his position is precarious in such a fashion as to lay him open to a notable increase of hardship, or to loss of the amenities of life, in the same relative degree as his well-to-do neighbour.

In point of fact it may well be doubted if this common man has anything to apprehend in the way of added hardship or loss of creature comforts under the contemplated regime of Imperial tutelage. He would presumably find himself in a precarious case under the arbitrary and irresponsible authority of an alien master working through an alien master class. The doubt which presents itself is as to whether this common man would be more precariously placed, or would come in for a larger and surer sum of hard usage and scant living, under this projected order of things, than what he already is exposed to in his pecuniary relations with his well-to-do compatriots under the current system of law and order.

Under this current regime of law and order, according to the equitable principles of Natural Rights, the man without means has no pecuniary rights which his well-to-do pecuniary master is bound to respect. This may have been an unintended, as it doubtless was an unforeseen, outcome of the move out of feudalism and prescriptive rights and immunities, into the system of individual liberty and manhood franchise; but as commonly happens in case of any substantial change in the scheme of institutional arrangements, unforeseen consequences come in along with those that have been intended. In that period of history when Western Europe was gathering that experience out of which the current habitual scheme of law and order has come, the right of property and free contract was a complement and safeguard to that individual initiative and masterless equality of men for which the spokesmen of the new era contended. That it is no longer so at every turn, or even in the main, in later time, is in great part due to changes of the pecuniary order, that have come on since then, and that seem not to have cast their shadow before.

In all good faith, and with none but inconsequential reservations, the material fortunes of modern civilised men--together with much else--have so been placed on a pecuniary footing, with little to safeguard them at any point except the inalienable right of pecuniary self-direction and initiative, in an environment where virtually all the indispensable means of pecuniary self-direction and initiative are in the hands of that contracted category of owners spoken of above. A numerical minority--under ten percent of the population--constitutes a conclusive pecuniary majority--over ninety percent of the means--under a system of law and order that turns on the inalienable right of owners to dispose of the means in hand as may suit their convenience and profit,--always barring recourse to illegal force or fraud. There is, however, a very appreciable margin of legal recourse to force and of legally protected fraud available in case of need. Of course the expedients here referred to as legally available force and fraud in the defense of pecuniary rights and the pursuit of pecuniary gain are not force and fraud *de jure* but only *de facto*.

They are further, and well known, illustrations of how the ulterior consequences of given institutional arrangements and given conventionalised principles (habits of thought) of conduct may in time come to run at cross purposes with the initial purpose that led to the acceptance of these institutions and to the confirmation and standardisation of these habitual norms of conduct. For the time being, however, they are "fundamentally and eternally right and good."

Being a pecuniary majority--what may be called a majority of the corporate stock--of the nation, it is also fundamentally and eternally right and good that the pecuniary interests of the owners of the material means of life should rule unabated in all those matters of public policy that touch on the material fortunes of the community at large. Barring a slight and intermittent mutter of discontent, this arrangement has also the cordial approval of popular sentiment in these modern democratic nations. One need only recall the paramount importance which is popularly attached to the maintenance and extension of the nation's trade--for the use of the investors--or the perpetuation of a protective tariff--for the use of the protected business concerns--or, again, the scrupulous regard with which such a body of public servants as the Interstate Commerce Commission will safeguard the legitimate claim of the railway companies to a "reasonable" rate of earnings on the capitalised value of the presumed earning-capacity of their property.

* * * * *

Again, in view of the unaccustomed freedom with which it is here necessary to speak of these delicate matters, it may be in place to disclaim all intention to criticise the established arrangements on their merits as details of public policy. All that comes in question here, touching these and the like features of the established law and order, is the bearing of all this on the material fortunes of the common man under the current regime, as contrasted with what he would reasonably have to look for under the projected regime of Imperial tutelage that would come in, consequent upon this national surrender to Imperial dominion.

* * * * *

In these democratic countries public policy is guided primarily by considerations of business expediency, and the administration, as well as the legislative power, is in the hands of businessmen, chosen avowedly on the ground of their businesslike principles and ability. There is no power in such a community that can over-rule the exigencies of business, nor would popular sentiment countenance any exercise of power that should traverse these exigencies, or that would act to restrain trade or discourage the pursuit of gain. An apparent exception to the rule occurs in wartime, when military exigencies may over-rule the current demands of business traffic; but the exception is in great part only apparent, in that the warlike operations are undertaken in whole or in part with a view to the protection or extension of business traffic.

National surveillance and regulation of business traffic in these countries hitherto, ever since and in so far as the modern democratic order of things has taken effect, has uniformly been of the nature of interference with trade and investment in behalf of the nation's mercantile community at large, as seen in port and shipping regulations and in the consular service, or in behalf of particular favored groups or classes of business concerns, as in protective tariffs and subsidies. In all this national management of pecuniary affairs, under modern democratic principles, the common man comes into the case only as raw material of business traffic,--as consumer or as laborer. He is one of the industrial agencies by use of which the businessman who employs him supplies himself with goods for the market, or he is one of the units of consumptive demand that make up this market in which the business man sells his goods, and so "realises" on his investment. He is, of course, free, under modern principles of the democratic order, to deal or not to deal with this business community, whether as laborer or as consumer, or as small-scale producer engaged in purveying materials or services on terms defined by the community of business interests engaged on so large a scale as to count in their determination. That is to say, he is free ***de jure*** to take or leave the terms offered. ***De facto*** he is only free to take them--with inconsequential exceptions--the alternative being obsolescence by disuse, not to choose a harsher name for a distasteful eventuality.

The general ground on which the business system, as it works under the overruling exigencies of the so-called "big business," so defines the terms of life for the common man, who works and buys, is the ground afforded by the principle of "charging what the traffic will bear;" that is to say, fixing the terms of hiring, buying and selling at such a figure as will yield the largest net return to the business concerns in whom, collectively or in severalty, the discretion vests. Discretion in these premises does not vest in any business concern that does not articulate with the system of "big business," or that does not dispose of resources sufficient to make it a formidable member of the system. Whether these concerns act in severalty or by collusion and conspiracy, in so defining the pecuniary terms of life for the community at large, is substantially an idle question, so far as bears on the material interest of the common man. The base-line is still what the traffic will bear, and it is still adhered to, so nearly as the human infirmity of the discretionary captains of industry will admit, whether the due approximation to this base-line is reached by a process of competitive bidding or by collusive advisement.

The generalisation so offered, touching the material conditions of life for the common man under the modern rule of big business, may seem unwarrantably broad. It may be worth while to take note of more than one point in qualification of it, chiefly to avoid the appearance of having overlooked any of the material circumstances of the case. The "system" of large business, working its material consequences through the system of large-scale industry, but more particularly by way of the large-scale and wide-reaching business of trade in the proper sense, draws into the net of its control all parts of the community and all its inhabitants, in some degree of dependence. But there is always, hitherto, an appreciable fraction of the inhabitants--as, e.g., outlying agricultural sections that are in a "backward" state--who are by no means closely bound in the orderly system of business, or closely dependent on the markets. They may be said to enjoy a degree of independence, by virtue of their foregoing as much as may be of the advantages offered by modern industrial specialisation. So also there are the minor and interstitial trades that are still carried on by handicraft methods; these, too, are still somewhat loosely held in the fabric of the business system. There is one thing and another in this way to be taken account of in any exhaustive survey, but the accounting for them will after all amount to nothing better than a gleaning of remnants and partial exceptions, such as will in no material degree derange the general proposition in hand.

Again, there runs through the length and breadth of this business community a certain measure of incompetence or inefficiency of management, as seen from the point of view of the conceivable perfect working of the system as a whole. It may be due to a slack attention here and there; or to the exigencies of business strategy which may constrain given business concerns to an occasional attitude of "watchful waiting" in the hope of catching a rival off his guard; or to a lack of perfect mutual understanding among the discretionary businessmen, due sometimes to an over-careful guarding of trade secrets or advance information; or, as also happens, and quite excusably, to a lack of perfect mutual confidence among these businessmen, as to one another's entire good faith or good-will. The system is after all a competitive one, in the sense that each of the discretionary directors of business is working for his own pecuniary gain, whether in cooperation with his fellows or not. "An honest man will bear watching." As in other collusive organisations for gain, confederates are apt to fall out when it comes to a division of what is in hand. In one way and another the system is beset with inherent infirmities, which hinder its perfect work; and in so far it will fall short of the full realisation of that rule of business that inculcates charging what the traffic will bear, and also in so far the pressure which the modern system of business management brings to bear on the common man will also fall short of the last straw--perhaps even of the next-to-the-last. Again it turns out to be a question not of the failure of the general proposition as formulated, but rather as to the closeness of approximation to its theoretically perfect work. It may be remarked by the way that vigilant and impartial surveillance of this system of business enterprise by an external authority interested only in aggregate results, rather than in the differential gains of the interested individuals, might hopefully be counted on to correct some of these shortcomings which the system shows when running loose under the guidance of its own multifarious incentives.

On the opposite side of the account, it is also worth noting that, while modern business management may now and again fall short of what the traffic will bear, it happens more commonly that its exactions will exceed that limit. This will particularly be true in businessmen's dealings with hired labour, as also and perhaps with equally far-reaching consequences in an excessive recourse to sophistications and adulterants and an excessively parsimonious provision for the safety, health or comfort of their customers--as, e.g., in passenger traffic by rail, water or tramway. The discrepancy to which attention is invited here is due to a discrepancy between business expediency, that is expediency for the purpose of gain by a given businessman, on the one hand, and serviceability to the common good, on the other hand. The business concern's interest in the traffic in which it engages is a short-term interest, or an interest in the short-term returns, as contrasted with the long-term or enduring interest which the community at large has in the public service over which any such given business concern disposes. The business incentive is that afforded by the prospective net pecuniary gain from the traffic, substantially an interest in profitable sales; while the community at large, or the common man that goes to make up such a community, has a material interest in this traffic only as regards the services rendered and the enduring effects that follow from it.

The businessman has not, or at least is commonly not influenced by, any interest in the ulterior consequences of the transactions in which he is immediately engaged. This appears to hold true in an accentuated degree in the domain of that large-scale business that draws its gains from the large-scale modern industry and is managed on the modern footing of corporation finance. This modern fashion of business organisation and management apparently has led to a substantial shortening of the term over which any given investor maintains an effective interest in any given corporate enterprise, in which his investments may be placed for the time being. With the current practice of organising industrial and mercantile enterprises on a basis of vendible securities, and with the nearly complete exemption from personal responsibility and enduring personal attachment to any one corporate enterprise which this financial expedient has brought, it has come about that in the common run of cases the investor, as well as the directorate, in any given enterprise, has an interest only for the time being. The average term over which it is (pecuniarily) incumbent on the modern businessman to take account of the working of any given enterprise has shortened so far that the old-fashioned accountability, that once was depended on to dictate a sane and considerate management with a view to permanent good-will, has in great measure become inoperative.

By and large, it seems unavoidable that the pecuniary interests of the businessmen on the one hand and the material interests of the community on the other hand are diverging in a more and more pronounced degree, due to institutional circumstances over which no prompt control can be had without immediate violation of that scheme of personal rights in which the constitution of modern democratic society is grounded. The quandary in which these communities find themselves, as an outcome of their entrance upon "the simple and obvious system of Natural Liberty," is shown in a large and instructive way by what is called "labor trouble," and in a more recondite but no less convincing fashion by the fortunes of the individual workman under the modern system.

The cost of production of a modern workman has constantly increased, with the advance of the industrial arts. The period of preparation, of education and training, necessary to turn out competent workmen, has been increasing; and the period of full workmanlike efficiency has been shortening, in those industries that employ the delicate and exacting processes of the modern technology. The shortening of this working-life of the workman is due both to a lengthening of the necessary period of preparation, and to the demand of these processes for so full a use of the workman's forces that even the beginning of senescence will count as a serious disability,--in many occupations as a fatal disability. It is also a well ascertained fact that effectual old age will be brought on at an earlier period by overwork; overwork shortens the working life-time of the workman. Thorough speeding-up ("Scientific Management"?) will unduly shorten this working life-time, and so it may, somewhat readily, result in an uneconomical consumption of the community's man-power, by consuming the workmen at a higher rate of speed, a higher pressure, with a more rapid rate of deterioration, than would give the largest net output of product per unit of man-power available, or per unit of cost of production of such man-power.

On this head the guiding incentives of the businessman and the material interest of the community at large--not to speak of the selfish interest of the individual workman--are systematically at variance. The cost of production of workmen does not fall on the business concern which employs them, at least not in such definite fashion as to make it appear that the given business concern or businessman has a material interest in the economical consumption of the man-power embodied in this given body of employees. Some slight and exceptional qualification of this statement is to be noted, in those cases where the processes in use are such as to require special training, not to be had except by a working habituation to these processes in the particular industrial plant in question. So far as such special training, to be had only as employees of the given concern, is a necessary part of the workman's equipment for this particular work, so far the given employer bears a share and an interest in the cost of production of the workmen employed; and so far, therefore, the employer has also a pecuniary interest in the economical use of his employees; which usually shows itself in the way of some special precautions being taken to prevent the departure of these workmen so long as there is a clear pecuniary loss involved in replacing them with men who have not yet had the special training required. Evidently this qualifying consideration covers no great proportion of the aggregate man-power consumed in industrial enterprises under business management. And apart from the instances, essentially exceptional, where such a special consideration comes in, the businessmen in charge will, quite excusably as things go, endeavour to consume the man-power of which they dispose in the persons of their employees, not at the rate that would be most economical to the community at large, in view of the cost of their replacement, nor at such a rate as would best suit the taste or the viability of the particular workman, but at such a rate as will yield the largest net pecuniary gain to the employer.

There is on record an illustrative, and indeed an illustrious, instance of such cannily gainful consumption of man-power carried out systematically and with consistently profitable effect in one of the staple industries of the country. In this typical, though exceptionally thoroughgoing and lucrative enterprise, the set rule of the management was, to employ none but select workmen, in each respective line of work; to procure such select workmen and retain them by offering wages slightly over the ordinary standard; to work them at the highest pace and pressure attainable with such a picked body; and to discharge them on the first appearance of aging or of failing powers. In the rules of the management was also included the negative proviso that the concern assumed no responsibility for the subsequent fortunes of discharged workmen, in the way of pension, insurance or the like.

This enterprise was highly successful and exceedingly profitable, even beyond the high average of profits among enterprises in the same line of business. Out of it came one of the greater and more illustrious fortunes that have been accumulated during the past century; a fortune which has enabled one of the most impressive and most gracious of this generation's many impressive philanthropists, never weary in well-doing; but who, through this cannily gainful consumption of man-power, has been placed in the singular position of being unable, in spite of avowedly unremitting endeavour, to push his continued disbursements in the service of humanity up to the figure of his current income. The case in question is one of the most meritorious known to the records of modern business, and while it will conveniently serve to illustrate many an other, and perhaps more consequential truth come to realisation in the march of Triumphant Democracy, it will also serve to show the gainfulness of an unreservedly canny consumption of man-power with an eye single to one's own net gain in terms of money.

* * * * *

Evidently this is a point in the articulation of the modern economic system where a sufficiently ruthless outside authority, not actuated by a primary regard for the pecuniary interests of the employers, might conceivably with good effect enforce a more economical consumption of the country's man-power. It is not a matter on which one prefers to dwell, but it can do no harm to take note of the fact for once in a way, that these several national establishments of the democratic order, as they are now organised and administered, do somewhat uniformly and pervasively operate with an effectual view to the advantage of a class, so far as may plausibly be done. They are controlled by and administered in behalf of those elements of the population that, for the purpose in hand, make up a single loose-knit class,--the class that lives by income rather than by work. It may be called the class of the business interests, or of capital, or of gentlemen. It all comes to much the same, for the purpose in hand.

The point in speaking of this contingent whose place in the economy of human affairs it is to consume, or to own, or to pursue a margin of profit, is simply that of contrasting this composite human contingent with the common man; whose numbers account for some nine-tenths or more of the community, while his class accounts for something less than one-tenth of the invested wealth, and appreciably less than that proportion of the discretionary national establishment,--the government, national or local, courts, attorneys, civil service, diplomatic and consular, military and naval. The arrangement may be called a gentlemen's government, if one would rather have it that way; but a gentleman is necessarily one who lives on free income from invested wealth--without such a source of free, that is to say unearned, income he becomes a decayed gentleman. Again, pushing the phrasing back a step farther toward the ground facts, there are those who would speak of the current establishments as "capitalistic;" but this term is out of line in that it fails to touch the human element in the case, and institutions, such as governmental establishments and their functioning, are after all nothing but the accustomed ways and means of human behaviour; so that "capitalistic" becomes a synonym for "businessmen's" government so soon as it is designated in terms of the driving incentives and the personnel. It is an organisation had with a view to the needs of business (i.e. pecuniary) enterprise, and is made up of businessmen and gentlemen, which comes to much the same, since a gentleman is only a businessman in the second or some later generation. Except for the slightly odious suggestion carried by the phrase, one might aptly say that the gentleman, in this bearing, is only a businessman gone to seed.

By and large, and taking the matter naively at the simple face value of the material gain or loss involved, it should seem something of an idle question to the common man whether his collective affairs are to be managed by a home-bred line of businessmen and their successive filial generations of gentlemen, with a view to accelerate the velocity and increase the volume of competitive gain and competitive spending, on the one hand, or by an alien line of officials, equally aloof from his common interests, and managing affairs with a view to the usufruct of his productive powers in furtherance of the Imperial dominion.

Not that the good faith or the generous intentions of these governments of gentlemen is questioned or is in any degree questionable; what is here spoken of is only the practical effect of the policies which they pursue, doubtless with benevolent intentions and well-placed complacency. In effect, things being as they are today in the civilised world's industry and trade, it happens, as in some sort an unintended but all-inclusive accident, that the guidance of affairs by business principles works at cross purposes with the material interests of the common man.

So ungraceful a view of the sacred core of this modern democratic organisation will need whatever evidence can be cited to keep it in countenance. Therefore indulgence is desired for one further count in this distasteful recital of ineptitudes inherent in this institutional scheme of civilised life. This count comes under the head of what may be called capitalistic sabotage. "Sabotage" is employed to designate a wilful retardation, interruption or obstruction of industry by peaceable, and ordinarily by legally defensible, measures. In its present application, particularly, there is no design to let the term denote or insinuate a recourse to any expedients or any line of conduct that is in any degree legally dubious, or that is even of questionable legitimacy.

Sabotage so understood, as not comprising recourse to force or fraud, is a necessary and staple expedient of business management, and its employment is grounded in the elementary and indefeasible rights of ownership. It is simply that the businessman, like any other owner, is vested with the right freely to use or not to use his property for any given purpose. His decision, for reasons of his own, not to employ the property at his disposal in a particular way at a particular time, is well and blamelessly within his legitimate discretion, under the rights of property as universally accepted and defended by modern nations. In the particular instance of the American nation he is protected in this right by a constitutional provision that he must not be deprived of his property without due process of law. When the property at his disposal is in the shape of industrial plant or industrial material, means of transportation or stock of goods awaiting distribution, then his decision not to employ this property, or to limit its use to something less than full capacity, in the way for which it is adapted, becomes sabotage, normally and with negligible exceptions. In so doing he hinders, retards or obstructs the working of the country's industrial forces by so much. It is a matter of course and of absolute necessity to the conduct of business, that any discretionary businessman must be free to deal or not to deal in any given case; to limit or to withhold the equipment under his control, without reservation. Business discretion and business strategy, in fact, has no other means by which to work out its aims. So that, in effect, all business sagacity reduces itself in the last analysis to a judicious use of sabotage. Under modern conditions of large business, particularly, the relation of the discretionary businessman to industry is that of authoritative permission and of authoritative limitation or stoppage, and on his shrewd use of this authority depends the gainfulness of his enterprise.

If this authority were exercised with an eye single to the largest and most serviceable output of goods and services, or to the most economical use of the country's material resources and man-power, regardless of pecuniary consequences, the course of management so carried out would be not sabotage but industrial strategy. But business is carried on for pecuniary gain, not with an unreserved view to the largest and most serviceable output or to the economical use of resources. The volume and serviceability of the output must wait unreservedly on the very particular pecuniary question of what quantity and what degree of serviceability will yield the largest net return in terms of price. Uneconomical use of equipment, labor and resources is necessarily an everyday matter under these circumstances, as in the duplication of plant and processes between rival concerns, and in the wasteful use of all resources that do not involve expenditure on the part of the given concern.

It has been the traditional dogma among economists and publicists in these modern communities that free competition between the businessmen in charge will indefeasibly act to bring the productiveness of industry to the highest practicable pitch and would lead to the most unreserved and vigilant endeavour to serve the community's material needs at all points. The reasons for the failure of this genial expectation, particularly under latterday business management, might be shown in some detail, if that were needed to enforce the argument as it runs in the present connection. But a summary indication of the commoner varieties and effects of sabotage as it is systematically applied in the businesslike conduct of industry will serve the purpose as well and with less waste of words and patience.

It is usual to notice, and not unusual to deplore the duplication of plant and appliances in many lines of industry, due to competitive management, as in factories engaged in the same class of manufacture, in parallel or otherwise competing railways and boat lines, in retail merchandising, and in some degree also in the wholesale trade. The result, of course, is sabotage; in the sense that this volume of appliances, materials and workmen are not employed to the best advantage for the community. One effect of the arrangement is an increased necessary cost of the goods and services supplied by these means. The reason for it is competition for gain to be got from the traffic. That all this is an untoward state of things is recognised on all hands; but no lively regret is commonly spent on the matter, since it is commonly recognised that under the circumstances there is no help for it except at the cost of a more untoward remedy.

The competitive system having been tried and found good--or at least so it is assumed--it is felt that the system will have to be accepted with the defects of its qualities. Its characteristic qualities are held to be good, acceptable to the tastes of modern men whose habits of thought have been standardised in its terms; and it would be only reluctantly and by tardy concession that these modern men could bring themselves to give up that scheme of "Natural Liberty" within the framework of which runs this competitive system of business management and its wasteful manifolding of half-idle equipment and nugatory work. The common man, at the worst, comforts himself and his neighbour with the sage reflection that "It might have been worse." The businessmen, on the other hand, have also begun to take note of this systematic waste by duplication and consequent incompetence, and have taken counsel how to intercept the waste and divert it to their own profit. The businessmen's remedy is consolidation of competing concerns, and monopoly control. To the common man, with his preconceptions on the head of "restraint of trade," the proposed remedy seems more vicious than the evil it is designed to cure. The fault of the remedy plainly is not that the mismanagement of affairs due to competitive business can not be corrected by recourse to monopoly, but only that the community, it is presumed, would still suffer all the burdens and discomforts of the regime of competition and sabotage, with, possibly, further inconveniences and impositions at the hands of the businesslike monopoly; which, men are agreed, may fairly be depended on to use its advantage unsparingly under the business principle of charging what the traffic will bear.

There is also this other singular phenomenon in this modern industrial world, that something not very far short of one-half the industrial equipment systematically lies idle for something approaching one-half the time, or is worked only to one-half its capacity half the time; not because of competition between these several industrial concerns, but because business conditions will not allow its continued productive use; because the volume of product that would be turned out if the equipment were working uninterruptedly at its full capacity could not be sold at remunerative prices. From time to time one establishment and another will shut down during a period of slack times, for the same reason.

This state of things is singular only as seen from the point of view of the community's material interest, not that it is in any degree unfamiliar or that any serious fault is found with the captains of industry for so shutting off the industrial process and letting the industrial equipment lie waste. As all men know, the exigencies of business will not tolerate production to supply the community's needs under these circumstances; although, as is equally notorious, these slack times, when production of goods is unadvisable on grounds of business expediency, are commonly times of wide-spread privation, "hard times," in the community at large, when the failure of the supply is keenly felt.

It is not that the captains of industry are at fault in so failing, or refusing, to supply the needs of the community under these circumstances, but only that they are helpless under the exigencies of business. They can not supply the goods except for a price, indeed not except for a remunerative price, a price which will add something to the capital values which they are venturing in their various enterprises. So long as the exigencies of price and of pecuniary gain rule the case, there is manifestly no escaping this enforced idleness of the country's productive forces.

It may not be out of place also to remark, by way of parenthesis, that this highly productive state of the industrial arts, which is embodied in the industrial plant and processes that so are systematically and advisedly retarded or arrested under the rule of business, is at the same time the particular pride of civilised men and the most tangible achievement of the civilised world.

A conservative estimate of this one item of capitalistic sabotage could scarcely appraise it at less than a twenty-five percent reduction from the normally possible productive capacity of the community, at an average over any considerable period; and a somewhat thorough review of the pertinent facts would probably persuade any impartial observer that, one year with another, such businesslike enforced idleness of plant and personnel lowers the actual output of the country's industry by something nearer fifty percent of its ordinary capacity when fully employed. To many, such an assertion may seem extravagant, but with further reflection on the well-known facts in the case it will seem less so in proportion as the unfamiliarity of it wears off.

However, the point of attention in the case is not the precise, nor the approximate, percentages of this arrest and retardation, this partial neutralisation of modern improvements in the industrial arts; it is only the notorious fact that such arrest occurs, systematically and advisedly, under the rule of business exigencies, and that there is no corrective to be found for it that will comport with those fundamental articles of the democratic faith on which the businessmen necessarily proceed. Any effectual corrective would break the framework of democratic law and order, since it would have to traverse the inalienable right of men who are born free and equal, each freely to deal or not to deal in any pecuniary conjuncture that arises.

But it is at the same time plain enough that this, in the larger sense untoward, discrepancy between productive capacity and current productive output can readily be corrected, in some appreciable degree at least, by any sufficient authority that shall undertake to control the country's industrial forces without regard to pecuniary profit and loss. Any authority competent to take over the control and regulate the conduct of the community's industry with a view to maximum output as counted by weight and tale, rather than by net aggregate price-income over price-cost, can readily effect an appreciable increase in the effectual productive capacity; but it can be done only by violating that democratic order of things within which business enterprise runs. The several belligerent nations of Europe are showing that it can be done, that the sabotage of business enterprise can be put aside by sufficiently heroic measures. And they are also showing that they are all aware, and have always been aware, that the conduct of industry on business principles is incompetent to bring the largest practicable output of goods and services; incompetent to such a degree, indeed, as not to be tolerable in a season of desperate need, when the nation requires the full use of its productive forces, equipment and man-power, regardless of the pecuniary claims of individuals.

*   *   *   *   *

Now, the projected Imperial dominion is a power of the character required to bring a sufficient corrective to bear, in case of need, on this democratic situation in which the businessmen in charge necessarily manage the country's industry at cross purposes with the community's--that is the common man's--material interest. It is an extraneous power, to whom the continued pecuniary gain of these nations' businessmen is a minor consideration, a negligible consideration in case it shall appear that the Imperial usufruct of the underlying nation's productive forces is in any degree impaired by the businessmen's management of it for their own net gain. It is difficult to see on what grounds of self-interest such an Imperial government could consent to tolerate the continued management of these underlying nations' industries on business principles, that is to say on the principle of the maximum pecuniary gain to the businesslike managers; and recent experience seems to teach that no excessive, that is to say no inconvenient, degree of consideration for vested rights, and the like, would long embarrass the Imperial government in its administration of its usufruct.

It should be a reasonable expectation that, without malice and with an unprejudiced view to its own usufruct of these underlying countries, the Imperial establishment would take due care that no systematically, and in its view gratuitously, uneconomical methods should continue in the ordinary conduct of their industry. Among other considerations of weight in this connection is the fact that a contented, well-fed, and not wantonly over-worked populace is a valuable asset in such a case. Similarly, by contraries, as an asset in usufruct to such an alien power, a large, wealthy, spendthrift, body of gentlefolk, held in high esteem by the common people, would have but a slight value, conceivably even a negative value, in such a case. A wise administration would presumably look to their abatement, rather than otherwise. At this point the material interest of the common man would seem to coincide with that of the Imperial establishment. Still, his preconceived notions of the wisdom and beneficence of his gentlefolk would presumably hinder his seeing the matter in that reasonable light.

Under the paramount surveillance of such an alien power, guided solely by its own interest in the usufruct of the country and its population, it is to be presumed that class privileges and discrimination would be greatly abated if not altogether discontinued. The point is in some doubt, partly because this alien establishment whose dominion is in question is itself grounded in class prerogatives and discrimination, and so, not improbably, it would carry over into its supervision of the underlying nations something of a bias in favor of class privileges. And a similar order of things might also result by choice of a class-system as a convenient means of control and exploitation. The latter consideration is presumably the more cogent, since the Imperial establishment in question is already, by ancient habit, familiar with the method of control by class and privilege; and, indeed, unfamiliar with any other method. Such a government, which governs without effectual advice or formal consent of the governed, will almost necessarily rest its control of the country on an interested class, of sufficient strength and bound by sufficiently grave interest to abet the Imperial establishment effectually in all its adventures and enterprises.

But such a privileged order, that is to be counted in to share dynastic usufruct and liabilities, in good days and evil, will be of a feudalistic complexion rather than something after the fashion of a modern business community doing business by investment and pecuniary finesse. It would still be a reasonable expectation that discrimination between pecuniary classes should fall away under this projected alien tutelage; more particularly all such discrimination as is designed to benefit any given class or interest at the cost of the whole, as, e.g., protective tariffs, monopolistic concessions and immunities, engrossing of particular lines of material resources, and the like. The character of the economic policy to be pursued should not be difficult of apprehension, if only these underlying peoples are conceived as an estate in tail within the dynastic line of descent. The Imperial establishment which so is prospectively to take over the surveillance of these modern peoples under this projected enterprise in dominion, may all the more readily be conceived as handling its new and larger resources somewhat unreservedly as an estate to be administered with a shrewd eye to the main chance, since such has always been its relation to the peoples and territories whose usufruct it already enjoys. It is only that the circumstances of the case will admit a freer and more sagacious application of those principles of usufruct that lie at the root of the ancient Culture of the Fatherland.

* * * * *

This excessively long, and yet incomplete, review of the presumptive material advantages to accrue to the common man under a regime of peace by unconditional surrender to an alien dynasty, brings the argument apparently to the conclusion that such an eventuality might be fortunate rather than the reverse; or at least that it has its compensations, even if it is not something to be desired. Such should particularly appear to be the presumption in case one is at all inclined to make much of the cultural gains to be brought in under the new regime. And more particularly should a policy of non-resistant submission to the projected new order seem expedient in view of the exceedingly high, not to say prohibitive, cost of resistance, or even of materially retarding its fulfillment.

CHAPTER V
PEACE AND NEUTRALITY

Considered simply on the face of the tangible material interests involved, the choice of the common man in these premises should seem very much of a foregone conclusion, if he could persuade himself to a sane and perspicuous consideration of these statistically apparent merits of the case alone. It is at least safely to be presumed that he has nothing to lose, in a material way, and there is reason to look for some slight gain in creature comforts and in security of life and limb, consequent upon the elimination, or at least the partial disestablishment, of pecuniary necessity as the sole bond and criterion of use and wont in economic concerns.

But man lives not by bread alone. In point of fact, and particularly as touches the springs of action among that common run that do not habitually formulate their aspirations and convictions in extended and grammatically defensible documentary form, and the drift of whose impulses therefore is not masked or deflected by the illusive consistencies of set speech,--as touches the common run, particularly, it will hold true with quite an unacknowledged generality that the material means of life are, after all, means only; and that when the question of what things are worth while is brought to the final test, it is not these means, nor the life conditioned on these means, that are seen to serve as the decisive criterion; but always it is some ulterior, immaterial end, in the pursuit of which these material means find their ulterior ground of valuation. Neither the overt testimony nor the circumstantial evidence to this effect is unequivocal; but seen in due perspective, and regard being had chiefly to the springs of concerted action as shown in any massive movement of this common run of mankind, there is, after all, little room to question that the things which commend themselves as indefeasibly worth while are the things of the human spirit.

These ideals, aspirations, aims, ends of endeavour, are by no means of a uniform or homogeneous character throughout the modern communities, still less throughout the civilised world, or throughout the checkered range of classes and conditions of men; but, with such frequency and amplitude that it must be taken as a major premise in any attempted insight into human behaviour, it will hold true that they are of a spiritual, immaterial nature.

The caution may, parenthetically, not be out of place, that this characterisation of the ulterior springs of action as essentially not of the nature of creature comforts, need be taken in no wider extension than that which so is specifically given it. It will be found to apply as touches the conduct of the common run; what modification of it might be required to make it at all confidently applicable to the case of one and another of those classes into whose scheme of life creature comforts enter with more pronounced effect may be more of a delicate point. But since it is the behaviour, and the grounds of behaviour, of the common run that are here in question, the case of their betters in this respect may conveniently be left on one side.

The question in hand touches the behavior of the common man, taken in the aggregate, in face of the quandary into which circumstances have led him; since the question of what these modern peoples will do is after all a question of what the common man in the aggregate will do, of his own motion or by persuasion. His betters may be in a position to guide, persuade, cajole, mislead, and victimise him; for among the many singular conceits that beset the common man is the persuasion that his betters are in some way better than he, wiser, more beneficent. But the course that may so be chosen, with or without guidance or persuasion from the superior classes, as well as the persistence and energy with which this course is pursued, is conditioned on the frame of mind of the common run.

Just what will be the nature and the concrete expression of these ideal aspirations that move the common run is a matter of habitual preconceptions; and habits of thought vary from one people to another according to the diversity of experience to which they have been exposed. Among the Western nations the national prestige has come to seem worth while as an ulterior end, perhaps beyond all else that is comprised in the secular scheme of things desirable to be had or to be achieved. And in the apprehension of such of them as have best preserved the habits of thought induced by a long experience in feudal subjection, the service of the sovereign or the dynasty still stands over as the substantial core of the cultural scheme, upon which sentiment and endeavour converge. In the past ages of the democratic peoples, as well as in the present-day use and wont among subjects of the dynastic States--as e.g., Japan or Germany--men are known to have resolutely risked, and lost, their life for the sake of the sovereign's renown, or even to save the sovereign's life; whereas, of course, even the slightest and most nebulous reflection would make it manifest that in point of net material utility the sovereign's decease is an idle matter as compared with the loss of an able-bodied workman. The sovereign may always be replaced, with some prospect of public advantage, or failing that, it should be remarked that a regency or inter-regnum will commonly be a season of relatively economical administration. Again, religious enthusiasm, and the furtherance of religious propaganda, may come to serve the same general purpose as these secular ideals, and will perhaps serve it just as well. Certain "principles," of personal liberty and of opportunity for creative self-direction and an intellectually worthy life, perhaps may also become the idols of the people, for which they will then be willing to risk their material fortune; and where this has happened, as among the democratic peoples of Christendom, it is not selfishly for their own personal opportunity to live untroubled under the light of these high principles that these opinionated men are ready to contend, but rather impersonally for the human right which under these principles is the due of all mankind, and particularly of the incoming and of later generations.

On these and the like intangible ends the common man is set with such inveterate predilection that he will, on provocation, stick at nothing to put the project through. For such like ends the common man will lay down his life; at least, so they say. There may always be something of rhetorical affectation in it all; but, after all, there is sufficient evidence to hand of such substance and tenacity in the common man's hold on these ideal aspirations, on these idols of his human spirit, as to warrant the assertion that he is, rather commonly, prepared to go to greater lengths in the furtherance of these immaterial gains that are to inure to someone else than for any personal end of his own, in the way of creature comforts or even of personal renown.

For such ends the common man, in democratic Christendom is, on provocation, willing to die; or again, the patient and perhaps more far-seeing common man of pagan China is willing to live for these idols of an inveterate fancy, through endless contumely and hard usage. The conventional Chinese preconceptions, in the way of things that are worth while in their own right, appear to differ from those current in the Occident in such a way that the preconceived ideal is not to be realised except by way of continued life. The common man's accountability to the cause of humanity, in China, is of so intimately personal a character that he can meet it only by tenaciously holding his place in the sequence of generations; whereas among the peoples of Christendom there has arisen out of their contentious past a preconception to the effect that this human duty to mankind is of the nature of a debt, which can be cancelled by bankruptcy proceedings, so that the man who unprofitably dies fighting for the cause has thereby constructively paid the reckoning in full.

Evidently, if the common man of these modern nations that are prospectively to be brought under tutelage of the Imperial government could be brought to the frame of mind that is habitual with his Chinese counterpart, there should be a fair hope that pacific counsels would prevail and that Christendom would so come in for a regime of peace by submission under this Imperial tutelage. But there are always these preconceptions of self-will and insubordination to be counted with among these nations, and there is the ancient habit of a contentious national solidarity in defense of the nation's prestige, more urgent among these peoples than any sentiment of solidarity with mankind at large, or any ulterior gain in civilisation that might come of continued discipline in the virtues of patience and diligence under distasteful circumstances.

The occidental conception of manhood is in some considerable measure drawn in negative terms. So much so that whenever a question of the manly virtues comes under controversy it presently appears that at least the indispensable minimum, and indeed the ordinary marginal modicum, of what is requisite to a worthy manner of life is habitually formulated in terms of what not. This appearance is doubtless misleading if taken without the universally understood postulate on the basis of which negative demands are formulated. There is a good deal of what would be called historical accident in all this. The indispensable demands of this modern manhood take the form of refusal to obey extraneous authority on compulsion; of exemption from coercive direction and subservience; of insubordination, in short. But it is always understood as a matter of course that this insubordination is a refusal to submit to irresponsible or autocratic rule. Stated from the positive side it would be freedom from restraint by or obedience to any authority not constituted by express advice and consent of the governed. And as near as it may be formulated, when reduced to the irreducible minimum of concrete proviso, this is the final substance of things which neither shame nor honour will permit the modern civilised man to yield. To no arrangement for the abrogation of this minimum of free initiative and self-direction will he consent to be a party, whether it touches the conditions of life for his own people who are to come after, or as touches the fortunes of such aliens as are of a like mind on this head and are unable to make head against invasion of these human rights from outside.

As has just been remarked, the negative form so often taken by these demands is something of an historical accident, due to the fact that these modern peoples came into their highly esteemed system of Natural Liberty out of an earlier system of positive checks on self-direction and initiative; a system, in effect, very much after the fashion of that Imperial jurisdiction that still prevails in the dynastic States--as, e.g., Germany or Japan--whose projected dominion is now the immediate object of apprehension and repugnance. How naively the negative formulation gained acceptance, and at the same time how intrinsic to the new dispensation was the aspiration for free initiative, appears in the confident assertion of its most genial spokesman, that when these positive checks are taken away, "The simple and obvious system of Natural Liberty establishes itself of its own accord."

The common man, in these modern communities, shows a brittle temper when any overt move is made against this heritage of civil liberty. He may not be altogether well advised in respect of what liberties he will defend and what he will submit to; but the fact is to be counted with in any projected peace, that there is always this refractory residue of terms not open to negotiation or compromise. Now it also happens, also by historical accident, that these residual principles of civil liberty have come to blend and coalesce with a stubborn preconception of national integrity and national prestige. So that in the workday apprehension of the common man, not given to analytic excursions, any infraction of the national integrity or any abatement of the national prestige has come to figure as an insufferable infringement on his personal liberty and on those principles of humanity that make up the categorical articles of the secular creed of Christendom. The fact may be patent on reflection that the common man's substantial interest in the national integrity is slight and elusive, and that in sober common sense the national prestige has something less than a neutral value to him; but this state of the substantially pertinent facts is not greatly of the essence of the case, since his preconceptions in these premises do not run to that effect, and since they are of too hard and fast a texture to suffer any serious abatement within such a space of time as can come in question here and now.

*   *   *   *   *

The outlook for a speedy settlement of the world's peace on a plan of unconditional surrender to the projected Imperial dominion seems unpromisingly dubious, in view of the stubborn temper shown by these modern peoples wherever their preconceived ideas of right and honest living appear to be in jeopardy; and the expediency of entering into any negotiated compact of diplomatic engagements and assurances designed to serve as groundwork to an eventual enterprise of that kind must therefore also be questionable in a high degree. It is even doubtful if any allowance of time can be counted on to bring these modern peoples to a more reasonable, more worldly-wise, frame of mind; so that they would come to see their interest in such an arrangement, or would divest themselves of their present stubborn and perhaps fantastic prejudice against an autocratic regime of the kind spoken for. At least for the present any such hope of a peaceable settlement seems illusive. What may be practicable in this way in the course of time is of course still more obscure; but argument on the premises which the present affords does not point to a substantially different outcome in the calculable future.

For the immediate future--say, within the life-time of the oncoming generation--the spiritual state of the peoples concerned in this international quandary is not likely to undergo so radical a change as to seriously invalidate an argument that proceeds on the present lie of the land in this respect. Preconceptions are a work of habit impinging on a given temperamental bent; and where, as in these premises, the preconceptions have taken on an institutionalised form, have become conventionalised and commonly accepted, and so have been woven into the texture of popular common sense, they must needs be a work of protracted and comprehensive habituation impinging on a popular temperamental bent of so general a prevalence that it may be called congenital to the community at large. A heritable bent pervading the group within which inheritance runs, does not change, so long as the racial complexion of the group remains passably intact; a conventionalised, commonly established habit of mind will change only slowly, commonly not without the passing of at least one generation, and only by grace of a sufficiently searching and comprehensive discipline of experience. For good or ill, the current situation is to be counted on not to lose character over night or with a revolution of the seasons, so far as concerns these spiritual factors that make or mar the fortunes of nations.

At the same time these spiritual assets, being of the nature of habit, are also bound to change character more or less radically, by insensible shifting of ground, but incontinently,--provided only that the conditions of life, and therefore the discipline of experience, undergo any substantial change. So the immediate interest shifts to the presumptive rate and character of those changes that are in prospect, due to the unremitting change of circumstances under which these modern peoples live and to the discipline of which they are unavoidably exposed. For the present and for the immediate future the current state of things is a sufficiently stable basis of argument; but assurance as to the sufficiency of the premises afforded by the current state of things thins out in proportion as the perspective of the argument runs out into the succeeding years. The bearing of it all is two-fold, of course. This progressive, cumulative habituation under changing circumstances affects the case both of those democratic peoples whose fortunes are in the hazard, and also of those dynastic States by whom the projected enterprise in dominion is to be carried into effect.

* * * * *

The case of the two formidable dynastic States whose names have been coupled together in what has already been said is perhaps the more immediately interesting in the present connection. As matters stand, and in the measure in which they continue so to stand, the case of these is in no degree equivocal. The two dynastic establishments seek dominion, and indeed they seek nothing else, except incidentally to and in furtherance of the main quest. As has been remarked before, it lies in the nature of a dynastic State to seek dominion, that being the whole of its nature in so far as it runs true to form. But a dynastic State, like any other settled, institutionalised community of men, rests on and draws its effectual driving force from the habit of mind of its underlying community, the common man in the aggregate, his preconceptions and ideals as to what things are worth while. Without a suitable spiritual ground of this kind such a dynastic State passes out of the category of formidable Powers and into that of precarious despotism.

In both of the two States here in question the dynastic establishment and its bodyguard of officials and gentlefolk may be counted on to persevere in the faith that now animates them, until an uneasy displacement of sentiment among the underlying populace may in time induce them judiciously to shift their footing. Like the ruling classes elsewhere, they are of a conservative temper and may be counted on so to continue. They are also not greatly exposed to the discipline of experience that makes for adaptive change in habits of life, and therefore in the correlated habits of thought. It is always the common man that is effectually reached by any exacting or wide-reaching change in the conditions of life. He is relatively unsheltered from any forces that make for adaptive change, as contrasted with the case of his betters; and however sluggish and reluctant may be his response to such discipline as makes for a displacement of outworn preconceptions, yet it is always out of the mass of this common humanity that those movements of disaffection and protest arise, which lead, on occasion, to any material realignment of the institutional fabric or to any substantial shift in the line of policy to be pursued under the guidance of their betters.

The common mass of humanity, it may be said in parenthesis, is of course not a homogeneous body. Uncommon men, in point of native gifts of intelligence, sensibility, or personal force, will occur as frequently, in proportion to the aggregate numbers, among the common mass as among their betters. Since in any one of these nations of Christendom, with their all-inclusive hybridisation, the range, frequency and amplitude of variations in hereditary endowment is the same throughout all classes. Class differentiation is a matter of habit and convention; and in distinction from his betters the common man is common only in point of numbers and in point of the more general and more exacting conditions to which he is exposed. He is in a position to be more hardly ridden by the discipline of experience, and is at the same time held more consistently to such a body of preconceptions, and to such changes only in this body of preconceptions, as fall in with the drift of things in a larger mass of humanity. But all the while it is the discipline which impinges on the sensibilities of this common mass that shapes the spiritual attitude and temper of the community and so defines what may and what may not be undertaken by the constituted leaders. So that, in a way, these dynastic States are at the mercy of that popular sentiment whose creatures they are, and are subject to undesired changes of direction and efficiency in their endeavors, contingent on changes in the popular temper; over which they have only a partial, and on the whole a superficial control.

A relatively powerful control and energetic direction of the popular temper is and has been exercised by these dynastic establishments, with a view to its utilisation in the pursuit of the dynastic enterprise; and much has visibly been accomplished in that way; chiefly, perhaps, by military discipline in subordination to personal authority, and also by an unsparing surveillance of popular education, with a view to fortify the preconceptions handed down from the passing order as well as to eliminate all subversive innovation. Yet in spite of all the well-conceived and shrewdly managed endeavors of the German Imperial system in this direction, e.g., there has been evidence of an obscurely growing uneasiness, not to say disaffection, among the underlying mass. So much so that hasty observers, and perhaps biased, have reached the inference that one of the immediate contributory causes that led to the present war was the need of a heroic remedy to correct this untoward drift of sentiment.

For the German people the government of the present dynastic incumbent has done all that could (humanly speaking) be expected in the way of endeavoring to conserve the passing order and to hold the popular imagination to the received feudalistic ideals of loyal service. And yet the peoples of the Empire are already caught in the net of that newer order which they are now endeavoring to break by force of arms. They are inextricably implicated in the cultural complex of Christendom; and within this Western culture those peoples to whom it fell to lead the exodus out of the Egypt of feudalism have come quite naturally to set the pace in all the larger conformities of civilised life. Within the confines of Christendom today, for good or ill, whatever usage or customary rule of conduct falls visibly short of the precedent set by these cultural pioneers is felt to fall beneath the prescriptive commonplace level of civilisation. Failure to adopt and make use of those tried institutional expedients on which these peoples of the advance guard have set their mark of authentication is today presumptively a mistake and an advantage foregone; and a people who are denied the benefit of these latterday ways and means of civic life are uneasy with a sense of grievance at the hands of their rulers. Besides which, the fashion in articles of institutional equipage so set by the authentic pioneers of culture has also come to be mandatory, as a punctilio of the governmental proprieties; so that no national establishment which aspires to a decorous appearance in the eyes of the civilised world can longer afford to be seen without them. The forms at least must be observed. Hence the "representative" and pseudo-representative institutions of these dynastic States.

These dynastic States among the rest have partly followed the dictates of civilised fashion, partly yielded to the, more or less intelligent, solicitations of their subjects, or the spokesmen of their subjects, and have installed institutional apparatus of this modern pattern--more in point of form than of substance, perhaps. Yet in time the adoption of the forms is likely to have an effect, if changing circumstances favor their taking effect. Such has on the whole been the experience of those peoples who have gone before along this trail of political advance. As instance the growth of discretionary powers under the hands of parliamentary representatives in those cases where the movement has gone on longest and farthest; and these instances should not be considered idle, as intimations of what may presumptively be looked for under the Imperial establishments of Germany or Japan. It may be true that hitherto, along with the really considerable volume of imitative gestures of discretionary deliberation delegated to these parliamentary bodies, they have as regards all graver matters brought to their notice only been charged with a (limited) power to talk. It may be true that, for the present, on critical or weighty measures the parliamentary discretion extends no farther than respectfully to say: "Ja wohl!" But then, *Ja wohl* is also something; and there is no telling where it may all lead to in the long course of years. One has a vague apprehension that this "Ja wohl!" may some day come to be a customarily necessary form of authentication, so that with-holding it (Behuet' es Gott!) may even come to count as an effectual veto on measures so pointedly neglected. More particularly will the formalities of representation and self-government be likely to draw the substance of such like "free institutions" into the effectual conduct of public affairs if it turns out that the workday experiences of these people takes a turn more conducive to habits of insubordination than has been the case hitherto.

Indications are, again, not wanting, that even in the Empire the discipline of workday experience is already diverging from that line that once trained the German subjects into the most loyal and unrepining subservience to dynastic ambitions. Of course, just now, under the shattering impact of warlike atrocities and patriotic clamour, the workday spirit of insubordination and critical scrutiny is gone out of sight and out of hearing.

Something of this inchoate insubordination has showed itself repeatedly during the present reign, sufficient to provoke many shrewd protective measures on the side of the dynastic establishment, both by way of political strategy and by arbitrary control. Disregarding many minor and inconsequential divisions of opinion and counsel among the German people during this eventful reign, the political situation has been moving on the play of three, incipiently divergent, strains of interest and sentiment: (a) the dynasty (together with the Agrarians, of whom in a sense the dynasty is a part); (b) the businessmen, or commercial interest (including investors); and (c) the industrial workmen. Doubtless it would be easier to overstate than to indicate with any nice precision what has been the nature, and especially the degree, of this alienation of sentiment and divergence of conscious interest among these several elements. It is not that there has at any point been a perceptible faltering in respect of loyalty to the crown as such. But since the crown belongs, by origin, tradition, interest and spiritual identity, in the camp of the Agrarians, the situation has been such as would inevitably take on a character of disaffection toward the dynastic establishment, in the conceivable absence of that strong surviving sentiment of dynastic loyalty that still animates all classes and conditions of men in the Fatherland. It would accordingly, again, be an overstatement to say that the crown has been standing precariously at the apex of a political triangle, the other two corners of which are occupied by these two divided and potentially recalcitrant elements of the body politic, held apart by class antipathy and divergent pecuniary interest, and held in check by divided counsels; but something after that fashion is what would have resulted under similar conditions of strain in any community where the modern spirit of insubordination has taken effect in any large measure.

Both of these elements of incipient disturbance in the dynastic economy, the modern commercial and working classes, are creatures of the new era; and they are systematically out of line with the received dynastic tradition of fealty, both in respect of their pecuniary interests and in respect of that discipline of experience to which their workday employment subjects them. They are substantially the same two classes or groupings that came forward in the modernisation of the British community, with a gradual segregation of interest and a consequent induced solidarity of class sentiment and class animosities. But with the difference that in the British case the movement of changing circumstances was slow enough to allow a fair degree of habituation to the altered economic conditions; whereas in the German case the move into modern economic conditions has been made so precipitately as to have carried the mediaeval frame of mind over virtually intact into this era of large business and machine industry. In the Fatherland the commercial and industrial classes have been called on to play their part without time to learn their lines.

The case of the English-speaking peoples, who have gone over this course of experience in more consecutive fashion than any others, teaches that in the long run, if these modern economic conditions persist, one or the other or both of these creatures of the modern era must prevail, and must put the dynastic establishment out of commission; although the sequel has not yet been seen in this British case, and there is no ground afforded for inference as to which of the two will have the fortune to survive and be invested with the hegemony. Meantime the opportunity of the Imperial establishment to push its enterprise in dominion lies in the interval of time so required for the discipline of experience under modern conditions to work out through the growth of modern habits of thought into such modern (i.e. civilised) institutional forms and such settled principles of personal insubordination as will put any effectual dynastic establishment out of commission. The same interval of time, that must so be allowed for the decay of the dynastic spirit among the German people under the discipline of life by the methods of modern trade and industry, marks the period during which no peace compact will be practicable, except with the elimination of the Imperial establishment as a possible warlike power. All this, of course, applies to the case of Japan as well, with the difference that while the Japanese people are farther in arrears, they are also a smaller, less formidable body, more exposed to outside forces, and their mediaevalism is of a more archaic and therefore more precarious type.

What length of time will be required for this decay of the dynastic spirit among the people of the Empire is, of course, impossible to say. The factors of the case are not of a character to admit anything like calculation of the rate of movement; but in the nature of the factors involved it is also contained that something of a movement in this direction is unavoidable, under Providence. As a preliminary consideration, these peoples of the Empire and its allies, as well as their enemies in the great war, will necessarily come out of their warlike experience in a more patriotic and more vindictive frame of mind than that in which they entered on this adventure. Fighting makes for malevolence. The war is itself to be counted as a set-back. A very large proportion of those who have lived through it will necessarily carry a warlike bent through life. By that much, whatever it may count for, the decay of the dynastic spirit--or the growth of tolerance and equity in national sentiment, if one chooses to put it that way--will be retarded from beforehand. So also the Imperial establishment, or whatever is left of it, may be counted on to do everything in its power to preserve the popular spirit of loyalty and national animosity, by all means at its disposal; since the Imperial establishment finally rests on the effectual body of national animosity. What hindrance will come in from this agency of retardation can at least vaguely be guessed at, in the light of what has been accomplished in that way under the strenuously reactionary rule of the present reign.

Again, there is the chance, as there always is a chance of human folly, that the neighboring peoples will undertake, whether jointly or severally, to restrict or prohibit trade relations between the people of the Empire and their enemies in the present war; thereby fomenting international animosity, as well as contributing directly to the economic readiness for war both on their own part and on that of the Empire. This is also, and in an eminent degree, an unknown factor in the case, on which not even a reasonable guess can be made beforehand. These are, all and several, reactionary agencies, factors of retardation, making for continuation of the current international situation of animosity, distrust, chicane, trade rivalry, competitive armament, and eventual warlike enterprise.

* * * * *

To offset these agencies of conservatism there is nothing much that can be counted on but that slow, random, and essentially insidious working of habituation that tends to the obsolescence of the received preconceptions; partly by supplanting them with something new, but more effectually by their falling into disuse and decay. There is, it will have to be admitted, little of a positive character that can be done toward the installation of a regime of peace and good-will. The endeavours of the pacifists should suffice to convince any dispassionate observer of the substantial futility of creative efforts looking to such an end. Much can doubtless be done in the way of precautionary measures, mostly of a negative character, in the way especially of removing sources of infection and (possibly) of so sterilising the apparatus of national life that its working shall neither maintain animosities and interests at variance with the conditions of peace nor contribute to their spread and growth.

There is necessarily little hope or prospect that any national establishment will contribute materially or in any direct way to the obsolescence of warlike sentiments and ambitions; since such establishments are designed for the making of war by keeping national jealousies intact, and their accepted place in affairs is that of preparation for eventual hostilities, defensive or offensive. Except for the contingency of eventual hostilities, no national establishment could be kept in countenance. They would all fall into the decay of desuetude, just as has happened to the dynastic establishments among those peoples who have (passably) lost the spirit of dynastic aggression.

The modern industrial occupations, the modern technology, and that modern empirical science that runs so close to the frontiers of technology, all work at cross purposes with the received preconceptions of the nationalist order; and in a more pronounced degree they are at cross purposes with that dynastic order of preconceptions that converges on Imperial dominion. The like is true, with a difference, of the ways, means and routine of business enterprise as it is conducted in the commercialised communities of today. The working of these agencies runs to this effect not by way of deliberate and destructive antagonism, but almost wholly by force of systematic, though unintended and incidental, neglect of those values, standards, verities, and grounds of discrimination and conviction that make up the working realities of the national spirit and of dynastic ambition. The working concepts of this new, essentially mechanistic, order of human interests, do not necessarily clash with those of the old order, essentially the order of personages and personalities; the two are incommensurable, and they are incompatible only in the sense and degree implied in that state of the case. The profoundest and most meritorious truths of dynastic politics can on no provocation and by no sleight of hand be brought within the logic of that system of knowledge and appraisal of values by which the mechanistic technology proceeds. Within the premises of this modern mechanistic industry and science all the best values and verities of the dynastic order are simply "incompetent, irrelevant and impertinent."

There is accordingly no unavoidable clash and no necessary friction between the two schemes of knowledge or the two habits of mind that characterise the two contrasted cultural eras. It is only that a given individual--call him the common man--will not be occupied with both of these incommensurable systems of logic and appreciation at the same time or bearing on the same point; and further that in proportion as his waking hours and his mental energy are fully occupied within the lines of one of these systems of knowledge, design and employment, in much the same measure he will necessarily neglect the other, and in time he will lose proficiency and interest in its pursuits and its conclusions. The man who is so held by his daily employment and his life-long attention within the range of habits of thought that are valid in the mechanistic technology, will, on an average and in the long run, lose his grip on the spiritual virtues of national prestige and dynastic primacy; "for they are foolishness unto him; neither can he know them, because they are spiritually discerned."

Not that the adepts in this modern mechanistic system of knowledge and design may not also be very good patriots and devoted servants of the dynasty. The artless and, on the whole, spontaneous riot of dynastic avidity displayed to the astonished eyes of their fellow craftsmen in the neutral countries by the most eminent scientists of the Fatherland during the early months of the war should be sufficient warning that the archaic preconceptions do not hurriedly fly out of the window when the habits of thought of the mechanistic order come in at the door. But with the passage of time, pervasively, by imperceptible displacement, by the decay of habitual disuse, as well as by habitual occupation with these other and unrelated ways and means of knowledge and belief, dynastic loyalty and the like conceptions in the realm of religion and magic pass out of the field of attention and fall insensibly into the category of the lost arts. Particularly will this be true of the common man, who lives, somewhat characteristically, in the mass and in the present, and whose waking hours are somewhat fully occupied with what he has to do.

With the commercial interests the Imperial establishment can probably make such terms as to induce their support of the dynastic enterprise, since they can apparently always be made to believe that an extension of the Imperial dominion will bring correspondingly increased opportunities of trade. It is doubtless a mistake, but it is commonly believed by the interested parties, which is just as good for the purpose as if it were true. And it should be added that in this, as in other instances of the quest of larger markets, the costs are to be paid by someone else than the presumed commercial beneficiaries; which brings the matter under the dearest principle known to businessmen: that of getting something for nothing. It will not be equally easy to keep the affections of the common man loyal to the dynastic enterprise when he begins to lose his grip on the archaic faith in dynastic dominion and comes to realise that he has also--individually and in the mass--no material interest even in the defense of the Fatherland, much less in the further extension of Imperial rule.

But the time when this process of disillusionment and decay of ideals shall have gone far enough among the common run to afford no secure footing in popular sentiment for the contemplated Imperial enterprise,--this time is doubtless far in the future, as compared with the interval of preparation required for a new onset. Habituation takes time, particularly such habituation as can be counted on to derange the habitual bent of a great population in respect of their dearest preconceptions. It will take a very appreciable space of time even in the case of a populace so accessible to new habits of thought as the German people are by virtue of their slight percentage of illiteracy, the very large proportion engaged in those modern industries that constantly require some intelligent insight into mechanistic facts, the density of population and the adequate means of communication, and the extent to which the whole population is caught in the web of mechanically standardised processes that condition their daily life at every turn. As regards their technological situation, and their exposure to the discipline of industrial life, no other population of nearly the same volume is placed in a position so conducive to a rapid acquirement of the spirit of the modern era. But, also, no other people comparable with the population of the Fatherland has so large and well-knit a body of archaic preconceptions to unlearn. Their nearest analogue, of course, is the Japanese nation.

In all this there is, of course, no inclination to cast a slur on the German people. In point of racial characteristics there is no difference between them and their neighbours. And there is no reason to question their good intentions. Indeed, it may safely be asserted that no people is more consciously well-meaning than the children of the Fatherland. It is only that, with their archaic preconceptions of what is right and meritorious, their best intentions spell malevolence when projected into the civilised world as it stands today. And by no fault of theirs. Nor is it meant to be intimated that their rate of approach to the accepted Occidental standard of institutional maturity will be unduly slow or unduly reluctant, so soon as the pertinent facts of modern life begin effectively to shape their habits of thought. It is only that, human nature--and human second nature--being what it always has been, the rate of approach of the German people to a passably neutral complexion in matters of international animosity and aggression must necessarily be slow enough to allow ample time for the renewed preparation of a more unsparing and redoubtable endeavour on the part of the Imperial establishment.

What makes this German Imperial establishment redoubtable, beyond comparison, is the very simple but also very grave combination of circumstances whereby the German people have acquired the use of the modern industrial arts in the highest state of efficiency, at the same time that they have retained unabated the fanatical loyalty of feudal barbarism.[9] So long, and in so far, as this conjunction of forces holds there is no outlook for peace except on the elimination of Germany as a power capable of disturbing the peace.

It may seem invidious to speak so recurrently of the German Imperial establishment as the sole potential disturber of the peace in Europe. The reason for so singling out the Empire for this invidious distinction--of merit or demerit, as one may incline to take it--is that the facts run that way. There is, of course, other human material, and no small volume of it in the aggregate, that is of much the same

---

9 For an extended discussion of this point, see *Imperial Germany and the Industrial Revolution*, especially ch. v. and vi.

character, and serviceable for the same purposes as the resources and man-power of the Empire. But this other material can come effectually into bearing as a means of disturbance only in so far as it clusters about the Imperial dynasty and marches under his banners. In so speaking of the Imperial establishment as the sole enemy of a European peace, therefore, these outlying others are taken for granted, very much as one takes the nimbus for granted in speaking of one of the greater saints of God.

* * * * *

So the argument returns to the alternative: Peace by unconditional surrender and submission, or peace by elimination of Imperial Germany (and Japan). There is no middle course apparent. The old-fashioned--that is to say nineteenth-century--plan of competitive defensive armament and a balance of powers has been tried, and it has not proved to be a success, even so early in the twentieth century. This plan offers a substitute (Ersatz) for peace; but even as such it has become impracticable. The modern, or rather the current late-modern, state of the industrial arts does not tolerate it. Technological knowledge has thrown the advantage in military affairs definitively to the offensive, particularly to the offensive that is prepared beforehand with the suitable appliances and with men ready matured in that rigorous and protracted training by which alone they can become competent to make warlike use of these suitable appliances provided by the modern technology. At the same time, and by grace of the same advance in technology, any well-designed offensive can effectually reach any given community, in spite of distance or of other natural obstacles. The era of defensive armaments and diplomatic equilibration, as a substitute for peace, has been definitively closed by the modern state of the industrial arts.

Of the two alternatives spoken of above, the former--peace by submission under an alien dynasty--is presumably not a practicable solution, as has appeared in the course of the foregoing argument.

The modern nations are not spiritually ripe for it. Whether they have reached even that stage of national sobriety, or neutrality, that would enable them to live at peace among themselves after elimination of the Imperial Powers is still open to an uneasy doubt. It would be by a precarious margin that they can be counted on so to keep the peace in the absence of provocation from without the pale. Their predilection for peace goes to no greater lengths than is implied in the formula: Peace with Honour; which assuredly does not cover a peace of non-resistance, and which, in effect, leaves the distinction between an offensive and a defensive war somewhat at loose ends. The national prestige is still a live asset in the mind of these peoples; and the limit of tolerance in respect of this patriotic animosity appears to be drawn appreciably closer than the formula cited above would necessarily presume. They will fight on provocation, and the degree of provocation required to upset the serenity of these sportsmanlike modern peoples is a point on which the shrewdest guesses may diverge. Still, opinion runs more and more consistently to the effect that if these modern--say the French and the English-speaking--peoples were left to their own devices the peace might fairly be counted on to be kept between them indefinitely, barring unforeseen contingencies.

Experience teaches that warlike enterprise on a moderate scale and as a side interest is by no means incompatible with such a degree of neutral animus as these peoples have yet acquired,--e.g., the Spanish-American war, which was made in America, or the Boer war, which was made in England. But these wars, in spite of the dimensions which they presently took on, were after all of the nature of episodes,--the one chiefly an extension of sportsmanship, which engaged the best attention of only the more sportsmanlike elements, the other chiefly engineered by certain business interests with a callous view to getting something for nothing. Both episodes came to be serious enough, both in their immediate incidence and in their consequences; but neither commanded the deliberate and cordial support of the community at large. There is a meretricious air over both; and there is apparent a popular inclination to condone rather than to take pride in these *faits accomplis*. The one excursion was a product of sportsmanlike bravado, fed on boyish exuberance, fomented for mercenary objects by certain business interests and place-hunting politicians, and incited by meretricious newspapers with a view to increase their circulation. The other was set afoot by interested businessmen, backed by politicians, seconded by newspapers, and borne by the community at large, in great part under misapprehension and stung by wounded pride.

Opinions will diverge widely as to the chances of peace in a community of nations among whom episodes of this character, and of such dimensions, have been somewhat more than tolerated in the immediate past. But the consensus of opinion in these same countries appears to be setting with fair consistency to the persuasion that the popular spirit shown in these and in analogous conjunctures in the recent past gives warrant that peace is deliberately desired and is likely to be maintained, barring unforeseen contingencies.

* * * * *

In the large, the measures conducive to the perpetuation of peace, and necessary to be taken, are simple and obvious; and they are largely of a negative character, exploits of omission and neglect. Under modern conditions, and barring aggression from without, the peace is kept by avoiding the breaking of it. It does not break of itself,--in the absence of such national establishments as are organised with the sole ulterior view of warlike enterprise. A policy of peace is obviously a policy of avoidance,--avoidance of offense and of occasion for annoyance.

What is required to insure the maintenance of peace among pacific nations is the neutralisation of all those human relations out of which international grievances are wont to arise. And what is necessary to assure a reasonable expectation of continued peace is the neutralisation of so much of these relations as the patriotic self-conceit and credulity of these peoples will permit. These two formulations are by no means identical; indeed, the disparity between what could advantageously be dispensed with in the way of national rights and pretensions, and what the common run of modern patriots could be induced to relinquish, is probably much larger than any sanguine person would like to believe. It should be plain on slight reflection that the greater part, indeed substantially the whole, of those material interests and demands that now engage the policy of the nations, and that serve on occasion to set them at variance, might be neutralised or relinquished out of hand, without detriment to any one of the peoples concerned.

The greater part of these material interests over which the various national establishments keep watch and hold pretensions are, in point of historical derivation, a legacy from the princely politics of what is called the "Mercantilist" period; and they are uniformly of the nature of gratuitous interference or discrimination between the citizens of the given nation and outsiders. Except (doubtfully) in the

English case, where mercantilist policies are commonly believed to have been adopted directly for the benefit of the commercial interest, measures of this nature are uniformly traceable to the endeavours of the crown and its officers to strengthen the finances of the prince and give him an advantage in warlike enterprise. They are kept up essentially for the same eventual end of preparation for war. So, e.g., protective tariffs, and the like discrimination in shipping, are still advocated as a means of making the nation self-supporting, self-contained, self-sufficient; with a view to readiness in the event of hostilities.

A nation is in no degree better off in time of peace for being self-sufficient. In point of patent fact no nation can be industrially self-sufficient except at the cost of foregoing some of the economic advantages of that specialisation of industry which the modern state of the industrial arts enforces. In time of peace there is no benefit comes to the community at large from such restraint of trade with the outside world, or to any class or section of the community except those commercial concerns that are favored by the discrimination; and these invariably gain their special advantage at the cost of their compatriots. Discrimination in trade--export, import or shipping--has no more beneficial effect when carried out publicly by the national authorities than when effected surreptitiously and illegally by a private conspiracy in restraint of trade within a group of interested business concerns.

Hitherto the common man has found it difficult to divest himself of an habitual delusion on this head, handed down out of the past and inculcated by interested politicians, to the effect that in some mysterious way he stands to gain by limiting his own opportunities. But the neutralisation of international trade, or the abrogation of all discrimination in trade, is the beginning of wisdom as touches the perpetuation of peace. The first effect of such a neutral policy would be wider and more intricately interlocking trade relations, coupled with a further specialisation and mutual dependence of industry between the several countries concerned; which would mean, in terms of international comity, a lessened readiness for warlike operations all around.

It used to be an argument of the free-traders that the growth of international commercial relations under a free-trade policy would greatly conduce to a spirit of mutual understanding and forbearance between the nations. There may or may not be something appreciable in the contention; it has been doubted, and there is no considerable evidence to be had in support of it. But what is more to the point is the tangible fact that such specialisation of industry and consequent industrial interdependence would leave all parties to this relation less capable, materially and spiritually, to break off amicable relations. So again, in time of peace and except with a view to eventual hostilities, it would involve no loss, and presumably little pecuniary gain, to any country, locality, town or class, if all merchant shipping were registered indiscriminately under neutral colors and sailed under the neutral no-man's flag, responsible indiscriminately to the courts where they touched or where their business was transacted.

Neither producers, shippers, merchants nor consumers have any slightest interest in the national allegiance of the carriers of their freight, except such as may artificially be induced by discriminatory shipping regulations. In all but the name--in time of peace--the world's merchant shipping already comes near being so neutralised, and the slight further simplification required to leave it on a neutral peace footing would be little else than a neglect of such vexatious discrimination as is still in force. If no nation could claim the allegiance, and therefore the usufruct, of any given item of merchant shipping in case of eventual hostilities, on account of the domicile of the owners or the port of registry, that would create a further handicap on eventual warlike enterprise and add so much to the margin of tolerance. At the same time, in the event of hostilities, shipping sailing under the neutral no-man's flag and subject to no national allegiance would enjoy such immunities as still inure to neutral shipping. It is true, neutrality has not carried many immunities lately.

Cumulatively effective usage and the exigencies of a large, varied, shifting and extensive maritime trade have in the course of time brought merchant shipping to something approaching a neutral footing. For most, one might venture to say for virtually all, routine purposes of business and legal liability the merchant shipping comes under the jurisdiction of the local courts, without reservation. It is true, there still are formalities and reservations which enable questions arising out of incidents in the shipping trade to become subject of international conference and adjustment, but they are after all not such as would warrant the erection of national apparatus to take care of them in case they were not already covered by usage to that effect. The visible drift of usage toward neutralisation in merchant shipping, in maritime trade, and in international commercial transactions, together with the similarly visible feasibility of a closer approach to unreserved neutralisation of this whole range of traffic, suggests that much the same line of considerations should apply as regards the personal and pecuniary rights of citizens traveling or residing abroad. The extreme,--or, as seen from the present point of view, the ultimate--term in the relinquishment of national pretensions along this line would of course be the neutralisation of citizenship.

This is not so sweeping a move as a patriotically-minded person might imagine on the first alarm, so far as touches the practical status of the ordinary citizen in his ordinary relations, and particularly among the English-speaking peoples. As an illustrative instance, citizenship has sat somewhat lightly on the denizens of the American republic, and with no evident damage to the community at large or to the inhabitants in detail. Naturalisation has been easy, and has been sought with no more eagerness, on the whole, than the notably low terms of its acquirement would indicate. Without loss or discomfort many law-abiding aliens have settled in this country and spent the greater part of a life-time under its laws without becoming citizens, and no one the worse or the wiser for it. Not infrequently the decisive inducement to naturalisation on the part of immigrant aliens has been, and is, the desirability of divesting themselves of their rights of citizenship in the country of their origin. Not that the privilege and dignity of citizenship, in this or in any other country, is to be held of little account. It is rather that under modern civilised conditions, and among a people governed by sentiments of humanity and equity, the stranger within our gates suffers no obloquy and no despiteful usage for being a stranger. It may be admitted that of late, with the fomentation of a more accentuated nationalism by politicians seeking a *raison d'etre*, additional difficulties have been created in the way of naturalisation and the like incidents. Still, when all is told of the average American citizen, *qua* citizen, there is not much to tell. The like is true throughout the English-speaking peoples, with inconsequential allowance for local color. A definitive neutralisation of citizenship within the range of these English-speaking countries would scarcely ripple the surface of things as they are--in time of peace.

All of which has not touched the sore and sacred spot in the received scheme of citizenship and its rights and liabilities. It is in the event of hostilities that the liabilities of the citizen at home come into the foreground, and it is as a source of patriotic grievance looking to warlike retaliation that the rights of the citizen abroad chiefly come into the case.

If, as was once, almost inaudibly, hinted by a well-regarded statesman, the national establishment should refuse to jeopardise the public peace for the safeguarding of the person and property of citizens who go out *in partes infidelium* on their own private concerns, and should so leave them under the uncurbed jurisdiction of the authorities in those countries into which they have intruded, the result might in many cases be hardship to such individuals. This would, of course, be true almost exclusively of such instances only as occur in such localities as are, temporarily or permanently, outside the pale of modern law and order. And, it may be in place to remark, instances of such hardship, with the accompanying hazard of national complications, would, no doubt, greatly diminish in frequency consequent upon the promulgation of such a disclaimer of national responsibility for the continued well-being of citizens who so expatriate themselves in the pursuit of their own advantage or amusement. Meantime, let it not seem inconsiderate to recall that to the community at large the deplorable case of such expatriates under hardship involves no loss or gain in the material respect; and that, except for the fortuitous circumstance of his being a compatriot, the given individual's personal or pecuniary fortune in foreign parts has no special claim on his compatriots' sympathy or assistance; from which it follows also that with the definitive neutralisation of citizenship as touches expatriates, the sympathy which is now somewhat unintelligently confined to such cases, on what may without offense be called extraneous grounds, would somewhat more impartially and humanely extend to fellowmen in distress, regardless of nativity or naturalisation.

What is mainly to the point here, however, is the fact that if citizenship were so neutralised within the range of neutral countries here contemplated, one further source of provocation to international jealousy and distrust would drop out of the situation. And it is not easy to detect any element of material loss involved in such a move. In the material respect no individual would be any the worse off, with the doubtful and dubious exception of the expatriate fortune-hunter, who aims to fish safely in troubled waters at his compatriots' expense. But the case stands otherwise as regards the balance of immaterial assets. The scaffolding of much highly-prized sentiment would collapse, and the world of poetry and pageantry--particularly that of the tawdrier and more vendible poetry and pageantry--would be poorer by so much. The Man Without a Country would lose his pathetic appeal, or would at any rate lose much of it. It may be, of course, that in the sequel there would result no net loss even in respect of these immaterial assets of sentimental animation and patriotic self-complacency, but it is after all fairly certain that something would be lost, and it is by no means clear what if anything would come in to fill its place.

An historical parallel may help to illustrate the point. In the movement out of what may be called the royal age of dynasties and chivalric service, those peoples who have moved out of that age and out of its spiritual atmosphere have lost much of the conscious magnanimity and conviction of merit that once characterised that order of things, as it still continues to characterise the prevalent habit of mind in the countries that still continue under the archaic order of dynastic mastery and service. But it is also to be noted that these peoples who so have moved out of the archaic order appear to be well content with this change of spiritual atmosphere, and they are even fairly well persuaded, in the common run, that the move has brought them some net gain in the way of human dignity and neighbourly tolerance, such as to offset any loss incurred on the heroic and invidious side of life. Such is the tempering force of habit. Whereas, e.g., on the other hand, the peoples of these surviving dynastic States, to which it is necessary continually to recur, who have not yet moved out of that realm of heroics, find themselves unable to see anything in such a prospective shift but net loss and headlong decay of the spirit; that modicum of forbearance and equity that is requisite to the conduct of life in a community of ungraded masterless men is seen by these stouter stomachs as a loosening of the moral fiber and a loss of nerve.

* * * * *

What is here tentatively projected under the phrase, "neutralization of citizenship," is only something a little more and farther along the same general line of movement which these more modern peoples have been following in all that sequence of institutional changes that has given them their present distinctive character of commonwealths, as contrasted with the dynastic States of the mediaeval order. What may be in prospect--if such a further move away from the mediaeval landmarks is to take effect--may best be seen in the light of the later moves in the same direction hitherto, more particularly as regards the moral and aesthetic merits at large of such an institutional mutation. As touches this last previous shifting of ground along this line, just spoken of, the case stands in this singular but significant posture, in respect of the spiritual values and valuations involved: These peoples who have, even in a doubtful measure, made this transition from the archaic institutional scheme, of fealty and dynastic exploit and coercion, to the newer scheme of the ungraded commonwealth, are convinced, to the point of martyrdom, that anything like a return to the old order is morally impossible as well as insufferably shameful and irksome; whereas those people, of the retarded division of the race, who have had no experience of this new order, are equally convinced that it is all quite incompatible with a worthy life.

Evidently, there should be no disputing about tastes. Evidently, too, these retarded others will not move on into the later institutional phase, of the ungraded commonwealth, by preconceived choice; but only, if at all, by such schooling of experience as will bring them insensibly to that frame of mind out of which the ideal of the ungraded commonwealth emerges by easy generalisation of workday practice. Meantime, having not yet experienced that phase of sentiment and opinion on civic rights and immunities that is now occupied by their institutionally maturer neighbours, the subjects of the Imperial Fatherland, e.g., in spite of the most laudable intentions and the best endeavour, are, by failure of this experience, unable to comprehend either the ground of opposition to their well-meaning projects of dominion or the futility of trying to convert these their elder brothers to their own prescriptive acceptation of what is worth while. In time, and with experience, this retarded division of Christendom may come to the same perspective on matters of national usage and ideals as has been enforced on the more modern peoples by farther habituation. So, also, in time and with experience, if the drift of circumstance shall turn out to set that way, the further move away from mediaeval discriminations and constraint and into the unspectacular scheme of neutralisation may come to seem as right, good and beautiful as the democratic commonwealth now seems to the English-speaking peoples, or as the Hohenzollern Imperial State now seems to the subjects of the Fatherland. There is, in effect, no disputing about tastes.

There is little that is novel, and nothing that is to be rated as constructive innovation, in this sketch of what might not inaptly be called peace by neglect. The legal mind, which commonly takes the initiative in counsels on what to do, should scarcely be expected to look in that direction for a way out, or to see its way out in that direction in any case; so that it need occasion no surprise if the many current projects of pacification turn on ingenious and elaborate provisions of apparatus and procedure, rather than on that simpler line of expedients which the drift of circumstance, being not possessed of a legal mind, has employed in the sequence of institutional change hitherto. The legal mind that dominates in the current deliberations on peace is at home in exhaustive specifications and meticulous demarkations, and it is therefore prone to seek a remedy for the burden of supernumerary devices by recourse to further excesses of regulation.

This trait of the legal mind is not a bad fault at the worst, and the quality in which this defect inheres is of the greatest moment in any project of constructive engineering on the legal and political plane. But it is less to the purpose, indeed it is at cross purposes, in such a conjuncture as the present; when the nations are held up in their quest of peace chiefly by an accumulation of institutional apparatus that has out-stayed its usefulness. It is the fortune even of good institutions to become imbecile with the change of conditioning circumstances, and it then becomes a question of their disestablishment, not of their rehabilitation. If there is anywhere a safe negative conclusion, it is that an institution grown mischievous by obsolescence need not be replaced by a substitute.

Instances of such mischievous institutional arrangements, obsolete or in process of obsolescence, would be, e.g., the French monarchy of the ancient regime, the Spanish Inquisition, the British corn laws and the "rotten boroughs," the Barbary pirates, the Turkish rule in Armenia, the British crown, the German Imperial Dynasty, the European balance of powers, the Monroe Doctrine. In some sense, at least in the sense and degree implied in their selective survival, these various articles of institutional furniture, and many like them, have once presumably been suitable to some end, in the days of their origin and vigorous growth; and they have at least in some passable fashion met some felt want; but if they ever had a place and use in the human economy they have in time grown imbecile and mischievous by force of changing circumstances, and the question is not how to replace them with something else to the same purpose after their purpose is outworn. A man who loses a wart off the end of his nose does not apply to the *Ersatz* bureau for a convenient substitute.

Now, a large proportion, perhaps even substantially the whole, of the existing apparatus of international rights, pretensions, discriminations, covenants and provisos, visibly fall in that class, in so far as concerns their material serviceability to the nation at large, and particularly as regards any other than a warlike purpose, offensive or defensive. Of course, the national dignity and diplomatic punctilio, and the like adjuncts and instrumentalities of the national honour, all have their prestige value; and they are not likely to be given up out of hand. In point of fact, however solicitous for a lasting peace these patriotically-minded modern peoples may be, it is doubtful if they could be persuaded to give up any appreciable share of these appurtenances of national jealousy even when their retention implies an imminent breach of the peace. Yet it is plain that the peace will be secure in direct proportion to the measure in which national discrimination and prestige are allowed to pass into nothingness and be forgot.

* * * * *

By so much as it might amount to, such neutralisation of outstanding interests between these pacific nations should bring on a degree of coalescence of these nationalities. In effect, they are now held apart in many respects by measures of precaution against their coming to a common plan of use and wont. The degree of coalescence would scarcely be extreme; more particularly it could not well become onerous, since it would rest on convenience, inclination and the neglect of artificial discrepancies. The more intimate institutions of modern life, that govern human conduct locally and in detail, need not be affected, or not greatly affected, for better or worse. Yet something appreciable in that way might also fairly be looked for in time.

The nature, reach and prescriptive force of this prospective coalescence through neutralisation may perhaps best be appreciated in the light of what has already come to pass, without design or mandatory guidance, in those lines of human interest where the national frontiers interpose no bar, or at least no decisive bar, whether by force of unconcern or through impotence. Fashions of dress, equipage and decorous usage, e.g., run with some uniformity throughout these modern nations, and indeed with some degree of prescriptive force. There is, of course, nothing mandatory, in the simpler sense, about all this; nor is the degree of conformity extreme or uniform throughout. But it is a ready-made generalisation that only those communities are incorporated in this cosmopolitan coalescence of usage that are moved by their own incitement, and only so far as they have an effectually felt need of conformity in these premises. It is true, a dispassionate outsider, if such there be, would perhaps be struck by the degree of such painstaking conformity to canons of conduct which it frequently must cost serious effort even to ascertain in such detail as the case calls for. Doubtless, or at least presumably, conformity under the jurisdiction of the fashions, and in related provinces of decorum, is obligatory in a degree that need not be looked for throughout the scheme of use and wont at large, even under the advisedly established non-interference of the authorities. Still, on a point on which the evidence hitherto is extremely scant it is the part of discretion to hold no settled opinion.

A more promising line of suggestion is probably that afforded by the current degree of contact and consistency among the modern nations in respect of science and scholarship, as also in the aesthetic or the industrial arts. Local color and local pride, with one thing and another in the way of special incitement or inhibition, may come in to vary the run of things, or to blur or hinder a common understanding and mutual furtherance and copartnery in these matters of taste and intellect. Yet it is scarcely misleading to speak of the peoples of Christendom as one community in these respects. The sciences and the arts are held as a joint stock among these peoples, in their elements, and measurably also in their working-out. It is true, these interests and achievements of the race are not cultivated with the same assiduity or with identical effect throughout; but it is equally true that no effectual bar could profitably be interposed, or would be tolerated in the long run in this field, where men have had occasion to learn that unlimited collusion is more to the purpose than a clannish discrimination.

* * * * *

It is, no doubt, beyond reasonable hope that these democratic peoples could be brought forthwith to concerted action on the lines of such a plan of peace by neutralisation of all outstanding national pretensions. Both the French and the English-speaking peoples are too eagerly set on national aims and national prestige, to allow such a plan to come to a hearing, even if something of the kind should be spoken for by their most trusted leaders. By settled habit they are thinking in terms of nationality, and just now they are all under the handicap of an inflamed national pride. Advocacy of such a plan, of course, does not enter seriously into the purpose of this inquiry; which is concerned with the conditions under which peace is sought today, with the further conditions requisite to its perpetuation, and with the probable effects of such a peace on the fortunes of these peoples in case peace is established and effectually maintained.

It is a reasonable question, and one to which a provisional answer may be found, whether the drift of circumstances in the present and for the immediate future may be counted on to set in the direction of a progressive neutralisation of the character spoken of above, and therefore possibly toward a perpetuation of that peace that is to follow the present season of war. So also is it an open and interesting question whether the drift in that direction, if such is the set of it, can be counted on to prove sufficiently swift and massive, so as not to be overtaken and overborne by the push of agencies that make for dissension and warlike enterprise.

Anything like a categorical answer to these questions would have to be a work of vaticination or of effrontery,--possibly as much to the point the one as the other. But there are certain conditions precedent to a lasting peace as the outcome of events now in train, and there are certain definable contingencies conditioned on such current facts as the existing state of the industrial arts and the state of popular sentiment, together with the conjuncture of circumstances under which these factors will come into action.

The state of the industrial arts, as it bears on the peace and its violation, has been spoken of above. It is of such a character that a judiciously prepared offensive launched by any Power of the first rank at an opportune time can reach and lay waste any given country of the habitable globe. The conclusive evidence of this is at hand, and it is the major premise underlying all current proposals and projects of peace, as well as the refusal of the nations now on the defensive to enter into negotiations looking to an "inconclusive peace." This state of the case is not commonly recognised in so many words, but it is well enough understood. So that all peace projects that shall hope to find a hearing must make up their account with it, and must show cause why they should be judged competent to balk any attempted offensive. In an inarticulate or inchoate fashion, perhaps, but none the less with ever-increasing certitude and increasing apprehension, this state of the case is also coming to be an article of popular "knowledge and belief," wherever much or little thought is spent on the outlook for peace. It has already had a visible effect in diminishing the exclusiveness of nationalities and turning the attention of the pacific peoples to the question of feasible ways and means of international cooperation in case of need; but it has not hitherto visibly lessened the militant spirit among these nations, nor has it lowered the tension of their national pride, at least not yet; rather the contrary, in fact.

The effect, upon the popular temper, of this inchoate realisation of the fatality that so lies in the modern state of the industrial arts, varies from one country to another, according to the varying position in which they are placed, or in which they conceive themselves to be placed. Among the belligerent nations it has put the spur of fear to their need of concerted action as well as to their efforts to strengthen the national defense. But the state of opinion and sentiment abroad in the nation in time of war is no secure indication of what it will be after the return to peace. The American people, the largest and most immediately concerned of the neutral nations, should afford more significant evidence of the changes in the popular attitude likely to follow from a growing realisation of this state of the case, that the advantage has passed definitively to any well prepared and resolute offensive, and that no precautions of diplomacy and no practicable measures of defensive armament will any longer give security,--provided always that there is anywhere a national Power actuated by designs of imperial dominion.

It is, of course, only little by little that the American people and their spokesmen have come to realise their own case under this late-modern situation, and hitherto only in an imperfect degree. Their first response to the stimulus has been a display of patriotic self-sufficiency and a move to put the national defense on a war-footing, such as would be competent to beat off all aggression. Those elements of the population who least realise the gravity of the situation, and who are at the same time commercially interested in measures of armament or in military preferment, have not begun to shift forward beyond this position of magniloquence and resolution; nor is there as yet much intimation that they see beyond it, although there is an ever-recurring hint that they in a degree appreciate the practical difficulty of persuading a pacific people to make adequate preparation beforehand, in equipment and trained man-power, for such a plan of self-sufficient self-defense. But increasingly among those who are, by force of temperament or insight or by lack of the pecuniary and the placeman's interest, less confident of an appeal to the nation's prowess, there is coming forward an evident persuasion that warlike preparations--"preparedness"--alone and carried through by the Republic in isolation, will scarcely serve the turn.

There are at least two lines of argument, or of persuasion, running to the support of such a view; readiness for a warlike defense, by providing equipment and trained men, might prove a doubtfully effectual measure even when carried to the limit of tolerance that will always be reached presently in any democratic country; and then, too, there is hope of avoiding the necessity of such warlike preparation, at least in the same extreme degree, by means of some practicable working arrangement to be effected with other nations who are in the same case. Hitherto the farthest reach of these pacific schemes for maintaining the peace, or for the common defense, has taken the shape of a projected league of neutral nations to keep the peace by enforcement of specified international police regulations or by compulsory arbitration of international disputes. It is extremely doubtful how far, if at all, popular sentiment of any effectual force falls in with this line of precautionary measures. Yet it is evident that popular sentiment, and popular apprehension, has been stirred profoundly by the events of the past two years, and the resulting change that is already visible in the prevailing sentiment as regards the national defense would argue that more far-reaching changes in the same connection are fairly to be looked for within a reasonable allowance of time.

In this American case the balance of effectual public opinion hitherto is to all appearance quite in doubt, but it is also quite unsettled. The first response has been a display of patriotic emotion and national self-assertion. The further, later and presumably more deliberate, expressions of opinion carry a more obvious note of apprehension and less of stubborn or unreflecting national pride. It may be too early to anticipate a material shift of base, to a more neutral, or less exclusively national footing in matters of the common defense.

The national administration has been moving at an accelerated rate in the direction not of national isolation and self-reliance resting on a warlike equipment formidable enough to make or break the peace at will--such as the more truculent and irresponsible among the politicians have spoken for--but rather in the direction of moderating or curtailing all national pretensions that are not of undoubted material consequence, and of seeking a common understanding and concerted action with those nationalities whose effectual interests in the matters of peace and war coincide with the American. The administration has grown visibly more pacific in the course of its exacting experience,--more resolutely, one might even say more aggressively pacific; but the point of chief attention in all this strategy of peace has also visibly been shifting somewhat from the maintenance of a running equilibrium between belligerents and a keeping of the peace from day to day, to the ulterior and altogether different question of what is best to be done toward a conclusive peace at the close of hostilities, and the ways and means of its subsequent perpetuation.

This latter is, in effect, an altogether different question from that of preserving neutrality and amicable relations in the midst of importunate belligerents, and it may even, conceivably, perhaps not unlikely, come to involve a precautionary breach of the current peace and a taking of sides in the war with an urgent view to a conclusive outcome. It would be going too far to impute to the administration, at the present stage, such an aggressive attitude in its pursuit of a lasting peace as could be called a policy of defensive offense; but it will shock no one's sensibilities to say that such a policy, involving a taking of sides and a renouncing of national isolation, is visibly less remote from the counsels of the administration today than it has been at any earlier period.

In this pacific attitude, increasingly urgent and increasingly far-reaching and apprehensive, the administration appears to be speaking for the common man rather than for the special interests or the privileged classes. Such would appear, on the face of the returns, to be the meaning of the late election. It is all the more significant on that account, since in the long run it is after all the common man that will have to pass on the expediency of any settled line of policy and to bear the material burden of carrying it into effect.

It may seem rash to presume that a popularly accredited administration in a democratic country must approximately reflect the effectual changes of popular sentiment and desire. Especially would it seem rash to anyone looking on from the point of view of an undemocratic nation, and therefore prone to see the surface fluctuations of excitement and shifting clamor. But those who are within the democratic pale will know that any administration in such a country, where official tenure and continued incumbency of the party rest on a popular vote,--any such administration is a political organisation and is guided by political expediency, in the tawdry sense of the phrase. Such a political situation has the defects of its qualities, as has been well and frequently expounded by its critics, but it has also the merits of its shortcomings. In a democracy of this modern order any incumbent of high office is necessarily something of a politician, quite indispensably so; and a politician at the same time necessarily is something of a demagogue. He yields to the popular drift, or to the set of opinion and demands among the effective majority on whom he leans; and he can not even appear to lead, though he may surreptitiously lead opinion in adroitly seeming to reflect it and obey it. Ostensible leadership, such as has been staged in this country from time to time, has turned out to be ostensible only. The politician must be adroit; but if he is also to be a statesman he must be something more. He is under the necessity of guessing accurately what the drift of events and opinion is going to be on the next reach ahead; and in taking coming events by the forelock he may be able to guide and shape the drift of opinion and sentiment somewhat to his own liking. But all the while he must keep within the lines of the long-term set of the current as it works out in the habits of thought of the common man.

Such foresight and flexibility is necessary to continued survival, but flexibility of convictions alone does not meet the requirements. Indeed, it has been tried. It is only the minor politicians--the most numerous and long-lived, it is true--who can hold their place in the crevices of the party organisation, and get their livelihood from the business of party politics, without some power of vision and some hazard of forecast. It results from this state of the case that the drift of popular sentiment and the popular response to the stimulus of current events is reflected more faithfully and more promptly by the short-lived administrations of a democracy than by the stable and formally irresponsible governmental establishments of the older order. It should also be noted that these democratic administrations are in a less advantageous position for the purpose of guiding popular sentiment and shaping it to their own ends.

*   *   *   *   *

Now, it happens that at no period within the past half-century has the course of events moved with such celerity or with so grave a bearing on the common good and the prospective contingencies of national life as during the present administration. This apparent congruity of the administration's policy with the drift of popular feeling and belief will incline anyone to put a high rating on the administration's course of conduct, in international relations as well as in national measures that have a bearing on international relations, as indicating the course taken by sentiment and second thought in the community at large,--for, in effect, whether or not in set form, the community at large reflects on any matters of such gravity and urgency as to force themselves upon the attention of the common man.

Two main lines of reflection have visibly been enforced on the administration by the course of events in the international field. There has been a growing apprehension, mounting in the later months to something like the rank of a settled conviction, that the Republic has been marked down for reduction to a vassal state by the dynastic Empire now engaged with its European adversaries. In so saying that the Republic has been marked down for subjection it is not intended to intimate that deliberate counsel has been had by the Imperial establishment on that prospective enterprise; still less that a resolution to such effect, with specification of ways and means, has been embodied in documentary form and deposited for future reference in the Imperial archives. All that is intended, and all that is necessary to imply, is that events are in train to such effect that the subjugation of the American republic will necessarily find its place in the sequence presently, provided that the present Imperial adventure is brought to a reasonably auspicious issue; though it does not follow that this particular enterprise need be counted on as the next large adventure in dominion to be undertaken when things again fall into promising shape. This latter point would, of course, depend on the conjuncture of circumstances, chief of which would have to be the exigencies of imperial dominion shaping the policy of the Empire's natural and necessary ally in the Far East. All this has evidently been coming more and more urgently into the workday deliberations of the American administration. Of course, it is not spoken of in set terms to this effect in official utterances, perhaps not even within doors; that sort of thing is not done. But it can do no harm to use downright expressions in a scientific discussion of these phenomena, with a view to understanding the current drift of things in this field.

Beyond this is the similar apprehension, similarly though more slowly and reluctantly rising to the level of settled conviction, that the American commonwealth is not fit to take care of its own case single-handed. This apprehension is enforced more and more unmistakably with every month that passes on the theatre of war. And it is reenforced by the constantly more obvious reflection that the case of the American commonwealth in this matter is the same as that of the democratic countries of Europe, and of the other European colonies. It is not, or at least one may believe it is not yet, that in the patriotic apprehension of the common man, or of the administration which speaks for him, the resources of the country would be inadequate to meet any contingencies of the kind that might arise, whether in respect of industrial capacity or in point of man-power, if these resources were turned to this object with the same singleness of purpose and the same drastic procedure that marks the course of a national establishment guided by no considerations short of imperial dominion. The doubt presents itself rather as an apprehension that the cost would be extravagantly high, in all respects in which cost can be counted; which is presently seconded, on very slight reflection and review of experience, by recognition of the fact that a democracy is, in point of fact, not to be persuaded to stand under arms interminably in mere readiness for a contingency, however distasteful the contingency may be.

In point of fact, a democratic commonwealth is moved by other interests in the main, and the common defense is a secondary consideration, not a primary interest,--unless in the exceptional case of a commonwealth so placed under the immediate threat of invasion as to have the common defense forced into the place of paramount consequence in its workday habits of thought. The American republic is not so placed. Anyone may satisfy himself by reasonable second thought that the people of this nation are not to be counted on to do their utmost in time of peace to prepare for war. They may be persuaded to do much more than has been their habit, and adventurous politicians may commit them to much more than the people at large would wish to undertake, but when all is done that can be counted on for a permanency, up to the limit of popular tolerance, it would be a bold guess that should place the result at more than one-half of what the country is capable of. Particularly would the people's patience balk at the extensive military training requisite to put the country in an adequate position of defense against a sudden and well-prepared offensive. It is otherwise with a dynastic State, to the directorate of which all other interests are necessarily secondary, subsidiary, and mainly to be considered only in so far as they are contributory to the nation's readiness for warlike enterprise.

America at the same time is placed in an extra-hazardous position, between the two seas beyond which to either side lie the two Imperial Powers whose place in the modern economy of nations it is to disturb the peace in an insatiable quest of dominion. This position is no longer defensible in isolation, under the later state of the industrial arts, and the policy of isolation that has guided the national policy hitherto is therefore falling out of date. The question is as to the manner of its renunciation, rather than the fact of it. It may end in a defensive copartnership with other nations who are placed on the defensive by the same threatening situation, or it may end in a bootless struggle for independence, but the choice scarcely extends beyond this alternative. It will be said, of course, that America is competent to take care of itself and its Monroe doctrine in the future as in the past. But that view, spoken for cogently by thoughtful men and by politicians looking for party advantage, overlooks the fact that the modern technology has definitively thrown the advantage to the offensive, and that intervening seas can no longer be counted on as a decisive obstacle. On this latter head, what was reasonably true fifteen years ago is doubtful today, and it is in all reasonable expectation invalid for the situation fifteen years hence.

The other peoples that are of a neutral temper may need the help of America sorely enough in their endeavours to keep the peace, but America's need of cooperation is sorer still, for the Republic is coming into a more precarious place than any of the others. America is also, at least potentially, the most democratic of the greater Powers, and is handicapped with all the disabilities of a democratic commonwealth in the face of war. America is also for the present, and perhaps for the calculable future, the most powerful of these greater Powers, in point of conceivably available resources, though not in actually available fighting-power; and the entrance of America unreservedly into a neutral league would consequently be decisive both of the purposes of the league and of its efficiency for the purpose; particularly if the neutralisation of interests among the members of the league were carried so far as to make withdrawal and independent action disadvantageous.

On the establishment of such a neutral league, with such neutralisation of national interests as would assure concerted action in time of stress, the need of armament on the part of the American republic would disappear, at least to the extent that no increase of armed force would be advisable. The strength of the Republic lies in its large and varied resources and the unequalled industrial capacity of its population,--a capacity which is today seriously hampered by untoward business interests and business methods sheltered under national discrimination, but which would come more nearly to its own so soon as these national discriminations were corrected or abrogated in the neutralisation of national pretensions. The neutrally-minded countries of Europe have been constrained to learn the art of modern war, as also to equip themselves with the necessary appliances, sufficient to meet all requirements for keeping the peace through such a period as can or need be taken into account,--provided the peace that is to come on the conclusion of the present war shall be placed on so "conclusive" a footing as will make it anything substantially more than a season of recuperation for that warlike Power about whose enterprise in dominion the whole question turns. Provided that suitably "substantial guarantees" of a reasonable quiescence on the part of this Imperial Power are had, there need be no increase of the American armament. Any increased armament would in that case amount to nothing better than an idle duplication of plant and personnel already on hand and sufficient to meet the requirements.

To meet the contingencies had in view in its formation, such a league would have to be neutralised to the point that all pertinent national pretensions would fall into virtual abeyance, so that all the necessary resources at the disposal of the federated nations would automatically come under the control of the league's appointed authorities without loss of time, whenever the need might arise. That is to say, national interests and pretensions would have to give way to a collective control sufficient to insure prompt and concerted action. In the face of such a neutral league Imperial Japan alone would be unable to make a really serious diversion or to entertain much hope of following up its quest of dominion. The Japanese Imperial establishment might even be persuaded peaceably to let its unoffending neighbours live their own life according to their own light. It is, indeed, possibly the apprehension of some such contingency that has hurried the rapacity of the Island Empire into the headlong indecencies of the past year or two.

CHAPTER VI
ELIMINATION OF THE UNFIT

It may seem early (January 1917) to offer a surmise as to what must be the manner of league into which the pacific nations are to enter and by which the peace will be kept, in case such a move is to be made. But the circumstances that are to urge such a line of action, and that will condition its carrying out in case it is entered on, have already come into bearing and should, on the whole, no longer be especially obscure to anyone who will let the facts of the case rather than his own predilections decide what he will believe. By and large, the pressure of these conditioning circumstances may be seen, and the line of least resistance under this pressure may be calculated, with due allowance of a margin of error owing to unknown contingencies of time and minor variables.

Time is of the essence of the case. So that what would have been dismissed as idle vapour two years ago has already become subject of grave deliberation today, and may rise to paramount urgency that far hence. Time is needed to appreciate and get used to any innovation of appreciable gravity, particularly where the innovation depends in any degree on a change in public sentiment, as in this instance. The present outlook would seem to be that no excess of time is allowed in these premises; but it should also be noted that events are moving with unexampled celerity, and are impinging on the popular apprehension with unexampled force,--unexampled on such a scale. It is hoped that a recital of these circumstances that provoke to action along this line will not seem unwarrantably tedious, and that a tentative definition of the line of least resistance under pressure of these circumstances may not seem unwarrantably presumptuous.

The major premise in the case is the felt need of security from aggression at the hands of Imperial Germany and its auxiliary Powers; seconded by an increasingly uneasy apprehension as to the prospective line of conduct on the part of Imperial Japan, bent on a similar quest of dominion. There is also the less articulate apprehension of what, if anything, may be expected from Imperial Russia; an obscure and scarcely definable factor, which comes into the calculation chiefly by way of reenforcing the urgency of the situation created by the dynastic ambitions of these other two Imperial States. Further, the pacific nations, the leading ones among them being the French and English-speaking peoples, are coming to recognise that no one among them can provide for its own security single-handed, even at the cost of their utmost endeavour in the way of what is latterly called "preparedness;" and they are at the same time unwilling to devote their force unreservedly to warlike preparation, having nothing to gain. The solution proposed is a league of the pacific nations, commonly spoken of at the present stage as a league to enforce peace, or less ambitiously as a league to enforce arbitration. The question being left somewhat at loose ends, whether the projected league is to include the two or three Imperial Powers whose pacific intentions are, euphemistically, open to doubt.

Such is the outline of the project and its premises. An attempt to fill in this outline will, perhaps, conduce to an appreciation of what is sought and of what the conditioning circumstances will enforce in the course of its realisation. As touches the fear of aggression, it has already been indicated, perhaps with unnecessary iteration, that these two Imperial Powers are unable to relinquish the quest of dominion through warlike enterprise, because as dynastic States they have no other ulterior aim; as has abundantly appeared in the great volume of expository statements that have come out of the Fatherland the past few years, official, semi-official, inspired, and spontaneous. "Assurance of the nation's future" is not translatable into any other terms. The Imperial dynasty has no other ground to stand on, and can not give up the enterprise so long as it can muster force for any formidable diversion, to get anything in the way of dominion by seizure, threat or chicane.

This is coming to be informally and loosely, but none the less definitively, realised by the pacific nations; and the realisation of it is gaining in clearness and assurance as time passes. And it is backed by the conviction that, in the nature of things, no engagement on the part of such a dynastic State has any slightest binding force, beyond the material constraint that would enforce it from the outside. So the demand has been diplomatically phrased as a demand for "substantial guarantees."

Any gain in resources on the part of these Powers is to be counted as a gain in the ways and means of disturbing the peace, without reservation.

The pacific nations include among them two large items, both of which are indispensable to the success of the project, the United States and the United Kingdom. The former brings in its train, virtually without exception or question, the other American republics, none of which can practically go in or stay out except in company and collusion with the United States. The United Kingdom after the same fashion, and with scarcely less assurance, may be counted on to carry the British colonies. Evidently, without both of these groups the project would not even make a beginning. Beyond this is to be counted in as elements of strength, though scarcely indispensable, France, Belgium, the Netherlands and the Scandinavian countries. The other west-European nations would in all probability be found in the league, although so far as regards its work and its fortunes their adhesion would scarcely be a matter of decisive consequence; they may therefore be left somewhat on one side in any consideration of the circumstances that would shape the league, its aims and its limitations. The Balkan states, in the wider acceptance, they that frequent the Sign of the Double Cross, are similarly negligible in respect of the organisation of such a league or its resources and the mutual concessions necessary to be made between its chief members. Russia is so doubtful a factor, particularly as regards its place and value in industry, culture and politics, in the near future, as to admit nothing much more than a doubt on what its relation to the situation will be. The evil intentions of the Imperial-bureaucratic establishment are probably no more to be questioned than the good intentions of the underlying peoples of Russia. China will have to be taken in, if for no other reason than the use to which the magnificent resources of that country would be turned by its Imperial neighbour in the absence of insurmountable interference from outside. But China will come in on any terms that include neutrality and security.

The question then arises as to the Imperial Powers whose dynastic enterprise is primarily to be hedged against by such a league. Reflection will show that if the league is to effect any appreciable part of its purpose, these Powers will also be included in the league, or at least in its jurisdiction. A pacific league not including these Powers, or not extending its jurisdiction and surveillance to them and their conduct, would come to the same thing as a coalition of nations in two hostile groups, the one standing on the defensive against the warlike machinations of the other, and both groups bidding for the favor of those minor Powers whose traditions and current aspirations run to national (dynastic) aggrandizement by way of political intrigue. It would come to a more articulate and accentuated form of that balance of power that has latterly gone bankrupt in Europe, with the most corrupt and unreliable petty monarchies of eastern Europe vested with a casting vote; and it would also involve a system of competitive armaments of the same general character as what has also shown itself bankrupt. It would, in other words, mean a virtual return to the ***status quo ante***, but with an overt recognition of its provisional character, and with the lines of division more sharply drawn. That is to say, it would amount to reinstating the situation which the projected league is intended to avert. It is evidently contained in the premises that the projected league must be all-inclusive, at least as regards its jurisdiction and surveillance. The argument will return to this point presently.

The purpose of the projected league is peace and security, commonly spoken of under patriotic preconceptions as "national" peace and security. This will have to mean a competent enforcement of peace, on such a footing of overmastering force at the disposal of the associated pacific nations as to make security a matter of ordinary routine. It is true, the more genial spokesmen of the project are given to the view that what is to come of it all is a comity of neutral nations, amicably adjusting their own relations among themselves in a spirit of peace and good-will. But this view is over-sanguine, in that it overlooks the point that into this prospective comity of nations Imperial Germany (and Imperial Japan) fit like a drunken savage with a machine gun. It also overlooks the patent fatality that these two are bound to come into a coalition at the next turn, with whatever outside and subsidiary resources they can draw on; provided only that a reasonable opening for further enterprise presents itself. The league, in other terms, must be in a position to enforce peace by overmastering force, and to anticipate any move at cross purposes with the security of the pacific nations.

This end can be reached by either one of two ways. If the dynastic States are left to their own devices, it will be incumbent on the associated nations to put in the field a standing force sufficient to prevent a recourse to arms; which means competitive armament and universal military rule. Or the dynastic States may be taken into partnership and placed under such surveillance and constraint as to practically disarm them; which would admit virtual disarmament of the federated nations. The former arrangement has nothing in its favour, except the possibility that no better or less irksome arrangement can be had under existing circumstances; that is to say that the pacific nations may not be able to bring these dynastic states to terms of disarmament under surveillance. They assuredly can not except by force; and this is the precise point on which the continued hostilities in Europe turn today. In diplomatic parable the German Imperial spokesmen say that they can accept (or as they prefer to phrase it, grant) no terms that do not fully safeguard the Future of the Fatherland; and in similarly diplomatic parable the spokesmen of the Entente insist that Prussian militarism must be permanently put out of commission; but it all means the same thing, viz. that the Imperial establishment is to be (or is not to be) disabled beyond the possibility of its entering on a similar warlike enterprise again, when it has had time for recuperation. The dynastic statesmen, and the lay subjects of the Imperial establishment, are strenuously set on securing a fair opportunity for recuperation and a wiser endeavour to achieve that dominion which the present adventure promises to defeat; while the Entente want no recurrence, and are persuaded that a recurrence can be avoided only on the footing of a present collapse of the Imperial power and a scrupulously enforced prostration of it henceforth.

Without the definitive collapse of the Imperial power no pacific league of nations can come to anything much more than armistice. On the basis of such a collapse the league may as well administer its affairs economically by way of an all-around reduction of armaments, as by the costlier and more irksome way of "preparedness." But a sensible reduction of armaments on the part of the neutral nations implies disarmament of the dynastic States. Which would involve a neutral surveillance of the affairs of these dynastic States in such detail and with such exercise of authority as would reduce their governments to the effective status of local administrative officials. Out of which, in turn, would arise complications that would lead to necessary readjustments all along the line. It would involve the virtual, if not also the formal, abolition of the monarchy, since the monarchy has no other use than that of international war and intrigue; or at least it would involve the virtual abrogation of its powers, reducing it to the same status of *faineantise* as now characterises the British crown. Evidently this means a serious intermeddling in the domestic concerns and arrangements of the Fatherland, such as is not admissible under the democratic principle that any people must be left free to follow their own inclinations and devices in their own concerns; at the same time that this degree of interference is imperative if the peace is to be kept on any other footing than that of eternal vigilance and superior armed force, with a people whose own inclinations and devices are of the kind now grown familiar in the German case,--all of which also applies, with accentuation, in the case of Imperial Japan.

* * * * *

Some such policy of neutral surveillance in the affairs of these peoples whose pacific temper is under suspicion, is necessarily involved in a plan to enforce peace by concert of the pacific nations, and it will necessarily carry implications and farther issues, touching not only these supposedly recalcitrant peoples, but also as regards the pacific nations themselves. Assuming always that the prime purpose and consistent aim of the projected league is the peace and security of those pacific nations on whose initiative it is to be achieved, then it should be reasonable to assume that the course of procedure in its organisation, administration and further adaptations and adjustments must follow the logic of necessities leading to that end. He who wills the end must make up his account with the means.

The end in this case is peace and security; which means, for practical purposes, peace and good-will. Ill-will is not a secure foundation of peace. Even the military strategists of the Imperial establishment recommend a programme of "frightfulness" only as a convenient military expedient, essentially a provisional basis of tranquility. In the long run and as a permanent peace measure it is doubtless not to the point. Security is finally to be had among or between modern peoples only on the ground of a common understanding and an impartially common basis of equity, or something approaching that basis as nearly as circumstances will permit. Which means that in so far as the projected peace-compact is to take effect in any enduring way, and leave the federated nations some degree of freedom from persistent apprehension and animosity, as well as from habitual insecurity of life and limb, the league must not only be all-inclusive, but it must be inclusively uniform in all its requirements and regulations.

The peoples of the quondam Imperial nations must come into the league on a footing of formal equality with the rest. This they can not do without the virtual abdication of their dynastic governmental establishments and a consequent shift to a democratic form of organisation, and a formal abrogation of class privileges and prerogatives.

However, a virtual abdication or cancelment of the dynastic rule, such as to bring it formally into the same class with the British crown, would scarcely meet the requirements in the case of the German Imperial establishment; still more patently not in the case of Imperial Japan. If, following the outlines of the decayed British crown, one or the other of these Imperial establishments were by formal enactment reduced to a state of nominal desuetude, the effect would be very appreciably different from what happens in the British community, where the crown has lost its powers by failure of the requisite subordination on the part of the people, and not by a formal abdication of rights. In the German case, and even more in the Japanese case, the strength of the Imperial establishment lies in the unimpaired loyalty of the populace; which would remain nearly intact at the outset, and would thin out only by insensible degrees in the sequel; so that if only the Imperial establishment were left formally standing it would command the fealty of the common run in spite of any formal abrogation of its powers, and the course of things would, in effect, run as before the break. In effect, to bring about a shift to a democratic basis the dynastic slate would have to be wiped very clean indeed. And this shift would be indispensable to the successful conduct of such a pacific league of nations, since any other than an effectually democratic national establishment is to be counted on unfailingly to intrigue for dynastic aggrandizement, through good report and evil.

In a case like that of Imperial Germany, with its federated States and subsidiaries, where royalty and nobility still are potent preconceptions investing the popular imagination, and where loyal abnegation in the presence of authority still is the chief and staple virtue of the common man,--in all such cases virtual abdication of the dynastic initiative under constitutional forms can be had only by a formal and scrupulously complete abrogation of all those legal and customary arrangements on which this irresponsible exercise of authority has rested and through which it has taken effect. Neutralisation in these instances will mean reduction to an unqualified democratic footing; which will, at least at the outset, not be acceptable to the common people, and will be wholly intolerable to the ruling classes. Such a regime, therefore, while it is indispensable as a working basis for a neutral league of peace, would from the outset have to be enforced against the most desperate resistance of the ruling classes, headed by the dynastic statesmen and warlords, and backed by the stubborn loyalty of the subject populace. It would have to mean the end of things for the ruling classes and the most distasteful submission to an alien scheme of use and wont for the populace. And yet it is also an indispensable element in any scheme of pacification that aims at permanent peace and security. In time, it may well be believed, the people of the Fatherland might learn to do well enough without the gratuitous domination of their ruling classes, but at the outset it would be a heartfelt privation.

It follows that a league to enforce peace would have to begin its regime with enforcing peace on terms of the unconditional surrender of the formidable warlike nations; which could be accomplished only by the absolute and irretrievable defeat of these Powers as they now stand. The question will, no doubt, present itself, Is the end worth the cost? That question can, of course, not be answered in absolute terms, inasmuch as it resolves itself into a question of taste and prepossession. An answer to it would also not be greatly to the purpose here, since it would have no particular bearing on the course of action likely to be pursued by these pacific nations in their quest of a settled peace. It is more to the point to ask what is likely to be the practical decision of these peoples on that head when the question finally presents itself in a concrete form.

Again it is necessary to call to mind that any momentous innovation which rests on popular sentiment will take time; that consequently anything like a plebiscite on the question today would scarcely give a safe index of what the decision is likely to be when presently put to the test; and that as things go just now, swiftly and urgent, any time-allowance counts at something more than its ordinary workday coefficient. What can apparently be said with some degree of confidence is that just now, during these two years past, sentiment has been moving in the direction indicated, and that any growing inclination of the kind is being strongly reenforced by a growing realisation that nothing but heroic remedies will avail at this juncture. If it comes to be currently recognised that a settled peace can be had only at the cost of eradicating privilege and royalty from the warlike nations, it would seem reasonable to expect, from their present state of mind, that the pacific nations will scarcely hesitate to apply that remedy,--provided always that the fortunes of war fall out as that measure would require, and provided also that the conflict lasts long enough and severe enough to let them make up their mind to anything so drastic.

* * * * *

There is a certain side issue bearing on this question of the ulterior probabilities of popular sentiment and national policy as to what is to be done with the warlike nations in the event that the allied nations who fight for neutrality have the disposal of such matters. This side issue may seem remote, and it may not unlikely be overlooked among the mass of graver and more tangible considerations. It was remarked above that the United Kingdom is one of the two chief pillars of the projected house of peace; and it may be added without serious fear of contradiction or annoyance that the United Kingdom is also the one among these pacific nations that comes nearest being capable, in the event of such an emergency, to take care of its own case single-handed. For better or worse, British adhesion to the project is indispensable, and the British are in a position virtually to name their own terms of adhesion. The British commonwealth--a very inclusive phrase in this connection--must form the core of the pacific league, if any, and British sentiment will have a very great place in the terms of its formation and in the terms which it will be inclined to offer the Imperial coalition at the settlement.

Now, it happens that the British community entered on this war as a democratic monarchy ruled and officered by a body of gentlemen--doubtless the most correct and admirable muster of gentlemen, of anything approaching its volume, that the modern world can show. But the war has turned out not to be a gentlemen's war. It has on the contrary been a war of technological exploits, reenforced with all the beastly devices of the heathen. It is a war in which all the specific traits of the well-bred and gently-minded man are a handicap; in which veracity, gallantry, humanity, liberality are conducive to nothing but defeat and humiliation. The death-rate among the British gentlemen-officers in the early months, and for many months, ran extravagantly high, for the most part because they were gallant gentlemen as well as officers imbued with the good, old class spirit of ***noblesse*** *oblige*, that has made half the tradition and more than half the working theory of the British officer in the field,--good, but old, hopelessly out of date. That generation of officers died, for the most part; being unfit to survive or to serve the purpose under these modern conditions of warfare, to which their enemy on the other hand had adapted themselves with easy facility from beforehand. The gentlemanly qualifications, and the material apparatus of gentility, and, it will perhaps have to be admitted, the gentlemen, have fallen into the background, or perhaps rather have measurably fallen into abeyance, among the officers of the line. There may be more doubt as to the state of things in respect of the gentility of the staff, but the best that can confidently be said is that it is a point in doubt.

It is hoped that one may say without offense that in the course of time the personnel has apparently worked down to the level of vulgarity defined by the ways and means of this modern warfare; which means the level on which runs a familiar acquaintance with large and complex mechanical apparatus, railway and highway transport and power, reenforced concrete, excavations and mud, more particularly mud, concealment and ambush, and unlimited deceit and ferocity. It is not precisely that persons of pedigree and gentle breeding have ceased to enter or seek entrance to employment as officers, still less that measures have been taken to restrain their doing so or to eliminate from the service those who have come into it--though there may present itself a doubt on this point as touches the more responsible discretionary positions--but only that the stock of suitable gentlemen, uncommonly large as it is, has been overdrawn; that those who have latterly gone into service, or stayed in, have perforce divested themselves of their gentility in some appreciable measure, particularly as regards class distinction, and have fallen on their feet in the more commonplace role of common men.

Serviceability in this modern warfare is conditioned on much the same traits of temperament and training that make for usefulness in the modern industrial processes, where large-scale coordinations of movement and an effective familiarity with precise and far-reaching mechanical processes is an indispensable requirement,--indispensable in the same measure as the efficient conduct of this modern machine industry is indispensable. But the British gentleman, in so far as he runs true to type, is of no use to modern industry; quite the contrary, in fact. Still, the British gentleman is, in point of heredity, the same thing over again as the British common man; so that, barring the misdirected training that makes him a gentleman, and which can largely be undone under urgent need and pressure, he can be made serviceable for such uses as the modern warfare requires. Meantime the very large demand for officers, and the insatiable demand for capable officers, has brought the experienced and capable common man into the case and is in a fair way to discredit gentility as a necessary qualification of field officers.

But the same process of discredit and elimination is also extending to the responsible officials who have the administration of things in hand. Indeed, the course of vulgarisation among the responsible officials has now been under way for some appreciable time and with very perceptible effect, and the rate of displacement appears to be gathering velocity with every month that passes. Here, as in the field operations, it also appears that gentlemanly methods, standards, preconceptions, and knowledge of men and things, is no longer to the purpose. Here, too, it is increasingly evident that this is not a gentlemen's war. And the traditional qualifications that have sufficed in the past, at least to the extent of enabling the British management to "muddle through," as they are proudly in the habit of saying,--these qualifications are of slight account in this technological conjuncture of the nation's fortunes. It would perhaps be an under-statement to say that these gentlemanly qualifications are no longer of any account, for the purpose immediately in hand, and it would doubtless not do to say that they are wholly and unreservedly disserviceable as things run today; but captious critics might find at least a precarious footing of argument on such a proposition.

Through the course of the nineteenth century the British government had progressively been taking on the complexion of a "gentlemen's agreement;" a government by gentlemen, for gentlemen, and of gentlemen, too, beyond what could well be alleged in any other known instance, though never wholly so. No government could be a government of gentlemen exclusively, since there is no pecuniary profit in gentlemen as such, and therefore no object in governing them; more particularly could there never be any incentive in it for gentlemen, whose livelihood is, in the nature of the case, drawn from some one else. A gentlemen's government can escape death by inanition only in so far as it serves the material interest of its class, as contrasted with the underlying population from which the class draws its livelihood. This British arrangement of a government by prudent and humane gentlemen with a view to the conservation of that state of things that best conduced to the material well-being of their own class, has on the whole had the loyal support of the underlying populace, with an occasional floundering protest. But the protest has never taken the shape of an expressed distrust of gentlemen, considered as the staple ways and means of government; nor has the direction of affairs ever descended into the hands of any other or lower class or condition of men.

On the whole, this British arrangement for the control of national affairs by a body of interested gentlemen-investors has been, and perhaps still is, just as well at home in the affectionate preconceptions of the nineteenth-century British as the corresponding German usufruct by self-appointed swaggering aristocrats has been among the underlying German population, or as the American arrangement of national control by business men for business ends. The British and the American arrangements run very much to the same substantial effect, of course, inasmuch as the British gentlemen represent, as a class, the filial generations of a business community, and their aims and standards of conduct continue to be such as are enforced by the pecuniary interests on which their gentility is conditioned. They continue to draw the ways and means of a worthy life from businesslike arrangements of a "vested" character, made and provided with a view to their nourishment and repose. Their resulting usufruct of the community's productive efforts rests on a vested interest of a pecuniary sort, sanctioned by the sacred rights of property; very much as the analogous German dynastic and aristocratic usufruct rests on personal prerogative, sanctioned by the sacred rights of authentic prescription, without afterthought. The two, it will be noted are very much alike, in effect, "under the skin." The great distinguishing mark being that the German usufructuary gentlemen are, in theory at least, gentlemen-adventurers of prowess and proud words, whose place in the world's economy it is to glorify God and disturb the peace; whereas their British analogues are gentlemen-investors, of blameless propriety, whose place it is more simply to glorify God and enjoy Him forever.

All this arrangement of a usufruct with a view to the reputable consumption of the community's superfluous production has had the cordial support of British sentiment, perhaps fully as cordial as the German popular subservience in the corresponding German scheme; both being well embedded in the preconceptions of the common man. But the war has put it all to a rude test, and has called on the

British gentlemen's executive committee to take over duties for which it was not designed. The exigencies of this war of technological exploits have been almost wholly, and very insistently, of a character not contemplated in the constitution of such an executive committee of gentlemen-investors designed to safeguard class interests and promote their pecuniary class advantage by a blamelessly inconspicuous and indirect management of national affairs. The methods are of the class known colloquially among the vulgar-spoken American politicians as "pussyfooting" and "log-rolling"; but always with such circumstance of magnitude, authenticity and well-bred deference to precedent, as to give the resulting routine of subreption, trover and conversion, an air not only of benevolent consideration but of austere morality.

But the most austere courtesy and the most authentically dispassionate division of benefits will not meet the underbred exigencies of a war conducted on the mechanistic lines of the modern state of the industrial arts. So the blameless, and for the purpose imbecile, executive committee of gentlemen-investors has been insensibly losing the confidence and the countenance of the common man; who, when all is said, will always have to do what is to be done. The order of gentlemanly parleying and brokery has, therefore, with many apprehensions of calamity, been reluctantly and tardily giving ground before something that is of a visibly underbred order. Increasingly underbred, and thereby insensibly approaching the character of this war situation, but accepted with visible reluctance and apprehension both by the ruling class and by the underlying population. The urgent necessity of going to such a basis, and of working out the matter in hand by an unblushing recourse to that matter-of-fact logic of mechanical efficiency, which alone can touch the difficulties of the case, but which has no respect of persons,--this necessity has been present from the outset and has been vaguely apprehended for long past, but it is only tardily and after the chastening of heavy penalties on this gentlemanly imbecility that a substantial move in that direction has been made. It has required much British resolution to overcome the night-fear of going out into the unhallowed ground of matter-of-fact, where the farthest earlier excursions of the governmental agencies had taken them no farther than such financial transactions as are incident to the accomplishment of anything whatever in a commercial nation. And then, too, there is a pecuniary interest in being interested in financial transactions.

This shifting of discretionary control out of the hands of the gentlemen into those of the underbred common run, who know how to do what is necessary to be done in the face of underbred exigencies, may conceivably go far when it has once been started, and it may go forward at an accelerated rate if the pressure of necessity lasts long enough. If time be given for habituation to this manner of directorate in national affairs, so that the common man comes to realise how it is feasible to get along without gentlemen-investors holding the discretion, the outcome may conceivably be very grave. It is a point in doubt, but it is conceivable that in such a case the gentlemanly executive committee administering affairs in the light of the gentlemanly pecuniary interest, will not be fully reinstated in the discretionary control of the United Kingdom for an appreciable number of years after the return of peace. Possibly, even, the regime may be permanently deranged, and there is even a shadowy doubt possible to be entertained as to whether the vested pecuniary rights, on which the class of gentlemen rests, may not suffer some derangement, in case the control should pass into the hands of the underbred and unpropertied for so long a season as to let the common man get used to thinking that the vested interests and the sacred rights of gentility are so much ado about nothing.

Such an outcome would be extreme, but as a remote contingency it is to be taken into account. The privileged classes of the United Kingdom should by this time be able to see the danger there may be for them and their vested interests, pecuniary and moral, in an excessive prolongation of the war; in such postponement of peace as would afford time for a popular realisation of their incompetence and disserviceability as touches the nation's material well-being under modern conditions. To let the nation's war experience work to such an outcome, the season of war would have to be prolonged beyond what either the hopes or the fears of the community have yet contemplated; but the point is after all worth noting, as being within the premises of the case, that there is herein a remote contingency of losing, at least for a time, that unformulated clause in the British constitution which has hitherto restricted the holding of responsible office to men of pedigree and of gentle breeding, or at least of very grave pecuniary weight; so grave as to make the incumbents virtual gentlemen, with a virtual pedigree, and with a virtual gentleman's accentuated sense of class interest. Should such an eventuality overtake British popular sentiment and belief there is also the remote contingency that the rights of ownership and investment would lose a degree of sanctity.

It seems necessary to note a further, and in a sense more improbable, line of disintegration among modern fixed ideas. Among the best entrenched illusions of modern economic preconceptions, and in economic as well as legal theory, has been the indispensability of funds, and the hard and fast limitation of industrial operations by the supply or with-holding of funds. The war experience has hitherto gone tentatively to show that funds and financial transactions, of credit, bargain, sale and solvency, may be dispensed with under pressure of necessity; and apparently without seriously hindering that run of mechanical fact, on which interest in the present case necessarily centers, and which must be counted on to give the outcome. Latterly the case is clearing up a little further, on further experience and under further pressure of technological exigencies, to the effect that financial arrangements are indispensable in this connection only because and in so far as it has been arranged to consider them indispensable; as in international trade. They are an indispensable means of intermediation only in so far as pecuniary interests are to be furthered or safeguarded in the intermediation. When, as has happened with the belligerents in the present instance, the national establishment becomes substantially insolvent, it is beginning to appear that its affairs can be taken care of with less difficulty and with better effect without the use of financial expedients. Of course, it takes time to get used to doing things by the more direct method and without the accustomed circumlocution of accountancy, or the accustomed allowance for profits to go to interested parties who, under the financial regime, hold a power of discretionary permission in all matters that touch the use of the industrial arts. Under these urgent material exigencies, investment comes to have much of the appearance of a gratuitous drag and drain on the processes of industry.

Here, again, is a sinister contingency; sinister, that is, for those vested rights of ownership by force of which the owners of "capital" are enabled to permit or withhold the use of the industrial arts by the community at large, on pain of privation in case the accustomed toll to the owners of capital is not paid. It is, of course, not intended to find fault with this arrangement; which has the sanction of "time immemorial" and of a settled persuasion that it lies at the root of all civilised life and intercourse. It is only that in case of extreme need this presumed indispensable expedient of industrial control has broken down, and that experience is proving it to be, in these premises, an item of borrowed trouble. Should experience continue to run on the same lines for an appreciable period and at a high tension, it is at least conceivable that the vested right of owners to employ unlimited sabotage in the quest of profits might fall so far into disrepute as to leave them under a qualified doubt on the return of "normal" conditions. The common man, in other words, who gathers nothing but privation and anxiety from the owners' discretionary sabotage, may conceivably stand to lose his preconception that the vested rights of ownership are the cornerstone of his life, liberty and pursuit of happiness.

* * * * *

The considerations recited in this lengthy excursion on the war situation and its probable effects on popular habits of thought in the United Kingdom go to say that when peace comes to be negotiated, with the United Kingdom as the chief constituent and weightiest spokesman of the allied nations and of the league of pacific neutrals, the representatives of British aims and opinions are likely to speak in a different, chastened, and disillusioned fashion, as contrasted with what the British attitude was at the beginning of hostilities. The gentlemanly British animus of arrogant self-sufficiency will have been somewhat sobered, perhaps somewhat subdued. Concession to the claims and pretensions of the other pacific nations is likely to go farther than might once have been expected, particularly in the way of concession to any demand for greater international comity and less international discrimination; essentially concession looking to a reduction of national pretensions and an incipient neutralisation of national interests. Coupled with this will presumably be a less conciliatory attitude toward the members of the dynastic coalition against whom the war has been fought, owing to a more mature realisation of the impossibility of a lasting peace negotiated with a Power whose substantial core is a warlike and irresponsible dynastic establishment. The peace negotiations are likely to run on a lower level of diplomatic deference to constituted authorities, and with more of a view to the interests and sentiments of the underlying population, than was evident in the futile negotiations had at the outbreak of hostilities. The gentle art of diplomacy, that engages the talents of exalted personages and well-bred statesmen, has been somewhat discredited; and if it turns out that the vulgarisation of the directorate in the United Kingdom and its associated allies and neutrals will have time to go on to something like dominance and authenticity, then the deference which the spokesmen of these nations are likely to show for the prescriptive rights of dynasty, nobility, bureaucracy, or even of pecuniary aristocracy, in the countries that make up the party of the second part, may be expected to have shrunk appreciably, conceivably even to such precarious dimensions as to involve the virtual neglect or possible downright abrogation of them, in sum and substance.

Indeed, the chances of a successful pacific league of neutrals to come out of the current situation appear to be largely bound up with the degree of vulgarisation due to overtake the several directorates of the belligerent nations as well as the popular habits of thought in these and in the neutral countries, during the further course of the war. It is too broad a generalisation, perhaps, to say that the longer the war lasts the better are the chances of such a neutral temper in the interested nations as will make a pacific league practicable, but the contrary would appear a much less defensible proposition. It is, of course, the common man that has the least interest in warlike enterprise, if any, and it is at the same time the common man that bears the burden of such enterprise and has also the most immediate interest in keeping the peace. If, slowly and pervasively, in the course of hard experience, he learns to distrust the conduct of affairs by his betters, and learns at the same move to trust to his own class to do what is necessary and to leave undone what is not, his deference to his betters is likely to suffer a decline, such as should show itself in a somewhat unguarded recourse to democratic ways and means.

In short, there is in this progressive vulgarisation of effectual use and wont and of sentiment, in the United Kingdom and elsewhere, some slight ground for the hope, or the apprehension, that no peace will be made with the dynastic Powers of the second part until they cease to be dynastic Powers and take on the semblance of democratic commonwealths, with dynasties, royalties and privileged classes thrown in the discard.

This would probably mean some prolongation of hostilities, until the dynasties and privileged classes had completely exhausted their available resources; and, by the same token, until the privileged classes in the more modern nations among the belligerents had also been displaced from direction and discretion by those underbred classes on whom it is incumbent to do what is to be done; or until a juncture were reached that comes passably near to such a situation. On the contingency of such a course of events and some such outcome appears also to hang the chance of a workable pacific league. Without further experience of the futility of upper-class and pecuniary control, to discredit precedent and constituted authority, it is scarcely conceivable, e.g., that the victorious allies would go the length of coercively discarding the German Imperial dynasty and the kept classes that with it constitute the Imperial State, and of replacing it with a democratic organisation of the people in the shape of a modern commonwealth; and without a change of that nature, affecting that nation and such of its allies as would remain on the map, no league of pacific neutrals would be able to manage its affairs, even for a time, except on a war-footing that would involve a competitive armament against future dynastic enterprises from the same quarter. Which comes to saying that a lasting peace is possible on no other terms than the disestablishment of the Imperial dynasty and the abrogation of all feudalistic remnants of privilege in the Fatherland and its allies, together with the reduction of those countries to the status of commonwealths made up of ungraded men.

* * * * *

It is easy to speculate on what the conditions precedent to such a pacific league of neutrals must of necessity be; but it is not therefore less difficult to make a shrewd guess as to the chances of these conditions being met. Of these conditions precedent, the chief and foremost, without which any other favorable circumstances are comparatively idle, is a considerable degree of neutralisation, extending to virtually all national interests and pretensions, but more particularly to all material and commercial interests of the federated peoples; and, indispensably and especially, such neutralisation would have to extend to the nations from whom aggression is now apprehended, as, e.g., the German people. But such neutralisation could not conceivably reach the Fatherland unless that nation were made over in the image of democracy, since the Imperial State is, by force of the terms, a warlike and unneutral power. This would seem to be the ostensibly concealed meaning of the allied governments in proclaiming that their aim is to break German militarism without doing harm to the German people.

As touches the neutralisation of the democratically rehabilitated Fatherland, or in default of that, as touches the peace terms to be offered the Imperial government, the prime article among the stipulations would seem to be abolition of all trade discrimination against Germany or by Germany against any other nationality. Such stipulation would, of course, cover all manner of trade discrimination,--e.g., import, export and excise tariff, harbor and registry dues, subsidy, patent right, copyright, trade mark, tax exemption whether partial or exclusive, investment preferences at home and abroad,--in short it would have to establish a thoroughgoing neutralisation of trade relations in the widest acceptation of the term, and to apply in perpetuity. The like applies, of course, to all that fringe of subsidiary and outlying peoples on whom Imperial Germany relies for much of its resources in any warlike enterprise. Such a move also disposes of the colonial question in a parenthesis, so far as regards any special bond of affiliation between the Empire, or the Fatherland, and any colonial possessions that are now thought desirable to be claimed. Under neutralisation, colonies would cease to be "colonial possessions," being necessarily included under the general abrogation of commercial discriminations, and also necessarily exempt from special taxation or specially favorable tax rates.

Colonies there still would be, though it is not easy to imagine what would be the meaning of a "German Colony" in such a case. Colonies would be free communities, after the fashion of New Zealand or Australia, but with the further sterilisation of the bond between colony and mother country involved in the abolition of all appointive offices and all responsibility to the crown or the imperial government. Now, there are no German colonies in this simpler British sense of the term, which implies nothing more than community of blood, institutions and language, together with that sense of solidarity between the colony and the mother country which this community of pedigree and institutions will necessarily bring; but while there are today no German colonies, in the sense of the term so given, there is no reason to presume that no such German colonies would come into bearing under the conditions of this prospective regime of neutrality installed by such a pacific league, when backed by the league's guarantee that no colony from the Fatherland will be exposed to the eventual risk of coming under the discretionary tutelage of the German Imperial establishment and so falling into a relation of step-childhood to the Imperial dynasty.

As is well known, and as has by way of superfluous commonplace been set forth by a sometime Colonial Secretary of the Empire, the decisive reason for there being no German colonies in existence is the consistently impossible colonial policy of the German government, looking to the usufruct of the colonies by the government, and the fear of further arbitrary control and nepotic discrimination at the pleasure of the self-seeking dynastic establishment. It is only under Imperial rule that no German colony, in this modern sense of the term, is possible; and only because Imperial rule does not admit of a free community being formed by colonists from the Fatherland; or of an ostensibly free community of that kind ever feeling secure from unsolicited interference with its affairs.

The nearest approach to a German Colony, as contrasted with a "Colonial Possession," hitherto have been the very considerable, number of escaped German subjects who have settled in English-speaking or Latin-speaking countries, particularly in North and South America. And considering that the chief common trait among them is their successful evasion of the Imperial government's heavy hand, they show an admirable filial piety toward the Imperial establishment; though troubled with no slightest regret at having escaped from the Imperial surveillance and no slightest inclination to return to the shelter of the Imperial tutelage. A colloquialism--"hyphenate"--has latterly grown up to meet the need of a term to designate these evasive and yet patriotic colonists. It is scarcely misleading to say that the German-American hyphenate, e.g., in so far as he runs true to form, is still a German subject with his heart, but he is an American citizen with his head. All of which goes to argue that if the Fatherland were to fall into such a state of democratic tolerance that no recidivist need carry a defensive hyphen to shield him from the importunate attentions of the Imperial government, German colonies would also come into bearing; although, it is true, they would have no value to the German government.

In the Imperial colonial policy colonies are conceived to stand to their Imperial guardian or master in a relation between that of a step-child and that of an indentured servant; to be dealt with summarily and at discretion and to be made use of without scruple. The like attitude toward colonies was once familiar matter-of-course with the British and Spanish statesmen. The British found the plan unprofitable, and also unworkable, and have given it up. The Spanish, having no political outlook but the dynastic one, could of course not see their way to relinquish the only purpose of their colonial enterprise, except in relinquishing their colonial possessions. The German (Imperial) colonial policy is and will be necessarily after the Spanish pattern, and necessarily, too, with the Spanish results.

Under the projected neutral scheme there would be no colonial policy, and of course, no inducement to the acquisition of colonies, since there would be no profit to be derived, or to be fancied, in the case. But while no country, as a commonwealth, has any material interest in the acquisition or maintenance of colonies, it is otherwise as regards the dynastic interests of an Imperial government; and it is also otherwise, at least in the belief of the interested parties, as regards special businessmen or business concerns who are in a position to gain something by help of national discrimination in their favor. As regards the pecuniary interests of favored businessmen or business concerns, and of investors favored by national discrimination in colonial relations, the case falls under the general caption of trade discrimination, and does not differ at all materially from such expedients as a protective tariff, a ship subsidy, or a bounty on exports. But as regards the warlike, that is to say dynastic, interest of an Imperial government the case stands somewhat different.

Colonial Possessions in such a case yield no material benefit to the country at large, but their possession is a serviceable plea for warlike preparations with which to retain possession of the colonies in the face of eventualities, and it is also a serviceable means of stirring the national pride and keeping alive a suitable spirit of patriotic animosity. The material service actually to be derived from such possessions in the event of war is a point in doubt, with the probabilities apparently running against their being of any eventual net use. But there need be no question that such possessions, under the hand of any national establishment infected with imperial ambitions, are a fruitful source of diplomatic complications, excuses for armament, international grievances, and eventual aggression. A pacific league of neutrals can evidently not tolerate the retention of colonial possessions by any dynastic State that may be drawn into the league or under its jurisdiction, as, e.g., the German Empire in case it should be left on an Imperial footing. Whereas, in case the German peoples are thrown back on a democratic status, as neutralised commonwealths without a crown or a military establishment, the question of their colonial possessions evidently falls vacant.

As to the neutralisation of trade relations apart from the question of colonies, and as bears on the case of Germany under the projected jurisdiction of a pacific league of neutrals, the considerations to be taken account of are of much the same nature. As it would have to take effect, e.g., in the abolition of commercial and industrial discriminations between Germany and the pacific nations, such neutralisation would doubtless confer a lasting material benefit on the German people at large; and it is not easy to detect any loss or detriment to be derived from such a move so long as peace prevails. Protective, that is to say discriminating, export, import, or excise duties, harbor and registry dues, subsidies, tax exemptions and trade preferences, and all the like devices of interference with trade and industry, are unavoidably a hindrance to the material interests of any people on whom they are imposed or who impose these disabilities on themselves. So that exemption from these things by a comprehensive neutralisation of trade relations would immediately benefit all the nations concerned, in respect of their material well-being in times of peace. There is no exception and no abatement to be taken account of under this general statement, as is well known to all men who are conversant with these matters.

But it is otherwise as regards the dynastic interest in the case, and as regards any national interest in warlike enterprise. It is doubtless true that all restraint of trade between nations, and between classes or localities within the national frontiers, unavoidably acts to weaken and impoverish the people on whose economic activities this restraint is laid; and to the extent to which this effect is had it will also be true that the country which so is hindered in its work will have a less aggregate of resources to place at the disposal of its enterprising statesmen for imperialist ends. But these restraints may yet be useful for dynastic, that is to say warlike, ends by making the country more nearly a "self-contained economic whole." A country becomes a "self-contained economic whole" by mutilation, in cutting itself off from the industrial system in which industrially it belongs, but in which it is unwilling nationally to hold its place. National frontiers are industrial barriers. But as a result of such mutilation of its industrial life such a country is better able--it has been believed--to bear the shock of severing its international trade relations entirely, as is likely to happen in case of war.

In a large country, such as America or Russia, which comprises within its national boundaries very extensive and very varied resources and a widely distributed and diversified population, the mischief suffered from restraints of trade that hinder industrial relations with the world at large will of course be proportionately lessened. Such a country comes nearer being a miniature industrial world; although none of the civilised nations, large or small, can carry on its ordinary industrial activities and its ordinary manner of life without drawing on foreign parts to some appreciable extent. But a country of small territorial extent and of somewhat narrowly restricted natural resources, as, e.g., Germany or France, can even by the most drastic measures of restraint and mutilation achieve only a very mediocre degree of industrial isolation and "self-sufficiency,"--as has, e.g., appeared in the present war. But in all cases, though in varying measure, the mitigated isolation so enforced by these restraints on trade will in their degree impair the country's industrial efficiency and lower the people's material well-being; yet, if the restrictions are shrewdly applied this partial isolation and partial "self-sufficiency" will go some way toward preparing the nation for the more thorough isolation that follows on the outbreak of hostilities.

The present plight of the German people under war conditions may serve to show how nearly that end may be attained, and yet how inadequate even the most unreserved measures of industrial isolation must be in face of the fact that the modern state of the industrial arts necessarily draws on the collective resources of the world at large. It may well be doubted, on an impartial view, if the mutilation of the country's industrial system by such measures of isolation does not after all rather weaken the nation even for warlike ends; but then, the discretionary authorities in the dynastic States are always, and it may be presumed necessarily, hampered with obsolete theories handed down from that cameralistic age, when the little princes of the Fatherland were making dynastic history. So, e.g., the current, nineteenth and twentieth century, economic policy of the Prussian-Imperial statesmen is still drawn on lines within which Frederick II, called the Great, would have felt well at home.

Like other preparation for hostilities this reduction of the country to the status of a self-contained economic organisation is costly, but like other preparation for hostilities it also puts the nation in a position of greater readiness to break off friendly relations with its neighbors. It is a war measure, commonly spoken for by its advocates as a measure of self-defense; but whatever the merits of the self-defenders' contention, this measure is a war measure. As such it can reasonably claim no hearing in the counsels of a pacific league of neutrals, whose purpose it is to make war impracticable. Particularly can there be no reasonable question of admitting a policy of trade discrimination and isolation on the part of a nation which has, for purposes of warlike aggression, pursued such a policy in the past, and which it is the immediate purpose of the league to bind over to keep the peace.

There has been a volume of loose talk spent on the justice and expediency of boycotting the trade of the peoples of the Empire after the return of peace, as a penalty and as a preventive measure designed to retard their recovery of strength with which to enter on a further warlike enterprise. Such a measure would necessarily be somewhat futile; since "Business is business," after all, and the practical limitations imposed on an unprofitable boycott by the moral necessity to buy cheap and sell dear that rests on all businessmen would surreptitiously mitigate it to the point of negligibility. It is inconceivable--or it would be inconceivable in the absence of imbecile politicians and self-seeking businessmen--that measures looking to the trade isolation of any one of these countries could be entertained as a point of policy to be pursued by a league of neutrals. And it is only in so far as patriotic jealousy and vindictive sentiments are allowed to displace the aspiration for peace and security, that such measures can claim consideration. Considered as a penalty to be imposed on the erring nations who set this warlike adventure afoot, it should be sufficiently plain that such a measure as a trade boycott could not touch the chief offenders, or even their responsible abettors. It would, rather, play into the hands of the militarist interests by keeping alive the spirit of national jealousy and international hatred, out of which wars arise and without which warlike enterprise might hopefully be expected to disappear out of the scheme of human intercourse. The punishment would fall, as all economic burdens and disabilities must always fall, on the common man, the underlying population.

The chief relation of this common run, this underlying population of German subjects, to the inception and pursuit of this Imperial warlike enterprise, is comprised in the fact that they are an underlying population of subjects, held in usufruct by the Imperial establishment and employed at will. It is true, they have lent themselves unreservedly to the uses for which the dynasty has use for them, and they have entered enthusiastically into the warlike adventure set afoot by the dynastic statesmen; but that they have done so is their misfortune rather than their fault. By use and wont and indoctrination they have for long been unremittingly, and helplessly, disciplined into a spirit of dynastic loyalty, national animosity and servile abnegation; until it would be nothing better than a pathetic inversion of all the equities of the case to visit the transgressions of their masters upon the common run; whose fault lies, after all, in their being an underlying population of subjects, who have not had a chance to reach that spiritual level on which they could properly be held accountable for the uses to which they are turned. It is true, men are ordinarily punished for their misfortunes; but the warlike enterprise of the Imperial dynasty has already brought what might fairly be rated as a good measure of punishment on this underlying populace, whose chief fault and chief misfortune lies in an habitual servile abnegation of those traits of initiative and discretion in man that constitute him an agent susceptible of responsibility or retribution.

It would be all the more of a pathetic mockery to visit the transgressions of their masters on these victims of circumstance and dynastic mendacity, since the conventionalities of international equity will scarcely permit the high responsible parties in the case to be chastised with any penalty harsher than a well-mannered figure of speech. To serve as a deterrent, the penalty must strike the point where vests the discretion; but servile use and wont is still too well intact in these premises to let any penalty touch the guilty core of a profligate dynasty. Under the wear and tear of continued war and its incident continued vulgarisation of the directorate and responsible staff among the pacific allies, the conventional respect of persons is likely to suffer appreciable dilapidation; but there need be no apprehension of such a loss of decent respect for personages as would compromise the creature comforts of that high syndicate of personages on whose initiative the Fatherland entered upon this enterprise in dominion.

Bygone shortcomings and transgressions can have no reasonable place in the arrangements by which a pacific league of neutrals designs to keep the peace. Neither can bygone prerogatives and precedents of magnificence and of mastery, except in so far as they unavoidably must come into play through the inability of men to divest themselves of their ingrained preconceptions, by virtue of which a Hohenzollern or a Hapsburger is something more formidable and more to be considered than a recruiting sergeant or a purveyor of light literature. The league can do its work of pacification only by elaborately forgetting differences and discrepancies of the kind that give rise to international grievances. Which is the same as saying that the neutralisation of national discriminations and pretensions will have to go all the way, if it is to serve. But this implies, as broadly as need be, that the pacific nations who make the league and provisionally administer its articles of agreement and jurisdiction, can not exempt themselves from any of the leveling measures of neutralisation to which the dynastic suspects among them are to be subject. It would mean a relinquishment of all those undemocratic institutional survivals out of which international grievances are wont to arise. As a certain Danish adage would have it, the neutrals of the league must all be shorn over the same comb.

* * * * *

What is to be shorn over this one comb of neutralisation and democracy is all those who go into the pacific league of neutrals and all who come under its jurisdiction, whether of their own choice or by the necessities of the case. It is of the substance of the case that those peoples who have been employed in the campaigns of the German-Imperial coalition are to come in on terms of impartial equality with those who have held the ground against them; to come under the jurisdiction, and prospectively into the copartnery, of the league of neutrals--all on the presumption that the Imperial coalition will be brought to make peace on terms of unconditional surrender.

Let it not seem presumptuous to venture on a recital of summary specifications intended to indicate the nature of those concrete measures which would logically be comprised in a scheme of pacification carried out with such a view to impartial equality among the peoples who are to make up the projected league. There is a significant turn of expression that recurs habitually in the formulation of terms put forth by the spokesmen of the Entente belligerents, where it is insisted that hostilities are carried on not against the German people or the other peoples associated with them, but only against the Imperial establishments and their culpable aids and abettors in the enterprise. So it is further insisted that there is no intention to bring pains and penalties on these peoples, who so have been made use of by their masters, but only on the culpable master class whose tools these peoples have been. And later, just now (January 1917), and from a responsible and disinterested spokesman for the pacific league, there comes the declaration that a lasting peace at the hands of such a league can be grounded only in a present "peace without victory."

The mutual congruity of these two declarations need not imply collusion, but they are none the less complementary propositions and they are none the less indicative of a common trend of convictions among the men who are best able to speak for those pacific nations that are looked to as the mainstay of the prospective league. They both converge to the point that the objective to be achieved is not victory for the Entente belligerents but defeat for the German-Imperial coalition; that the peoples underlying the defeated governments are not to be dealt with as vanquished enemies but as fellows in undeserved misfortune brought on by their culpable masters; and that no advantage is designed to be taken of these peoples, and no gratuitous hardship to be imposed on them. Their masters are evidently to be put away, not as defeated antagonists but as a public nuisance to be provided against as may seem expedient for the peace and security of those nations whom they have been molesting.

Taking this position as outlined, it should not be extremely difficult to forecast the general line of procedure which it would logically demand,--barring irrelevant regard for precedents and overheated resentment, and provided that the makers of these peace terms have a free hand and go to their work with an eye single to the establishment of an enduring peace. The case of Germany would be typical of all the rest; and the main items of the bill in this case would seem logically to run somewhat as follows:

(1) The definitive elimination of the Imperial establishment, together with the monarchical establishments of the several states of the Empire and the privileged classes;

(2) Removal or destruction of all warlike equipment, military and naval, defensive and offensive;

(3) Cancelment of the public debt, of the Empire and of its members--creditors of the Empire being accounted accessory to the culpable enterprise of the Imperial government;

(4) Confiscation of such industrial equipment and resources as have contrib-

uted to the carrying on of the war, as being also accessory;

(5) Assumption by the league at large of all debts incurred, by the Entente belligerents or by neutrals, for the prosecution or by reason of the war, and distribution of the obligation so assumed, impartially among the members of the league, including the peoples of the defeated nations;

(6) Indemnification for all injury done to civilians in the invaded territories; the means for such indemnification to be procured by confiscation of all estates in the defeated countries exceeding a certain very modest maximum, calculated on the average of property owned, say, by the poorer three-fourths of the population,--the kept classes being properly accounted accessory to the Empire's culpable enterprise.

The proposition to let the war debt be shared by all members of the league on a footing of impartial equality may seem novel, and perhaps extravagant. But all projects put forth for safeguarding the world's peace by a compact among the pacific nations run on the patent, though often tacit, avowal that the Entente belligerents are spending their substance and pledging their credit for the common cause. Among the Americans, the chief of the neutral nations, this is coming to be recognised more and more overtly. So that, in this instance at least, no insurmountable reluctance to take over their due share of the common burden should fairly be looked for, particularly when it appears that the projected league, if it is organised on a footing of neutrality, will relieve the republic of virtually all outlay for their own defense.

Of course, there is, in all this, no temerarious intention to offer advice as to what should be done by those who have it to do, or even to sketch the necessary course which events are bound to take. As has been remarked in another passage, that would have to be a work of prophesy or of effrontery, both of which, it is hoped, lie equally beyond the horizon of this inquiry; which is occupied with the question of what conditions will logically have to be met in order to an enduring peace, not what will be the nature and outcome of negotiations entered into by astute delegates pursuing the special advantage, each of his own nation. And yet the peremptory need of reaching some practicable arrangement whereby the peace may be kept, goes to say that even the most astute negotiations will in some degree be controlled by that need, and may reasonably be expected to make some approach to the simple and obvious requirements of the situation.

* * * * *

Therefore the argument returns to the United Kingdom and the probable limit of tolerance of that people, in respect of what they are likely to insist on as a necessary measure of democratisation in the nations of the second part, and what measure of national abnegation they are likely to accommodate themselves to. The United Kingdom is indispensable to the formation of a pacific league of neutrals. And the British terms of adhesion, or rather of initiation of such a league, therefore, will have to constitute the core of the structure, on which details may be adjusted and to which concessive adjustments will have to be made by all the rest. This is not saying that the projected league must or will be dominated by the United Kingdom or administered in the British interest. Indeed, it can not well be made to serve British particular interests in any appreciable degree, except at the cost of defeat to its main purpose; since the purposes of an enduring peace can be served only by an effectual neutralisation of national claims and interests. But it would mean that the neutralisation of national interests and discriminations to be effected would have to be drawn on lines acceptable to British taste in these matters, and would have to go approximately so far as would be dictated by the British notions of what is expedient, and not much farther. The pacific league of neutrals would have much of a British air, but "British" in this connection is to be taken as connoting the English-speaking countries rather than as applying to the United Kingdom alone; since the entrance of the British into the league would involve the entrance of the British colonies, and, indeed, of the American republic as well.

The temper and outlook of this British community, therefore, becomes a matter of paramount importance in any attempted analysis of the situation resulting after the war, or of any prospective course of conduct to be entered on by the pacific nations. And the question touches not so much the temper and preconceptions of the British community as known in recent history, but rather as it is likely to be modified by the war experience. So that the practicability of a neutral league comes to turn, in great measure, on the effect which this war experience is having on the habits of thought of the British people, or on that section of the British population which will make up the effectual majority when the war closes. The grave interest that attaches to this question must serve as justification for pursuing it farther, even though there can be no promise of a definite or confident answer to be found beforehand.

Certain general assertions may be made with some confidence. The experiences of the war, particularly among the immediate participants and among their immediate domestic connections--a large and increasing proportion of the people at large--are plainly impressing on them the uselessness and hardship of such a war. There can be no question but they are reaching a conviction that a war of this modern kind and scale is a thing to be avoided if possible. They are, no doubt, willing to go to very considerable lengths to make a repetition of it impossible, and they may reasonably be expected to go farther along that line before peace returns. But the lengths to which they are ready to go may be in the way of concessions, or in the way of contest and compulsion. There need be no doubt but a profound and vindictive resentment runs through the British community, and there is no reason to apprehend that this will be dissipated in the course of further hostilities; although it should fairly be expected to lose something of its earlier exuberant malevolence and indiscrimination, more particularly if hostilities continue for some time. It is not too much to expect, that this popular temper of resentment will demand something very tangible in the way of summary vengeance on those who have brought the hardships of war upon the nation.

The manner of retribution which would meet the popular demand for "justice" to be done on the enemy is likely to be affected by the fortunes of war, as also the incidence of it. Should the governmental establishment and the discretion still vest in the gentlemanly classes at the close of hostilities, the retribution is likely to take the accustomed gentlemanly shape of pecuniary burdens imposed on the people of the defeated country, together with diplomatically specified surrender of territorial and colonial possessions, and the like; such as to leave the ***de facto*** enemy courteously on one side, and to yield something in the way of pecuniary benefit to the gentlemen-investors in charge, and something more in the way of new emoluments of office to the office-holding class included in the same order of gentlemen. The retribution in the case would manifestly fall on the underlying population in the defeated country, without seriously touching the responsible parties, and would leave the defeated nation with a new grievance to nourish its patriotic animosity and with a new incentive to a policy of watchful waiting for a chance of retaliation.

But it is to be noted that under the stress of the war there is going forward in the British community a progressive displacement of gentlemanly standards and official procedure by standards and procedure of a visibly underbred character, a weakening of the hold of the gentlemanly classes on the control of affairs and a weakening of the hold which the sacred rights of property, investment and privilege have long had over the imagination of the British people. Should hostilities continue, and should the exigencies of the war situation continue to keep the futility of these sacred rights, as well as the fatuity of their possessors, in the public eye, after the same fashion as hitherto, it would not be altogether unreasonable to expect that the discretion would pass into the hands of the underbred, or into the hands of men immediately and urgently accountable to the underbred. In such a case, and with a constantly growing popular realisation that the directorate and responsible enemy in the war is the Imperial dynasty and its pedigreed aids and abettors, it is conceivable that the popular resentment would converge so effectually on these responsible instigators and directors of misfortune as to bring the incidence of the required retribution effectually to bear on them. The outcome might, not inconceivably, be the virtual erasure of the Imperial dynasty, together with the pedigreed-class rule on which it rests and the apparatus of irresponsible coercion through which it works, in the Fatherland and in its subsidiaries and dependencies.

With a sufficiently urgent realisation of their need of peace and security, and with a realisation also that the way to avoid war is to avoid the ways and means of international jealousy and of the national discriminations out of which international jealousy grows, it is conceivable that a government which should reflect the British temper and the British hopes might go so far in insisting on a neutralisation of the peoples of the Fatherland as would leave them without the dynastic apparatus with which warlike enterprise is set afoot, and so leave them also perforce in a pacific frame of mind. In time, in the absence of their dearly beloved leavings of feudalism, an enforced reliance on their own discretion and initiative, and an enforced respite from the rant and prance of warlike swagger, would reasonably be expected to grow into a popular habit. The German people are by no means less capable of tolerance and neighbourly decorum than their British or Scandinavian neighbours of the same blood,--if they can only be left to their own devices, untroubled by the maggoty conceit of national domination.

There is no intention herewith to express an expectation that this out-and-out neutralisation of the Fatherland's international relations and of its dynastic government will come to pass on the return of peace, or that the German people will, as a precaution against recurrent Imperial rabies, be organised on a democratic pattern by constraint of the pacific nations of the league. The point is only that this measure of neutralisation appears to be the necessary condition, in the absence of which no such neutral league can succeed, and that so long as the war goes on there is something of a chance that the British community may in time reach a frame of mind combining such settled determination to safeguard the peace at all costs, with such a degree of disregard for outworn conventions, that their spokesmen in the negotiations may push the neutralisation of these peoples to that length.

The achievement of such an outcome would evidently take time as well as harsh experience, more time and harsher experience, perhaps, than one likes to contemplate.

Most men, therefore, would scarcely rate the chance of such an outcome at all high. And yet it is to be called to mind that the war has lasted long and the effect of its demands and its experience has already gone far, and that the longer it lasts the greater are the chances of its prolongation and of its continued hardships, at least to the extent that with every month of war that passes the prospect of the allied nations making peace on any terms short of unconditional surrender grows less. And unconditional surrender is the first step in the direction of an unconditional dispossession of the Imperial establishment and its war prophets,--depending primarily on the state of mind of the British people at the time. And however unlikely, it is also always possible, as some contend, that in the course of further war experience the common man in the Fatherland may come to reflect on the use and value of the Imperial establishment, with the result of discarding and disowning it and all its works. Such an expectation would doubtless underrate the force of ancient habit, and would also involve a misapprehension of the psychological incidence of a warlike experience. The German people have substantially none of those preconceptions of independence and self-direction to go on, in the absence of which an effectual revulsion against dynastic rule can not come to pass.

Embedded in the common sense of the British population at large is a certain large and somewhat sullen sense of fair dealing. In this they are not greatly different from their neighbours, if at all, except that the body of common sense in which this British sense of fair dealing lies embedded is a maturer fashion of common sense than that which serves to guide the workday life of many of their neighbours. And the maturity in question appears to be chiefly a matter of their having unlearned, divested themselves of, or been by force of disuse divested of, an exceptionally large proportion of that burden of untoward conceits which western Europe, and more particularly middle Europe, at large has carried over from the Middle Ages. They have had time and occasion to forget more of what the exigencies of modern life make it expedient to have forgotten. And yet they are reputed slow, conservative. But they have been well placed for losing much of what would be well lost.

Among other things, their preconception of national animosity is not secure, in the absence of provocation. They are now again in a position to learn to do without some of the useless legacy out of the past,--useless, that is, for life as it runs today, however it may be rated in the setting in which it was all placed in that past out of which it has come. And the question is whether now, under the pressure of exigencies that make for a disestablishment of much cumbersome inherited apparatus for doing what need not be done, they will be ruled by their sense of expediency and of fair dealing to the extent of cancelling out of their own scheme of life so much of this legacy of conventional preconceptions as has now come visibly to hinder their own material well-being, and at the same time to defeat that peace and security for which they have shown themselves willing to fight. It is, of course, a simpler matter to fight than it is to put away a preconceived, even if it is a bootless, superstition; as, e.g., the prestige of hereditary wealth, hereditary gentility, national vainglory, and perhaps especially national hatred. But if the school is hard enough and the discipline protracted enough there is no reason in the nature of things why the common run of the British people should not unlearn these futilities that once were the substance of things under an older and outworn order. They have already shown their capacity for divesting themselves of outworn institutional bonds, in discarding the main substance of dynastic rule; and when they now come to face the exigencies of this new situation it should cause no great surprise if they are able to see their way to do what further is necessary to meet these exigencies.

* * * * *

At the hands of this British commonwealth the new situation requires the putting away of the German Imperial establishment and the military caste; the reduction of the German peoples to a footing of unreserved democracy with sufficient guarantees against national trade discriminations; surrender of all British tutelage over outlying possessions, except what may go to guarantee their local autonomy; cancelment of all extra-territorial pretensions of the several nations entering into the league; neutralisation of the several national establishments, to comprise virtual disarmament, as well as cancelment of all restrictions on trade and of all national defense of extra-territorial pecuniary claims and interests on the part of individual citizens. The naval control of the seas will best be left in British hands. No people has a graver or more immediate interest in the freedom and security of the sea-borne trade; and the United Kingdom has shown that it is to be trusted in that matter. And then it may well be that neither the national pride nor the apprehensions of the British people would allow them to surrender it; whereas, if the league is to be formed it will have to be on terms to which the British people are willing to adhere. A certain provision of armed force will also be needed to keep the governments of unneutral nations in check,--and for the purpose in hand all effectively monarchical countries are to be counted as congenitally unneutral, whatever their formal professions and whether they are members of the league or not. Here again it will probably appear that the people of the United Kingdom, and of the English-speaking countries at large, will not consent to this armed force and its discretionary use passing out of British hands, or rather out of French-British hands; and here again the practical decision will have to wait on the choice of the British people, all the more because the British community has no longer an interest, real or fancied, in the coercive use of this force for their own particular ends. No other power is to be trusted, except France, and France is less well placed for the purpose and would assuredly also not covet so invidious an honour and so thankless an office.

* * * * *

The theory, i.e. the logical necessities, of such a pacific league of neutral nations is simple enough, in its elements. War is to be avoided by a policy of avoidance. Which signifies that the means and the motives to warlike enterprise and warlike provocation are to be put away, so far as may be. If what may be, in this respect, does not come up to the requirements of the case, the experiment, of course, will fail. The preliminary requirement,--elimination of the one formidable dynastic State in Europe,--has been spoken of. Its counterpart in the Far East will cease to be formidable on the decease of its natural ally in Central Europe, in so far as touches the case of such a projected league. The ever increasingly dubious empire of the Czar would appear to fall in the same category. So that the pacific league's fortunes would seem to turn on what may be called its domestic or internal arrangements.

Now, the means of warlike enterprise, as well as of unadvised embroilment, is always in the last analysis the patriotic spirit of the nation. Given this patriotic spirit in sufficient measure, both the material equipment and the provocation to hostilities will easily be found. It should accordingly appear to be the first care of such a pacific league to reduce the sources of patriotic incitement to the practicable minimum. This can be done, in such measure as it can be done at all, by neutralisation of national pretensions. The finished outcome in this respect, such as would assure perpetual peace among the peoples concerned, would of course be an unconditional neutralisation of citizenship, as has already been indicated before. The question which, in effect, the spokesmen for a pacific league have to face is as to how nearly that outcome can be brought to pass. The rest of what they may undertake, or may come to by way of compromise and stipulation, is relatively immaterial and of relatively transient consequence.

A neutralisation of citizenship has of course been afloat in a somewhat loose way in the projects of socialistic and other "undesirable" agitators, but nothing much has come of it. Nor have specific projects for its realisation been set afoot. That anything conclusive along that line could now be reached would seem extremely doubtful, in view of the ardent patriotic temper of all these peoples, heightened just now by the experience of war. Still, an undesigned and unguided drift in that direction has been visible in all those nations that are accounted the vanguard among modern civilised peoples, ever since the dynastic rule among them began to be displaced by a growth of "free" institutions, that is to say institutions resting on an accepted ground of insubordination and free initiative.

The patriotism of these peoples, or their national spirit, is after all and at the best an attenuated and impersonalised remnant of dynastic loyalty, and it amounts after all, in effect, to nothing much else than a residual curtailment or partial atrophy of that democratic habit of mind that embodies itself in the formula: Live and let live. It is, no doubt, both an ancient and a very meritorious habit. It is easily acquired and hard to put away. The patriotic spirit and the national life (prestige) on which it centers are the subject of untiring eulogy; but hitherto its encomiasts have shown no cause and put forward no claim to believe that it all is of any slightest use for any purpose that does not take it and its paramount merit for granted. It is doubtless a very meritorious habit; at least so they all say. But under the circumstances of modern civilised life it is fruitful of no other net material result than damage and discomfort. Still it is virtually ubiquitous among civilised men, and in an admirable state of repair; and for the calculable future it is doubtless to be counted in as an enduring obstacle to a conclusive peace, a constant source of anxiety and unremitting care.

The motives that work out through this national spirit, by use of this patriotic ardor, fall under two heads: dynastic ambition, and business enterprise. The two categories have the common trait that neither the one nor the other comprises anything that is of the slightest material benefit to the community at large; but both have at the same time a high prestige value in the conventional esteem of modern men. The relation of dynastic ambition to warlike enterprise, and the uses of that usufruct of the nation's resources and man-power which the nation's patriotism places at the disposal of the dynastic establishment, have already been spoken of at length above, perhaps at excessive length, in the recurrent discussion of the dynastic State and its quest of dominion for dominion's sake. What measures are necessary to be taken as regards the formidable dynastic States that threaten the peace, have also been outlined, perhaps with excessive freedom.

But it remains to call attention to that mitigated form of dynastic rule called a constitutional monarchy. Instances of such a constitutional monarchy, designed to conserve the well-beloved abuses of dynastic rule under a cover of democratic formalities, or to bring in effectual democratic insubordination under cover of the ancient dignities of an outworn monarchical system,--the characterisation may run either way according to the fancy of the speaker, and to much the same practical effect in either case,--instances illustrative of this compromise monarchy at work today are to be had, as felicitously as anywhere, in the Balkan states; perhaps the case of Greece will be especially instructive. At the other, and far, end of the line will be found such other typical instances as the British, the Dutch, or, in pathetic and droll miniature, the Norwegian.

There is, of course, a wide interval between the grotesque effrontery that wears the Hellenic crown and the undeviatingly decorous self-effacement of the Dutch sovereign; and yet there is something of a common complexion runs through the whole range of establishments, all the way from the quasi-dynastic to the pseudo-dynastic. For reasons unavoidable and persistent, though not inscribed in the constituent law, the governmental establishment associated with such a royal concern will be made up of persons drawn from the kept classes, the nobility or lesser gentlefolk, and will be imbued with the spirit of these "better" classes rather than that of the common run.

With what may be uncanny shrewdness, or perhaps mere tropismatic response to the unreasoned stimulus of a "consciousness of kind," the British government--habitually a syndicate of gentlefolk--has uniformly insisted on the installation of a constitutional monarchy at the formation of every new national organisation in which that government has had a discretionary voice. And the many and various constitutional governments so established, commonly under British auspices in some degree, have invariably run true to form, in some appreciable degree. They may be quasi-dynastic or pseudo-dynastic, but at this nearest approach to democracy they always, and unavoidably, include at least a circumlocution office of gentlefolk, in the way of a ministry and court establishment, whose place in the economy of the nation's affairs it is to adapt the run of these affairs to the needs of the kept classes.

There need be no imputation of sinister designs to these gentlefolk, who so are elected by force of circumstances to guard and guide the nation's interests. As things go, it will doubtless commonly be found that they are as well-intentioned as need be. But a well-meaning gentleman of good antecedents means well in a gentlemanly way and in the light of good antecedents. Which comes unavoidably to an effectual bias in favor of those interests which honorable gentlemen of good antecedents have at heart. And among these interests are the interests of the kept classes, as contrasted with that common run of the population from which their keep is drawn.

Under the auspices, even if they are only the histrionic and decorative auspices, of so decorous an article of institutional furniture as royalty, it follows of logical necessity that the personnel of the effectual government must also be drawn from the better classes, whose place and station and high repute will make their association with the First Gentleman of the Realm not too insufferably incongruous. And then, the popular habit of looking up to this First Gentleman with that deference that royalty commands, also conduces materially to the attendant habitual attitude of deference to gentility more at large.

Even in so democratic a country, and with so exanimate a crown as is to be found in the United Kingdom, the royal establishment visibly, and doubtless very materially, conduces to the continued tenure of the effectual government by representatives of the kept classes; and it therefore counts with large effect toward the retardation of the country's further move in the direction of democratic insubordination and direct participation in the direction of affairs by the underbred, who finally pay the cost. And on the other hand, even so moderately royal an establishment as the Norwegian has apparently a sensible effect in the way of gathering the reins somewhat into the hands of the better classes, under circumstances of such meagerness as might be expected to preclude anything like a "better" class, in the conventional acceptation of that term. It would appear that even the extreme of pseudo-dynastic royalty, sterilised to the last degree, is something of an effectual hindrance to democratic rule, and in so far also a hindrance to the further continued neutralisation of nationalist pretensions, as also an effectual furtherance of upper-class rule for upper-class ends.

Now, a government by well-meaning gentlemen-investors will, at the nearest, come no nearer representing the material needs and interests of the common run than a parable comes to representing the concrete facts which it hopes to illuminate. And as bears immediately on the point in hand, these gentlemanly administrators of the nation's affairs who so cluster about the throne, vacant though it may be of all but the bodily presence of majesty, are after all gentlemen, with a gentlemanly sense of punctilio touching the large proprieties and courtesies of political life. The national honor is a matter of punctilio, always; and out of the formal exigencies of the national honor arise grievances to be redressed; and it is grievances of this character that commonly afford the formal ground of a breach of the peace. An appeal on patriotic grounds of wounded national pride, to the common run who have no trained sense of punctilio, by the gentlemanly responsible class who have such a sense, backed by assurances that the national prestige or the national interests are at stake, will commonly bring a suitable response. It is scarcely necessary that the common run should know just what the stir is about, so long as they are informed by their trusted betters that there is a grievance to redress. In effect, it results that the democratic nation's affairs are administered by a syndicate composed of the least democratic class in the population.

Excepting what is to be excepted, it will commonly hold true today that these gentlemanly governments are conducted in a commendably clean and upright fashion, with a conscious rectitude and a benevolent intention. But they are after all, in effect, class governments, and they unavoidably carry the bias of their class. The gentlemanly officials and law-givers come, in the main, from the kept classes, whose living comes to them in the way of income from investments, at home or in foreign parts, or from an equivalent source of accumulated wealth or official emolument. The bias resulting from this state of the case need not be of an intolerant character in order to bring its modicum of mischief into the national policy, as regards amicable relations with other nationalities. A slight bias running on a ground of conscious right and unbroken usage may go far. So, e.g., anyone of these gentlemanly governments is within its legitimate rights, or rather within its imperative duty, in defending the foreign investments of its citizens and enforcing due payment of its citizens' claims to income or principal of such property as they may hold in foreign parts; and it is within its ordinary lines of duty in making use of the nation's resources--that is to say of the common man and his means of livelihood--in enforcing such claims held by the investing classes. The community at large has no interest in the enforcement of such claims; it is evidently a class interest, and as evidently protected by a code of rights, duties and procedure that has grown out of a class bias, at the cost of the community at large.

This bias favoring the interests of invested wealth may also, and indeed it commonly does, take the aggressive form of aggressively forwarding enterprise in investment abroad, particularly in commercially backward countries abroad, by extension of the national jurisdiction and the active countenancing of concessions in foreign parts, by subventions, or by creation of offices to bring suitable emoluments to the younger sons of deserving families. The protective tariffs to which recourse is sometimes had, are of the same general nature and purpose. Of course, it is in this latter, aggressive or excursive, issue of the well-to-do bias in favor of investment and invested wealth that its most pernicious effect on international relations is traceable.

Free income, that is to say income not dependent on personal merit or exertion of any kind, is the breath of life to the kept classes; and as a corollary of the "First Law of Nature," therefore, the invested wealth which gives a legally equitable claim to such income has in their eyes all the sanctity that can be given by Natural Right. Investment--often spoken of euphemistically as "savings"--is consequently a meritorious act, conceived to be very serviceable to the community at large, and properly to be furthered by all available means. Invested wealth is so much added to the aggregate means at the community's disposal, it is believed. Of course, in point of fact, income from investment in the hands of these gentlefolk is a means of tracelessly consuming that much of the community's yearly product; but to the kept classes, who see the matter from the point of view of the recipient, the matter does not present itself in that light. To them it is the breath of life. Like other honorable men they are faithful to their bread; and by authentic tradition the common man, in whose disciplined preconceptions the kept classes are his indispensable betters, is also imbued with the uncritical faith that the invested wealth which enables these betters tracelessly to consume a due share of the yearly product is an addition to the aggregate means in hand.

The advancement of commercial and other business enterprise beyond the national frontiers is consequently one of the duties not to be neglected, and with which no trifling can be tolerated. It is so bound up with national ideals, under any gentlemanly government, that any invasion or evasion of the rights of investors in foreign parts, or of other business involved in dealings with foreign parts, immediately involves not only the material interest of the nation but the national honour as well. Hence international jealousies and eventual embroilment.

The constitutional monarchy that commonly covers a modern democratic community is accordingly a menace to the common peace, and any pacific league of neutrals will be laying up trouble and prospective defeat for itself in allowing such an institution to stand over in any instance. Acting with a free hand, if such a thing were possible, the projected league should logically eliminate all monarchical establishments, constitutional or otherwise, from among its federated nations. It is doubtless not within reason to look for such a move in the negotiations that are to initiate the projected league of neutrals; but the point is called to mind here chiefly as indicating one of the difficult passages which are to be faced in any attempted formation of such a league, as well as one of the abiding sources of international irritation with which the league's jurisdiction will be burdened so long as a decisive measure of the kind is not taken.

The logic of the whole matter is simple enough, and the necessary measures to be taken to remedy it are no less simple--barring sentimental objections which will probably prove insuperable. A monarchy, even a sufficiently inane monarchy, carries the burden of a gentlemanly governmental establishment--a government by and for the kept classes; such a government will unavoidably direct the affairs of state with a view to income on invested wealth, and will see the material interests of the country only in so far as they present themselves under the form of investment and business enterprise designed to eventuate in investment; these are the only forms of material interest that give rise to international jealousies, discriminations and misunderstanding, at the same time that they are interests of individuals only and have no material use or value to the community at large. Given a monarchical establishment and the concomitant gentlemanly governmental corps, there is no avoiding this sinister prime mover of international rivalry, so long as the rights of invested wealth continue in popular apprehension to be held inviolable.

Quite obviously there is a certain *tu quoque* ready to the hand of these "gentlemen of the old school" who see in the constitutional monarchy a God-given shelter from the unreserved vulgarisation of life at the hands of the unblest and unbalanced underbred and underfed. The formally democratic nations, that have not retained even a pseudo-dynastic royalty, are not much more fortunately placed in respect of national discrimination in trade and investment. The American republic will obviously come into the comparison as the type-form of economic policy in a democratic commonwealth. There is little to choose between the economic policy pursued by such republics as France or America on the one side and their nearest counterparts among the constitutional monarchies on the other. It is even to be admitted out of hand that the comparison does no credit to democratic institutions as seen at work in these republics. They are, in fact, somewhat the crudest and most singularly foolish in their economic policy of any peoples in Christendom. And in view of the amazing facility with which these democratic commonwealths are always ready to delude themselves in everything that touches their national trade policies, it is obvious that any league of neutrals whose fortunes are in any degree contingent on their reasonable compliance with a call to neutralise their trade regulations for the sake of peace, will have need of all the persuasive power it can bring to bear.

However, the powers of darkness have one less line of defense to shelter them and their work of malversation in these commonwealths than in the constitutional monarchies. The American national establishment, e.g., which may be taken as a fairly characteristic type-form in this bearing, is a government of businessmen for business ends; and there is no tabu of axiomatic gentility or of certified pedigree to hedge about this working syndicate of business interests. So that it is all nearer by one remove to the disintegrating touch of the common man and his commonplace circumstances. The businesslike regime of these democratic politicians is as undeviating in its advocacy and aid of enterprise in pursuit of private gain under shelter of national discrimination as the circumstances will permit; and the circumstances will permit them to do much and go far; for the limits of popular gullibility in all things that touch the admirable feats of business enterprise are very wide in these countries. There is a sentimental popular belief running to the curious effect that because the citizens of such a commonwealth are ungraded equals before the law, therefore somehow they can all and several become wealthy by trading at the expense of their neighbours.

Yet, the fact remains that there is only the one line of defense in these countries where the business interests have not the countenance of a time-honored order of gentlefolk, with the sanction of royalty in the background. And this fact is further enhanced by one of its immediate consequences. Proceeding upon the abounding faith which these peoples have in business enterprise as a universal solvent, the unreserved venality and greed of their businessmen--unhampered by the gentleman's ***noblesse oblige***--have pushed the conversion of public law to private gain farther and more openly here than elsewhere. The outcome has been divers measures in restraint of trade or in furtherance of profitable abuses, of such a crass and flagrant character that if once the popular apprehension is touched by matter-of-fact reflection on the actualities of this businesslike policy the whole structure should reasonably be expected to crumble. If the present conjuncture of circumstances should, e.g., present to the American populace a choice between exclusion from the neutral league, and a consequent probable and dubious war of self-defense, on the one hand; as against entrance into the league, and security at the cost of relinquishing their national tariff in restraint of trade, on the other hand, it is always possible that the people might be brought to look their protective tariff in the face and recognise it for a commonplace conspiracy in restraint of trade, and so decide to shuffle it out of the way as a good riddance. And the rest of the Republic's businesslike policy of special favors would in such a case stand a chance of going in the discard along with the protective tariff, since the rest is of substantially the same disingenuous character.

Not that anyone need entertain a confident expectation of such an exploit of common sense on the part of the American voters. There is little encouragement for such a hope in their past career of gullibility on this head. But this is again a point of difficulty to be faced in negotiations looking to such a pacific league of neutrals. Without a somewhat comprehensive neutralisation of national trade regulations, the outlook for lasting peace would be reduced by that much; there would be so much material for international jealousy and misunderstanding left standing over and requiring continued readjustment and compromise, always with the contingency of a breach that much nearer. The infatuation of the Americans with their protective tariff and other businesslike discriminations is a sufficiently serious matter in this connection, and it is always possible that their inability to give up this superstition might lead to their not adhering to this projected neutral league. Yet it is at least to be said that the longer the time that passes before active measures are taken toward the organisation of such a league--that is to say, in effect, the longer the great war lasts--the more amenable is the temper of the Americans likely to be, and the more reluctantly would they see themselves excluded. Should the war be protracted to some such length as appears to be promised by latterday pronunciamentos from the belligerents, or to something passably approaching such a duration; and should the Imperial designs and anomalous diplomacy of Japan continue to force themselves on the popular attention at the present rate; at the same time that the operations in Europe continue to demonstrate the excessive cost of defense against a well devised and resolute offensive; then it should reasonably be expected that the Americans might come to such a realisation of their own case as to let no minor considerations of trade discrimination stand in the way of their making common cause with the other pacific nations.

It appears already to be realised in the most responsible quarter that America needs the succor of the other pacific nations, with a need that is not to be put away or put off; as it is also coming to be realised that the Imperial Powers are disturbers of the peace, by force of their Imperial character. Of course, the politicians who seek their own advantage in the nation's embarrassment are commonly unable to see the matter in that light. But it is also apparent that the popular sentiment is affected with the same apprehension, more and more as time passes and the aims and methods of the Imperial Powers become more patent.

Hitherto the spokesmen of a pacific federation of nations have spoken for a league of such an (indeterminate) constitution as to leave all the federated nations undisturbed in all their conduct of their own affairs, domestic or international; probably for want of second thought as to the complications of copartnership between them in so grave and unwonted an enterprise. They have also spoken of America's share in the project as being that of an interested outsider, whose interest in any precautionary measures of this kind is in part a regard for his own tranquility as a disinterested neighbour, but in greater part a humane solicitude for the wellbeing of civilised mankind at large. In this view, somewhat self-complacent it is to be admitted, America is conceived to come into the case as initiator and guide, about whom the pacific nations are to cluster as some sort of queen-bee.

Now, there is not a little verisimilitude in this conception of America as a sort of central office and a tower of strength in the projected federation of neutral nations, however pharisaical an appearance it may all have in the self-complacent utterances of patriotic Americans. The American republic is, after all, the greatest of the pacific nations of Christendom, in resources, population and industrial capacity; and it is also not to be denied that the temper of this large population is, on the whole, as pacific as that of any considerable people--outside of China. The adherence of the American republic would, in effect, double the mass and powers of the projected league, and would so place it beyond all hazard of defeat from without, or even of serious outside opposition to its aims.

Yet it will not hold true that America is either disinterested or indispensable.

The unenviable position of the indispensable belongs to the United Kingdom, and carries with it the customary suspicion of interested motives that attaches to the stronger party in a bargain. To America, on the other hand, the league is indispensable, as a refuge from otherwise inevitable dangers ahead; and it is only a question of a moderate allowance of time for the American voters to realise that without an adequate copartnership with the other pacific nations the outlook of the Republic is altogether precarious. Single-handed, America can not defend itself, except at a prohibitive cost; whereas in copartnership with these others the national defense becomes a virtually negligible matter. It is for America a choice between a policy of extravagant armament and aggressive diplomacy, with a doubtful issue, on the one side, and such abatement of national pretensions as would obviate bootless contention, on the other side.

Yet, it must be admitted, the patriotic temper of the American people is of such a susceptible kind as to leave the issue in doubt. Not that the Americans will not endeavor to initiate some form of compact for the keeping of the peace, when hostilities are concluded; barring unforeseen contingencies, it is virtually a foregone conclusion that the attempt will be made, and that the Americans will take an active part in its promotion. But the doubt is as to their taking such a course as will lead to a compact of the kind needed to safeguard the peace of the country. The business interests have much to say in the counsels of the Americans, and these business interests look to short-term gains--American business interests particularly--to be derived from the country's necessities. It is likely to appear that the business interests, through representatives in Congress and elsewhere, will disapprove of any peace compact that does not involve an increase of the national armament and a prospective demand for munitions and an increased expenditure of the national funds.

With or without the adherence of America, the pacific nations of Europe will doubtless endeavour to form a league or alliance designed to keep the peace. If America does not come into the arrangement it may well come to nothing much more than a further continued defensive alliance of the belligerent nations now opposed to the German coalition. In any case it is still a point in doubt whether the league so projected is to be merely a compact of defensive armament against a common enemy--in which case it will necessarily be transient, perhaps ephemeral--or a more inclusive coalition of a closer character designed to avoid any breach of the peace, by disarmament and by disallowance and disclaimer of such national pretensions and punctilio as the patriotic sentiment of the contracting parties will consent to dispense with. The nature of the resulting peace, therefore, as well as its chances of duration, will in great measure be conditioned on the fashion of peace-compact on which it is to rest; which will be conditioned in good part on the degree in which the warlike coalition under German Imperial control is effectually to be eliminated from the situation as a prospective disturber of the peace; which, in turn, is a question somewhat closely bound up with the further duration of the war, as has already been indicated in an earlier passage.

CHAPTER VII
PEACE AND THE PRICE SYSTEM

Evidently the conception of peace on which its various spokesmen are proceeding is by no means the same for all of them. In the current German conception, e.g., as seen in the utterances of its many and urgent spokesmen, peace appears to be of the general nature of a truce between nations, whose God-given destiny it is, in time, to adjust a claim to precedence by wager of battle. They will sometimes speak of it, euphemistically, with a view to conciliation, as "assurance of the national future," in which the national future is taken to mean an opportunity for the extension of the national dominion at the expense of some other national establishment. In the same connection one may recall the many eloquent passages on the State and its paramount place and value in the human economy. The State is useful for disturbing the peace. This German notion may confidently be set down as the lowest of the current conceptions of peace; or perhaps rather as the notion of peace reduced to the lowest terms at which it continues to be recognisable as such. Next beyond in that direction lies the notion of armistice; which differs from this conception of peace chiefly in connoting specifically a definite and relatively short interval between warlike operations.

The conception of peace as being a period of preparation for war has many adherents outside the Fatherland, of course. Indeed, it has probably a wider vogue and a readier acceptance among men who interest themselves in questions of peace and war than any other. It goes hand in hand with that militant nationalism that is taken for granted, conventionally, as the common ground of those international relations that play a part in diplomatic intercourse. It is the diplomatist's ***metier*** to talk war in parables of peace. This conception of peace as a precarious interval of preparation has come down to the present out of the feudal age and is, of course, best at home where the feudal range of preconceptions has suffered least dilapidation; and it carries the feudalistic presumption that all national establishments are competitors for dominion, after the scheme of Macchiavelli. The peace which is had on this footing, within the realm, is a peace of subjection, more or less pronounced according as the given national establishment is more or less on the militant order; a warlike organisation being necessarily of a servile character, in the same measure in which it is warlike.

In much the same measure and with much the same limitations as the modern democratic nations have departed from the feudal system of civil relations and from the peculiar range of conceptions which characterise that system, they have also come in for a new or revised conception of peace. Instead of its being valued chiefly as a space of time in which to prepare for war, offensive or defensive, among these democratic and provisionally pacific nations it has come to stand in the common estimation as the normal and stable manner of life, good and commendable in its own right. These modern, pacific, commonwealths stand on the defensive, habitually. They are still pugnaciously national, but they have unlearned so much of the feudal preconceptions as to leave them in a defensive attitude, under the watch-word: Peace with honour. Their quasi-feudalistic national prestige is not to be trifled with, though it has lost so much of its fascination as ordinarily not to serve the purposes of an aggressive enterprise, at least not without some shrewd sophistication at the hands of militant politicians and their diplomatic agents. Of course, an exuberant patriotism may now and again take on the ancient barbarian vehemence and lead such a provisionally pacific nation into an aggressive raid against a helpless neighbour; but it remains characteristically true, after all, that these peoples look on the country's peace as the normal and ordinary course of things, which each nation is to take care of for itself and by its own force.

The ideal of the nineteenth-century statesmen was to keep the peace by a balance of power; an unstable equilibrium of rivalries, in which it was recognised that eternal vigilance was the price of peace by equilibration. Since then, by force of the object-lesson of the twentieth-century wars, it has become evident that eternal vigilance will no longer keep the peace by equilibration, and the balance of power has become obsolete. At the same time things have so turned that an effective majority of the civilised nations now see their advantage in peace, without further opportunity to seek further dominion. These nations have also been falling into the shape of commonwealths, and so have lost something of their national spirit.

With much reluctant hesitation and many misgivings, the statesmen of these pacific nations are accordingly busying themselves with schemes for keeping the peace on the unfamiliar footing of a stable equilibrium; the method preferred on the whole being an equilibration of make-believe, in imitation of the obsolete balance of power. There is a meticulous regard for national jealousies and discriminations, which it is thought necessary to keep intact. Of course, on any one of these slightly diversified plans of keeping the peace on a stable footing of copartnery among the pacific nations, national jealousies and national integrity no longer have any substantial meaning. But statesmen think and plan in terms of precedent; which comes to thinking and planning in terms of make-believe, when altered circumstances have made the precedents obsolete. So one comes to the singular proposal of the statesmen, that the peace is to be kept in concert among these pacific nations by a provision of force with which to break it at will. The peace that is to be kept on this footing of national discriminations and national armaments will necessarily be of a precarious kind; being, in effect, a statesmanlike imitation of the peace as it was once kept even more precariously by the pacific nations in severalty.

Hitherto the movement toward peace has not gone beyond this conception of it, as a collusive safeguarding of national discrepancies by force of arms. Such a peace is necessarily precarious, partly because armed force is useful for breaking the peace, partly because the national discrepancies, by which these current peace-makers set such store, are a constant source of embroilment. What the peace-makers might logically be expected to concern themselves about would be the elimination of these discrepancies that make for embroilment. But what they actually seem concerned about is their preservation. A peace by collusive neglect of those remnants of feudalistic make-believe that still serve to divide the pacific nations has hitherto not seriously come under advisement.

Evidently, hitherto, and for the calculable future, peace is a relative matter, a matter of more or less, whichever of the several working conceptions spoken of above may rule the case. Evidently, too, a peace designed to strengthen the national establishment against eventual war, will count to a different effect from a collusive peace of a defensive kind among the pacific peoples, designed by its projectors to conserve those national discrepancies on which patriotic statesmen like to dwell. Different from both would be the value of a peace by neglect of such useless national discriminations as now make for embroilment. A protracted season of peace should logically have a somewhat different cultural value according to the character of the public policy to be pursued under its cover. So that a safe and sane conservation of the received law and order should presumably best be effected under cover of a collusive peace of the defensive kind, which is designed to retain those national discrepancies intact that count for so much in the national life of today, both as a focus of patriotic sentiment and as an outlet for national expenditures. This plan would involve the least derangement of the received order among the democratic peoples, although the plan might itself undergo some change in the course of time.

* * * * *

Among the singularities of the latterday situation, in this connection, and brought out by the experiences of the great war, is a close resemblance between latterday warlike operations and the ordinary processes of industry. Modern warfare and modern industry alike are carried on by technological processes subject to surveillance and direction by mechanical engineers, or perhaps rather experts in engineering science of the mechanistic kind. War is not now a matter of the stout heart and strong arm. Not that these attributes do not have their place and value in modern warfare; but they are no longer the chief or decisive factors in the case. The exploits that count in this warfare are technological exploits; exploits of technological science, industrial appliances, and technological training. As has been remarked before, it is no longer a gentlemen's war, and the gentleman, as such, is no better than a marplot in the game as it is played.

Certain consequences follow from this state of the case. Technology and industrial experience, in large volume and at a high proficiency, are indispensable to the conduct of war on the modern plan, as well as a large, efficient and up-to-date industrial community and industrial plant to supply the necessary material of this warfare. At the same time the discipline of the campaign, as it impinges on the rank and file as well as on the very numerous body of officers and technicians, is not at cross purposes with the ordinary industrial employments of peace, or not in the same degree as has been the case in the past, even in the recent past. The experience of the campaign does not greatly unfit the men who survive for industrial uses; nor does it come in as a sheer interruption of their industrial training, or break the continuity of that range of habits of thought which modern industry of the technological order induces; not in the same degree as was the case under the conditions of war as carried on in the nineteenth century. The cultural, and particularly the technological, incidence of this modern warfare should evidently be appreciably different from what has been experienced in the past, and from what this past experience has induced students of these matters to look for among the psychological effects of warlike experience.

It remains true that the discipline of the campaign, however impersonal it may tend to become, still inculcates personal subordination and unquestioning obedience; and yet the modern tactics and methods of fighting bear somewhat more on the individual's initiative, discretion, sagacity and self-possession than once would have been true. Doubtless the men who come out of this great war, the common men, will bring home an accentuated and acrimonious patriotism, a venomous hatred of the enemies whom they have missed killing; but it may reasonably be doubted if they come away with a correspondingly heightened admiration and affection for their betters who have failed to make good as foremen in charge of this teamwork in killing. The years of the war have been trying to the reputation of officials and officers, who have had to meet uncharted exigencies with not much better chance of guessing the way through than their subalterns have had.

By and large, it is perhaps not to be doubted that the populace now under arms will return from the experience of the war with some net gain in loyalty to the nation's honour and in allegiance to their masters; particularly the German subjects,--the like is scarcely true for the British; but a doubt will present itself as to the magnitude of this net gain in subordination, or this net loss in self-possession. A doubt may be permitted as to whether the common man in the countries of the Imperial coalition, e.g., will, as the net outcome of this war experience, be in a perceptibly more pliable frame of mind as touches his obligations toward his betters and subservience to the irresponsible authority exercised by the various governmental agencies, than he was at the outbreak of the war. At that time, there is reason to believe, there was an ominous, though scarcely threatening, murmur of discontent beginning to be heard among the working classes of the industrial towns. It is fair to presume, however, that the servile discipline of the service and the vindictive patriotism bred of the fight should combine to render the populace of the Fatherland more amenable to the irresponsible rule of the Imperial dynasty and its subaltern royal establishments, in spite of any slight effect of a contrary character exercised by the training in technological methods and in self-reliance, with which this discipline of the service has been accompanied. As to the case of the British population, under arms or under compulsion of necessity at home, something has already been said in an earlier passage; and much will apparently depend, in their case, on the further duration of the war. The case of the other nationalities involved, both neutrals and belligerents, is even more obscure in this bearing, but it is also of less immediate consequence for the present argument.

* * * * *

The essentially feudal virtues of loyalty and bellicose patriotism would appear to have gained their great ascendency over all men's spirit within the Western civilisation by force of the peculiarly consistent character of the discipline of life under feudal conditions, whether in war or peace; and to the same uniformity of these forces that shaped the workday habits of thought among the feudal nations is apparently due that profound institutionalisation of the preconceptions of patriotism and loyalty, by force of which these preconceptions still hold the modern peoples in an unbreakable web of prejudice, after the conditions favoring their acquirement have in great part ceased to operate. These preconceptions of national solidarity and international enmity have come down from the past as an integral part of the unwritten constitution underlying all these modern nations, even those which have departed most widely from the manner of life to which the peoples owe these ancient preconceptions. Hitherto, or rather until recent times, the workday experience of these peoples has not seriously worked at cross purposes with the patriotic spirit and its bias of national animosity; and what discrepancy there has effectively been between the discipline of workday life and the received institutional preconceptions on this head, has hitherto been overborne by the unremitting inculcation of these virtues by interested politicians, priests and publicists, who speak habitually for the received order of things.

That order of things which is known on its political and civil side as the feudal system, together with that era of the dynastic States which succeeds the feudal age technically so called, was, on its industrial or technological side, a system of trained man-power organised on a plan of subordination of man to man. On the whole, the scheme and logic of that life, whether in its political (warlike) or its industrial doings, whether in war or peace, runs on terms of personal capacity, proficiency and relations. The organisation of the forces engaged and the constraining rules according to which this organisation worked, were of the nature of personal relations, and the impersonal factors in the case were taken for granted. Politics and war were a field for personal valor, force and cunning, in practical effect a field for personal force and fraud. Industry was a field in which the routine of life, and its outcome, turned on "the skill, dexterity and judgment of the individual workman," in the words of Adam Smith.

The feudal age passed, being done to death by handicraft industry, commercial traffic, gunpowder, and the state-making politicians. But the political States of the statemakers, the dynastic States as they may well be called, continued the conduct of political life on the personal plane of rivalry and jealousy between dynasties and between their States; and in spite of gunpowder and the new military engineering, warfare continued also to be, in the main and characteristically, a field in which man-power and personal qualities decided the outcome, by virtue of personal "skill, dexterity and judgment." Meantime industry and its technology by insensible degrees underwent a change in the direction of impersonalisation, particularly in those countries in which state-making and its warlike enterprise had ceased, or were ceasing, to be the chief interests and the controlling preconception of the people.

The logic of the new, mechanical industry which has supplanted handicraft in these countries, is a mechanistic logic, which proceeds in terms of matter-of-fact strains, masses, velocities, and the like, instead of the "skill, dexterity and judgment" of personal agents. The new industry does not dispense with the personal agencies, nor can it even be said to minimise the need of skill, dexterity and judgment in the personal agents employed, but it does take them and their attributes for granted as in some sort a foregone premise to its main argument. The logic of the handicraft system took the impersonal agencies for granted; the machine industry takes the skill, dexterity and judgment of the workmen for granted. The processes of thought, and therefore the consistent habitual discipline, of the former ran in terms of the personal agents engaged, and of the personal relations of discretion, control and subordination necessary to the work; whereas the mechanistic logic of the modern technology, more and more consistently, runs in terms of the impersonal forces engaged, and inculcates an habitual predilection for matter-of-fact statement, and an habitual preconception that the findings of material science alone are conclusive.

In those nations that have made up the advance guard of Western civilisation in its movement out of feudalism, the disintegrating effect of this matter-of-fact animus inculcated by the later state of the industrial arts has apparently acted effectively, in some degree, to discredit those preconceptions of personal discrimination on which dynastic rule is founded. But in no case has the discipline of this mechanistic technology yet wrought its perfect work or come to a definitive conclusion. Meantime war and politics have on the whole continued on the ancient plane; it may perhaps be fair to say that politics has so continued because warlike enterprise has continued still to be a matter of such personal forces as skill, dexterity and judgment, valor and cunning, personal force and fraud. Latterly, gradually, but increasingly, the technology of war, too, has been shifting to the mechanistic plane; until in the latest phases of it, somewhere about the turn of the century, it is evident that the logic of warfare too has come to be the same mechanistic logic that makes the modern state of the industrial arts.

What, if anything, is due by consequence to overtake the political strategy and the political preconceptions of the new century, is a question that will obtrude itself, though with scant hope of finding a ready answer. It may even seem a rash, as well as an ungraceful, undertaking to inquire into the possible manner and degree of prospective decay to which the received political ideals and virtues would appear to be exposed by consequence of this derangement of the ancient discipline to which men have been subjected. So much, however, would seem evident, that the received virtues and ideals of patriotic animosity and national jealousy can best be guarded against untimely decay by resolutely holding to the formal observance of all outworn punctilios of national integrity and discrimination, in spite of their increasing disserviceability,--as would be done, e.g., or at least sought to be done, in the installation of a league of neutral nations to keep the peace and at the same time to safeguard those "national interests" whose only use is to divide these nations and keep them in a state of mutual envy and distrust.

* * * * *

Those peoples who are subject to the constraining governance of this modern state of the industrial arts, as all modern peoples are in much the same measure in which they are "modern," are, therefore, exposed to a workday discipline running at cross purposes with the received law and order as it takes effect in national affairs; and to this is to be added that, with warlike enterprise also shifted to this same mechanistic-technological ground, war can no longer be counted on so confidently as before to correct all the consequent drift away from the ancient landmarks of dynastic, pseudo-dynastic, and national enterprise in dominion.

As has been noted above, modern warfare not only makes use of, and indeed depends on, the modern industrial technology at every turn of the operations in the field, but it draws on the ordinary industrial resources of the countries at war in a degree and with an urgency never equalled. No nation can hope to make a stand in modern warfare, much less to make headway in warlike enterprise, without the most thoroughgoing exploitation of the modern industrial arts. Which signifies for the purpose in hand that any Power that harbors an imperial ambition must take measures to let its underlying population acquire the ways and means of the modern machine industry, without reservation; which in turn signifies that popular education must be taken care of to such an extent as may be serviceable in this manner of industry and in the manner of life which this industrial system necessarily imposes; which signifies, of course, that only the thoroughly trained and thoroughly educated nations have a chance of holding their place as formidable Powers in this latterday phase of civilisation. What is needed is the training and education that go to make proficiency in the modern fashion of technology and in those material sciences that conduce to technological proficiency of this modern order. It is a matter of course that in these premises any appreciable illiteracy is an intolerable handicap. So is also any training which discourages habitual self-reliance and initiative, or which acts as a check on skepticism; for the skeptical frame of mind is a necessary part of the intellectual equipment that makes for advance, invention and understanding in the field of technological proficiency.

But these requirements, imperatively necessary as a condition of warlike success, are at cross purposes with that unquestioning respect of persons and that spirit of abnegation that alone can hold a people to the political institutions of the old order and make them a willing instrument in the hands of the dynastic statesmen. The dynastic State is apparently caught in a dilemma. The necessary preparation for warlike enterprise on the modern plan can apparently be counted on, in the long run, to disintegrate the foundations of the dynastic State. But it is only in the long run that this effect can be counted on; and it is perhaps not securely to be counted on even in a moderately long run of things as they have run hitherto, if due precautions are taken by the interested statesmen,--as would seem to be indicated by the successful conservation of archaic traits in the German peoples during the past half century under the archaising rule of the Hohenzollern. It is a matter of habituation, which takes time, and which can at the same time be neutralised in some degree by indoctrination.

Still, when all is told, it will probably have to be conceded that, e.g., such a nation as Russia will fall under this rule of inherent disability imposed by the necessary use of the modern industrial arts. Without a fairly full and free command of these modern industrial methods on the part of the Russian people, together with the virtual disappearance of illiteracy, and with the facile and far-reaching system of communication which it all involves, the Russian Imperial establishment would not be a formidable power or a serious menace to the pacific nations; and it is not easy to imagine how the Imperial establishment could retain its hold and its character under the conditions indicated.

The case of Japan, taken by itself, rests on somewhat similar lines as these others. In time, and in this case the time-allowance should presumably not be anything very large, the Japanese people are likely to get an adequate command of the modern technology; which would, here as elsewhere, involve the virtual disappearance of the present high illiteracy, and the loss, in some passable measure, of the current superstitiously crass nationalism of that people. There are indications that something of that kind, and of quite disquieting dimensions, is already under way; though with no indication that any consequent disintegrating habits of thought have yet invaded the sacred close of Japanese patriotic devotion.

Again, it is a question of time and habituation. With time and habituation the emperor may insensibly cease to be of divine pedigree, and the syndicate of statesmen who are doing business under his signature may consequently find their measures of Imperial expansion questioned by the people who pay the bills. But so long as the Imperial syndicate enjoy their present immunity from outside obstruction, and can accordingly carry on an uninterrupted campaign of cumulative predation in Korea, China and Manchuria, the patriotic infatuation is less likely to fall off, and by so much the decay of Japanese loyalty will be retarded. Yet, even if allowed anything that may seem at all probable in the way of a free hand for aggression against their hapless neighbours, the skepticism and insubordination to personal rule that seems inseparable in the long run from addiction to the modern industrial arts should be expected presently to overtake the Japanese spirit of loyal servitude. And the opportunity of Imperial Japan lies in the interval. So also does the menace of Imperial Japan as a presumptive disturber of the peace at large.

*　*　*　*　*

At the cost of some unavoidable tedium, the argument as regards these and similar instances may be summarised. It appears, in the (possibly doubtful) light of the history of democratic institutions and of modern technology hitherto, as also from the logical character of this technology and its underlying material sciences, that consistent addiction to the peculiar habits of thought involved in its carrying on will presently induce a decay of those preconceptions in which dynastic government and national ambitions have their ground. Continued addiction to this modern scheme of industrial life should in time eventuate in a decay of militant nationalism, with a consequent lapse of warlike enterprise. At the same time, popular proficiency in the modern industrial arts, with all that that implies in the way of intelligence and information, is indispensable as a means to any successful warlike enterprise on the modern plan. The menace of warlike aggression from such dynastic States, e.g., as Imperial Germany and Imperial Japan is due to their having acquired a competent use of this modern technology, while they have not yet had time to lose that spirit of dynastic loyalty which they have carried over from an archaic order of things, out of which they have emerged at a very appreciably later period (last half of the nineteenth century) than those democratic peoples whose peace they now menace. As has been said, they have taken over this modern state of the industrial arts without having yet come in for the defects of its qualities. This modern technology, with its underlying material sciences, is a novel factor in the history of human culture, in that addiction to its use conduces to the decay of militant patriotism, at the same time that its employment so greatly enhances the warlike efficiency of even a pacific people, at need, that they can not be seriously molested by any other peoples, however valorous and numerous, who have not a competent use of this technology. A peace at large among the civilised nations, by loss of the militant temper through addiction to this manner of arts of peace, therefore, carries no risk of interruption by an inroad of warlike barbarians,--always provided that those existing archaic peoples who might pass muster as barbarians are brought into line with the pacific nations on a footing of peace and equality. The disparity in point of outlook as between the resulting peace at large by neglect of bootless animosities, on the one hand, and those historic instances of a peaceable civilisation that have been overwhelmed by warlike barbarian invasions, on the other hand, should be evident.

* * * * *

It is always possible, indeed it would scarcely be surprising to find, that the projected league of neutrals or of nations bent on peace can not be brought to realisation at this juncture; perhaps not for a long time yet. But it should at the same time seem reasonable to expect that the drift toward a peaceable settlement of national discrepancies such as has been visible in history for some appreciable time past will, in the absence of unforeseen hindrances, work out to some such effect in the course of further experience under modern conditions. And whether the projected peace compact at its inception takes one form or another, provided it succeeds in its main purpose, the long-term drift of things under its rule should logically set toward some ulterior settlement of the general character of what has here been spoken of as a peace by neglect or by neutralisation of discrepancies.

It should do so, in the absence of unforeseen contingencies; more particularly if there were no effectual factor of dissension included in the fabric of institutions within the nation. But there should also, e.g., be no difficulty in assenting to the forecast that when and if national peace and security are achieved and settled beyond recall, the discrepancy in fact between those who own the country's wealth and those who do not is presently due to come to an issue. Any attempt to forecast the form which this issue is to take, or the manner, incidents, adjuncts and sequelae of its determination, would be a bolder and a more ambiguous, undertaking. Hitherto attempts to bring this question to an issue have run aground on the real or fancied jeopardy to paramount national interests. How, if at all, this issue might affect national interests and international relations, would obviously depend in the first instance on the state of the given national establishment and the character of the international engagements entered into in the formation of this projected pacific league. It is always conceivable that the transactions involving so ubiquitous an issue might come to take on an international character and that they might touch the actual or fanciful interests of these diverse nations with such divergent effect as to bring on a rupture of the common understanding between them and of the peace-compact in which the common understanding is embodied.

*   *   *   *   *

In the beginning, that is to say in the beginnings out of which this modern era of the Western civilisation has arisen, with its scheme of law and custom, there grew into the scheme of law and custom, by settled usage, a right of ownership and of contract in disposal of ownership,--which may or may not have been a salutary institutional arrangement on the whole, under the circumstances of the early days. With the later growth of handicraft and the petty trade in Western Europe this right of ownership and contract came to be insisted on, standardised under legal specifications, and secured against molestation by the governmental interests; more particularly and scrupulously among those peoples that have taken the lead in working out that system of free or popular institutions that marks the modern civilised nations. So it has come to be embodied in the common law of the modern world as an inviolable natural right. It has all the prescriptive force of legally authenticated immemorial custom.

Under the system of handicraft and petty trade this right of property and free contract served the interest of the common man, at least in much of its incidence, and acted in its degree to shelter industrious and economical persons from hardship and indignity at the hands of their betters. There seems reason to believe, as is commonly believed, that so long as that relatively direct and simple scheme of industry and trade lasted, the right of ownership and contract was a salutary custom, in its bearing on the fortunes of the common man. It appears also, on the whole, to have been favorable to the fuller development of the handicraft technology, as well as to its eventual outgrowth into the new line of technological expedients and contrivances that presently gave rise to the machine industry and the large-scale business enterprise.

The standard theories of economic science have assumed the rights of property and contract as axiomatic premises and ultimate terms of analysis; and their theories are commonly drawn in such a form as would fit the circumstances of the handicraft industry and the petty trade, and such as can be extended to any other economic situation by shrewd interpretation. These theories, as they run from Adam Smith down through the nineteenth century and later, appear tenable, on the whole, when taken to apply to the economic situation of that earlier time, in virtually all that they have to say on questions of wages, capital, savings, and the economy and efficiency of management and production by the methods of private enterprise resting on these rights of ownership and contract and governed by the pursuit of private gain. It is when these standard theories are sought to be applied to the later situation, which has outgrown the conditions of handicraft, that they appear nugatory or meretricious. The "competitive system" which these standard theories assume as a necessary condition of their own validity, and about which they are designed to form a defensive hedge, would, under those earlier conditions of small-scale enterprise and personal contact, appear to have been both a passably valid assumption as a premise and a passably expedient scheme of economic relations and traffic. At that period of its life-history it can not be said consistently to have worked hardship to the common man; rather the reverse. And the common man in that time appears to have had no misgivings about the excellence of the scheme or of that article of Natural Rights that underlies it.

This complexion of things, as touches the effectual bearing of the institution of property and the ancient customary rights of ownership, has changed substantially since the time of Adam Smith. The "competitive system," which he looked to as the economic working-out of that "simple and obvious system of natural liberty" that always engaged his best affections, has in great measure ceased to operate as a routine of natural liberty, in fact; particularly in so far as touches the fortunes of the common man, the impecunious mass of the people. ***De jure***, of course, the competitive system and its inviolable rights of ownership are a citadel of Natural Liberty; but ***de facto*** the common man is now, and has for some time been, feeling the pinch of it. It is law, and doubtless it is good law, grounded in immemorial usage and authenticated with statute and precedent. But circumstances have so changed that this good old plan has in a degree become archaic, perhaps unprofitable, or even mischievous, on the whole, and especially as touches the conditions of life for the common man. At least, so the common man in these modern democratic and commercial countries is beginning to apprehend the matter.

Some slight and summary characterisation of these changing circumstances that have affected the incidence of the rights of property during modern times may, therefore, not be out of place; with a view to seeing how far and why these rights may be due to come under advisement and possible revision, in case a state of settled peace should leave men's attention free to turn to these internal, as contrasted with national interests.

Under that order of handicraft and petty trade that led to the standardisation of these rights of ownership in the accentuated form which belongs to them in modern law and custom, the common man had a practicable chance of free initiative and self-direction in his choice and pursuit of an occupation and a livelihood, in so far as rights of ownership bore on his case. At that period the workman was the main factor in industry and, in the main and characteristically, the question of his employment was a question of what he would do. The material equipment of industry--the "plant," as it has come to be called--was subject of ownership, then as now; but it was then a secondary factor and, notoriously, subsidiary to the immaterial equipment of skill, dexterity and judgment embodied in the person of the craftsman. The body of information, or general knowledge, requisite to a workmanlike proficiency as handicraftsman was sufficiently slight and simple to fall within the ordinary reach of the working class, without special schooling; and the material equipment necessary to the work, in the way of tools and appliances, was also slight enough, ordinarily, to bring it within the reach of the common man. The stress fell on the acquirement of that special personal skill, dexterity and judgment that would constitute the workman a master of his craft. Given a reasonable measure of pertinacity, the common man would be able to compass the material equipment needful to the pursuit of his craft, and so could make his way to a livelihood; and the inviolable right of ownership would then serve to secure him the product of his own industry, in provision for his own old-age and for a fair start in behalf of his children. At least in the popular conception, and presumably in some degree also in fact, the right of property so served as a guarantee of personal liberty and a basis of equality. And so its apologists still look on the institution.

In a very appreciable degree this complexion of things and of popular conceptions has changed since then; although, as would be expected, the change in popular conceptions has not kept pace with the changing circumstances. In all the characteristic and controlling lines of industry the modern machine technology calls for a very considerable material equipment; so large an equipment, indeed, that this plant, as it is called, always represents a formidable amount of invested wealth; and also so large that it will, typically, employ a considerable number of workmen per unit of plant. On the transition to the machine technology the plant became the unit of operation, instead of the workman, as had previously been the case; and with the further development of this modern technology, during the past hundred and fifty years or so, the unit of operation and control has increasingly come to be not the individual or isolated plant but rather an articulated group of such plants working together as a balanced system and keeping pace in common, under a collective business management; and coincidently the individual workman has been falling into the position of an auxiliary factor, nearly into that of an article of supply, to be charged up as an item of operating expenses. Under this later and current system, discretion and initiative vest not in the workman but in the owners of the plant, if anywhere. So that at this point the right of ownership has ceased to be, in fact, a guarantee of personal liberty to the common man, and has come to be, or is coming to be, a guarantee of dependence. All of which engenders a feeling of unrest and insecurity, such as to instill a doubt in the mind of the common man as to the continued expediency of this arrangement and of the prescriptive rights of property on which the arrangement rests.

There is also an insidious suggestion, carrying a sinister note of discredit, that comes in from ethnological science at this point; which is adapted still further to derange the common man's faith in this received institution of ownership and its control of the material equipment of industry. To students interested in human culture it is a matter of course that this material equipment is a means of utilising the state of the industrial arts; that it is useful in industry and profitable to its owners only because and in so far as it is a creation of the current technological knowledge and enables its owner to appropriate the usufruct of the current industrial arts. It is likewise a matter of course that this technological knowledge, that so enables the material equipment to serve the purposes of production and of private gain, is a free gift of the community at large to the owners of industrial plant; and, under latter-day conditions, to them exclusively. The state of the industrial arts is a joint heritage of the community at large, but where, as in the modern countries, the work to be done by this technology requires a large material equipment, the usufruct of this joint heritage passes, in effect, into the hands of the owners of this large material equipment.

These owners have, ordinarily, contributed nothing to the technology, the state of the industrial arts, from which their control of the material equipment of industry enables them to derive a gain. Indeed, no class or condition of men in the modern community--with the possible exception of politicians and the clergy--can conceivably contribute less to the community's store of technological knowledge than the large owners of invested wealth. By one of those singular inversions due to production being managed for private gain, it happens that these investors are not only not given to the increase and diffusion of technological knowledge, but they have a well-advised interest in retarding or defeating improvements in the industrial arts in detail. Improvements, innovations that heighten productive efficiency in the general line of production in which a given investment is placed, are commonly to be counted on to bring "obsolescence by supersession" to the plant already engaged in that line; and therefore to bring a decline in its income-yielding capacity, and so in its capital or investment value.

Invested capital yields income because it enjoys the usufruct of the community's technological knowledge; it has an effectual monopoly of this usufruct because this machine technology requires large material appliances with which to do its work; the interest of the owners of established industrial plant will not tolerate innovations designed to supersede these appliances. The bearing of ownership on industry and on the fortunes of the common man is accordingly, in the main, the bearing which it has by virtue of its monopoly control of the industrial arts, and its consequent control of the conditions of employment and of the supply of vendible products. It takes effect chiefly by inhibition and privation; stoppage of production in case it brings no suitable profit to the investor, refusal of employment and of a livelihood to the workmen in case their product does not command a profitable price in the market.

The expediency of so having the nation's industry managed on a footing of private ownership in the pursuit of private gain, by persons who can show no equitable personal claim to even the most modest livelihood, and whose habitual method of controlling industry is sabotage--refusal to let production go on except it affords them an unearned income--the expediency of all this is coming to be doubted by those who have to pay the cost of it. And it does not go far to lessen their doubts to find that the cost which they pay is commonly turned to no more urgent or useful purpose than a conspicuously wasteful consumption of superfluities by the captains of sabotage and their domestic establishments.

This may not seem a veracious and adequate account of these matters; it may, in effect, fall short of the formulation: The truth, the whole truth, and nothing but the truth; nor does the question here turn on its adequacy as a statement of fact. Without prejudice to the question of its veracity and adequacy, it is believed to be such an account of these matters as will increasingly come easy and seem convincing to the common man who, in an ever increasing degree, finds himself pinched with privation and insecurity by a run of facts which will consistently bear this construction, and who perforce sees these facts from the prejudiced standpoint of a loser. To such a one, there is reason to believe, the view so outlined will seem all the more convincing the more attentively the pertinent facts and their bearing on his fortunes are considered. How far the contrary prejudice of those whose interest or training inclines them the other way may lead them to a different construction of these pertinent facts, does not concern the present argument; which has to do with this run of facts only as they bear on the prospective frame of mind of that unblest mass of the population who will have opportunity to present their proposals when peace at large shall have put national interests out of their preferential place in men's regard.

At the risk of what may seem an excessively wide digression, there is something further to be said of the capitalistic sabotage spoken of above. The word has by usage come to have an altogether ungraceful air of disapproval. Yet it signifies nothing more vicious than a deliberate obstruction or retardation of industry, usually by legitimate means, for the sake of some personal or partisan advantage. This morally colorless meaning is all that is intended in its use here. It is extremely common in all industry that is designed to supply merchantable goods for the market. It is, in fact, the most ordinary and ubiquitous of all expedients in business enterprise that has to do with supplying the market, being always present in the businessman's necessary calculations; being not only a usual and convenient recourse but quite indispensable as an habitual measure of business sagacity. So that no personal blame can attach to its employment by any given businessman or business concern. It is only when measures of this nature are resorted to by employees, to gain some end of their own, that such conduct becomes (technically) reprehensible.

Any businesslike management of industry is carried on for gain, which is to be got only on condition of meeting the terms of the market. The price system under which industrial business is carried on will not tolerate production in excess of the market demand, or without due regard to the expenses of production as determined by the market on the side of the supplies required. Hence any business concern must adjust its operations, by due acceleration, retardation or stoppage, to the market conditions, with a view to what the traffic will bear; that is to say, with a view to what will yield the largest obtainable net gain. So long as the price system rules, that is to say so long as industry is managed on investment for a profit, there is no escaping this necessity of adjusting the processes of industry to the requirements of a remunerative price; and this adjustment can be taken care of only by well-advised acceleration or curtailment of the processes of industry; which answers to the definition of sabotage. Wise business management, and more particularly what is spoken of as safe and sane business management, therefore, reduces itself in the main to a sagacious use of sabotage; that is to say a sagacious limitation of productive processes to something less than the productive capacity of the means in hand.

* * * * *

To anyone who is inclined to see these matters of usage in the light of their history and to appraise them as phenomena of habituation, adaptation and supersession in the sequence of cultural proliferation, there should be no difficulty in appreciating that this institution of ownership that makes the core of the modern institutional structure is a precipitate of custom, like any other item of use and wont; and that, like any other article of institutional furniture, it is subject to the contingencies of supersession and obsolescence. If prevalent habits of thought, enforced by the prevalent exigencies of life and livelihood, come to change in such a way as to make life under the rule imposed by this institution seem irksome, or intolerable, to the mass of the population; and if at the same time things turn in such a way as to leave no other and more urgent interest or exigency to take precedence of this one and hinder its being pushed to an issue; then it should reasonably follow that contention is due to arise between the unblest mass on whose life it is a burden and the classes who live by it. But it is, of course, impossible to state beforehand what will be the precise line of cleavage or what form the division between the two parties in interest will take. Yet it is contained in the premises that, barring unforeseen contingencies of a formidable magnitude, such a cleavage is due to follow as a logical sequel of an enduring peace at large. And it is also well within the possibilities of the case that this issue may work into an interruption or disruption of the peace between the nations.

In this connection it may be called to mind that the existing governmental establishments in these pacific nations are, in all cases, in the hands of the beneficiary, or kept classes,--beneficiaries in the sense in which a distinction to that effect comes into the premises of the case at this point. The responsible officials and their chief administrative officers,--so much as may at all reasonably be called the "Government" or the "Administration,"--are quite invariably and characteristically drawn from these beneficiary classes; nobles, gentlemen, or business men, which all comes to the same thing for the purpose in hand; the point of it all being that the common man does not come within these precincts and does not share in these counsels that assume to guide the destiny of the nations.

Of course, sporadically and ephemerally, a man out of the impecunious and undistinguished mass may now and again find his way within the gates; and more frequently will a professed "Man of the People" sit in council. But that the rule holds unbroken and inviolable is sufficiently evident in the fact that no community will let the emoluments of office for any of its responsible officials, even for those of a very scant responsibility, fall to the level of the habitual livelihood of the undistinguished populace, or indeed to fall below what is esteemed to be a seemly income for a gentleman. Should such an impecunious one be thrown up into a place of discretion in the government, he will forthwith cease to be a common man and will be inducted into the rank of gentleman,--so far as that feat can be achieved by taking thought or by assigning him an income adequate to a reputably expensive manner of life. So obvious is the antagonism between a vulgar station in life and a position of official trust, that many a "selfmade man" has advisedly taken recourse to governmental position, often at some appreciable cost, from no apparent motive other than its known efficacy as a Levitical corrective for a humble origin. And in point of fact, neither here nor there have the underbred majority hitherto learned to trust one of their own kind with governmental discretion; which has never yet, in the popular conviction, ceased to be a perquisite of the gently-bred and the well-to-do.

Let it be presumed that this state of things will continue without substantial alteration, so far as regards the complexion of the governmental establishments of these pacific nations, and with such allowance for overstatement in the above characterisation as may seem called for. These governmental establishments are, by official position and by the character of their personnel, committed more or less consistently to the maintenance of the existing law and order. And should no substantial change overtake them as an effect of the war experience, the pacific league under discussion would be entered into by and between governments of this complexion. Should difficulties then arise between those who own and those who do not, in any one of these countries, it would become a nice question whether the compact to maintain the peace and national integrity of the several nations comprised in the league should be held to cover the case of internal dissensions and possible disorders partaking of the character of revolt against the established authorities or against the established provisions of law. A strike of the scope and character of the one recently threatened, and narrowly averted, on the American railroads, e.g., might easily give rise to disturbances sufficiently formidable to raise a question of the peace league's jurisdiction; particularly if such a disturbance should arise in a less orderly and less isolated country than the American republic; so as unavoidably to carry the effects of the disturbance across the national frontiers along the lines of industrial and commercial intercourse and correlation. It is always conceivable that a national government standing on a somewhat conservative maintenance of the received law and order might feel itself bound by its conception of the peace to make common cause with the keepers of established rights in neighboring states, particularly if the similar interests of their own nation were thought to be placed in jeopardy by the course of events.

Antecedently it seems highly probable that the received rights of ownership and disposal of property, particularly of investment, will come up for advisement and revision so soon as a settled state of peace is achieved. And there should seem to be little doubt but this revision would go toward, or at least aim at the curtailment or abrogation of these rights; very much after the fashion in which the analogous vested rights of feudalism and the dynastic monarchy have been revised and in great part curtailed or abrogated in the advanced democratic countries. Not much can confidently be said as to the details of such a prospective revision of legal rights, but the analogy of that procedure by which these other vested rights have been reduced to a manageable disability, suggests that the method in the present case also would be by way of curtailment, abrogation and elimination. Here again, as in analogous movements of disuse and disestablishment, there would doubtless be much conservative apprehension as to the procuring of a competent substitute for the supplanted methods of doing what is no longer desirable to be done; but here as elsewhere, in a like conjuncture, the practicable way out would presumably be found to lie along the line of simple disuse and disallowance of class prerogative. Taken at its face value, without unavoidable prejudice out of the past, this question of a substitute to replace the current exploitation of the industrial arts for private gain by capitalistic sabotage is not altogether above a suspicion of drollery.

Yet it is not to be overlooked that private enterprise on the basis of private ownership is the familiar and accepted method of conducting industrial affairs, and that it has the sanction of immemorial usage, in the eyes of the common man, and that it is reenforced with the urgency of life and death in the apprehension of the kept classes. It should accordingly be a possible outcome of such a peace as would put away international dissension, that the division of classes would come on in a new form, between those who stand on their ancient rights of exploitation and mastery, and those who are unwilling longer to submit. And it is quite within the possibilities of the case that the division of opinion on these matters might presently shift back to the old familiar ground of international hostilities; undertaken partly to put down civil disturbances in given countries, partly by the more archaic, or conservative, peoples to safeguard the institutions of the received law and order against inroads from the side of the iconoclastic ones.

* * * * *

In the apprehension of those who are speaking for peace between the nations and planning for its realisation, the outlook is that of a return to, or a continuance of, the state of things before the great war came on, with peace and national security added, or with the danger of war eliminated. Nothing appreciable in the way of consequent innovation, certainly nothing of a serious character, is contemplated as being among the necessary consequences of such a move into peace and security. National integrity and autonomy are to be preserved on the received lines, and international division and discrimination is to be managed as before, and with the accustomed incidents of punctilio and pecuniary equilibration. Internationally speaking, there is to dawn an era of diplomacy without afterthought, whatever that might conceivably mean.

There is much in the present situation that speaks for such an arrangement, particularly as an initial phase of the perpetual peace that is aimed at, whatever excursive variations might befall presently, in the course of years. The war experience in the belligerent countries and the alarm that has disturbed the neutral nations have visibly raised the pitch of patriotic solidarity in all these countries; and patriotism greatly favors the conservation of established use and wont; more particularly is it favorable to the established powers and policies of the national government. The patriotic spirit is not a spirit of innovation. The chances of survival, and indeed of stabilisation, for the accepted use and wont and for the traditional distinctions of class and prescriptive rights, should therefore seem favorable, at any rate in the first instance.

Presuming, therefore, as the spokesmen of such a peace-compact are singularly ready to presume, that the era of peace and good-will which they have in view is to be of a piece with the most tranquil decades of the recent past, only more of the same kind, it becomes a question of immediate interest to the common man, as well as to all students of human culture, how the common man is to fare under this regime of law and order,--the mass of the population whose place it is to do what is to be done, and thereby to carry forward the civilisation of these pacific nations. It may not be out of place to recall, by way of parenthesis, that it is here taken for granted as a matter of course that all governmental establishments are necessarily conservative in all their dealings with this heritage of culture, except so far as they may be reactionary. Their office is the stabilisation of archaic institutions, the measure of archaism varying from one to another.

With due stabilisation and with a sagacious administration of the established scheme of law and order, the common man should find himself working under conditions and to results of the familiar kind; but with the difference that, while legal usage and legal precedent remain unchanged, the state of the industrial arts can confidently be expected to continue its advance in the same general direction as before, while the population increases after the familiar fashion, and the investing business community pursues its accustomed quest of competitive gain and competitive spending in the familiar spirit and with cumulatively augmented means. Stabilisation of the received law and order will not touch these matters; and for the present it is assumed that these matters will not derange the received law and order. The assumption may seem a violent one to the students of human culture, but it is a simple matter of course to the statesmen.

To this piping time of peace the nearest analogues in history would seem to be the Roman peace, say, of the days of the Antonines, and passably the British peace of the Victorian era. Changes in the scheme of law and order supervened in both of these instances, but the changes were, after all, neither unconscionably large nor were they of a subversive nature. The scheme of law and order, indeed, appears in neither instance to have changed so far as the altered circumstances would seem to have called for. To the common man the Roman peace appears to have been a peace by submission, not widely different from what the case of China has latterly brought to the appreciation of students. The Victorian peace, which can be appreciated more in detail, was of a more genial character, as regards the fortunes of the common man. It started from a reasonably low level of hardship and ***de facto*** iniquity, and was occupied with many prudent endeavours to improve the lot of the unblest majority; but it is to be admitted that these prudent endeavours never caught up with the march of circumstances. Not that these prudent measures of amelioration were nugatory, but it is clear that they were not an altogether effectual corrective of the changes going on; they were, in effect, systematically so far in arrears as always to leave an uncovered margin of discontent with current conditions. It is a fact of history that very appreciable sections of the populace were approaching an attitude of revolt against what they considered to be intolerable conditions when that era closed. Much of what kept them within bounds, that is to say within legal bounds, was their continued loyalty to the nation; which was greatly, and for the purpose needfully, reenforced by a lively fear of warlike aggression from without. Now, under the projected ***pax orbis terrarum*** all fear of invasion, it is hopefully believed, will be removed; and with the disappearance of this fear should also disappear the drag of national loyalty on the counsels of the underbred.

If this British peace of the nineteenth century is to be taken as a significant indication of what may be looked for under a regime of peace at large, with due allowance for what is obviously necessary to be allowed for, then what is held in promise would appear to be an era of unexampled commercial prosperity, of investment and business enterprise on a scale hitherto not experienced. These developments will bring their necessary consequences affecting the life of the community, and some of the consequences it should be possible to foresee. The circumstances conditioning this prospective era of peace and prosperity will necessarily differ from the corresponding circumstances that conditioned the Victorian peace, and many of these points of difference it is also possible to forecast in outline with a fair degree of confidence. It is in the main these economic factors going to condition the civilisation of the promised future that will have to be depended on to give the cue to any student interested in the prospective unfolding of events.

The scheme of law and order governing all modern nations, both in the conduct of their domestic affairs and in their national policies, is in its controlling elements the scheme worked out through British (and French) experience in the eighteenth century and earlier, as revised and further accommodated in the nineteenth century. Other peoples, particularly the Dutch, have of course had their part in the derivation and development of this modern scheme of institutional principles, but it has after all been a minor part; so that the scheme at large would not differ very materially, if indeed it should differ sensibly, from what it is, even if the contribution of these others had not been had. The backward nations, as e.g., Germany, Russia, Spain, etc., have of course contributed substantially nothing but retardation and maladjustment to this modern scheme of civil life; whatever may be due to students resident in those countries, in the way of scholarly formulation. This nineteenth century scheme it is proposed to carry over into the new era; and the responsible spokesmen of the projected new order appear to contemplate no provision touching this scheme of law and order, beyond the keeping of it intact in all substantial respects.

When and in so far as the projected peace at large takes effect, international interests will necessarily fall somewhat into the background, as being no longer a matter of precarious equilibration, with heavy penalties in the balance; and diplomacy will consequently become even more of a make-believe than today--something after the fashion of a game of bluff played with irredeemable "chips." Commercial, that is to say business, enterprise will consequently come in for a more undivided attention and be carried on under conditions of greater security and of more comprehensive trade relations. The population of the pacified world may be expected to go on increasing somewhat as in the recent past; in which connection it is to be remarked that not more than one-half, presumably something less than one-half, of the available agricultural resources have been turned to account for the civilised world hitherto. The state of the industrial arts, including means of transport and communication, may be expected to develop farther in the same general direction as before, assuming always that peace conditions continue to hold. Popular intelligence, as it is called,--more properly popular education,--may be expected to suffer a further advance; necessarily so, since it is a necessary condition of any effectual advance in the industrial arts,--every appreciable technological advance presumes, as a requisite to its working-out in industry, an augmented state of information and of logical facility in the workmen under whose hands it is to take effect.

Of the prescriptive rights carried over into the new era, under the received law and order, the rights of ownership alone may be expected to have any material significance for the routine of workday life; the other personal rights that once seemed urgent will for everyday purposes have passed into a state of half-forgotten matter-of-course. As now, but in an accentuated degree, the rights of ownership will, in effect, coincide and coalesce with the rights of investment and business management. The market--that is to say the rule of the price-system in all matters of production and livelihood--may be expected to gain in volume and inclusiveness; so that virtually all matters of industry and livelihood will turn on questions of market price, even beyond the degree in which that proposition holds today. The progressive extension and consolidation of investments, corporate solidarity, and business management may be expected to go forward on the accustomed lines, as illustrated by the course of things during the past few decades. Market conditions should accordingly, in a progressively increased degree, fall under the legitimate discretionary control of businessmen, or syndicates of businessmen, who have the disposal of large blocks of invested wealth,--"big business," as it is called, should reasonably be expected to grow bigger and to exercise an increasingly more unhampered control of market conditions, including the money market and the labor market.

With such improvements in the industrial arts as may fairly be expected to come forward, and with the possible enhancement of industrial efficiency which should follow from a larger scale of organisation, a wider reach of transport and communication, and an increased population,--with these increasing advantages on the side of productive industry, the per-capita product as well as the total product should be increased in a notable degree, and the conditions of life should possibly become notably easier and more attractive, or at least more conducive to efficiency and personal comfort, for all concerned. Such would be the first and unguarded inference to be drawn from the premises of the case as they offer themselves in the large; and something of that kind is apparently what floats before the prophetic vision of the advocates of a league of nations for the maintenance of peace at large. These premises, and the inferences so drawn from them, may be further fortified and amplified in the same sense on considering that certain very material economies also become practicable, and should take effect "in the absence of disturbing causes," on the establishment of such a peace at large. It will of course occur to all thoughtful persons that armaments must be reduced, perhaps to a minimum, and that the cost of these things, in point of expenditures as well as of man-power spent in the service, would consequently fall off in a corresponding measure. So also, as slight further reflection will show, would the cost of the civil service presumably fall off very appreciably; more particularly the cost of this service per unit of service rendered. Some such climax of felicities might be looked for by hopeful persons, in the absence of disturbing causes.

Under the new dispensation the standard of living, that is to say the standard of expenditure, would reasonably be expected to advance in a very appreciable degree, at least among the wealthy and well-to-do; and by pressure of imitative necessity a like effect would doubtless also be had among the undistinguished mass. It is not a question of the standard of living considered as a matter of the subsistence minimum, or even a standard of habitually prevalent creature comfort, particularly not among the wealthy and well-to-do. These latter classes have long since left all question of material comfort behind in their accepted standards of living and in the continued advance of these standards. For these classes who are often spoken of euphemistically as being "in easy circumstances," it is altogether a question of a standard of reputable expenditure, to be observed on pain of lost self-respect and of lost reputation at large. As has been remarked in an earlier passage, wants of this kind are indefinitely extensible. So that some doubt may well be entertained as to whether the higher productive efficiency spoken of will necessarily make the way of life easier, in view of this need of a higher standard of expenditure, even when due account is taken of the many economies which the new dispensation is expected to make practicable.

One of the effects to be looked for would apparently be an increased pressure on the part of aspiring men to get into some line of business enterprise; since it is only in business, as contrasted with the industrial occupations, that anyone can hope to find the relatively large income required for such an expensive manner of life as will bring any degree of content to aspirants for pecuniary good repute. So it should follow that the number of businessmen and business concerns would increase up to the limit of what the traffic could support, and that the competition between these rival, and in a sense over-numerous, concerns would push the costs of competition to the like limit. In this respect the situation would be of much the same character as what it now is, with the difference that the limit of competitive expenditures would be rather higher than at present, to answer to the greater available margin of product that could be devoted to this use; and that the competing concerns would be somewhat more numerous, or at least that the aggregate expenditure on competitive enterprise would be somewhat larger; as, e.g., costs of advertising, salesmanship, strategic litigation, procuration of legislative and municipal grants and connivance, and the like.

It is always conceivable, though it may scarcely seem probable, that these incidents of increased pressure of competition in business traffic might eventually take up all the slack, and leave no net margin of product over what is available under the less favorable conditions of industry that prevail today; more particularly when this increased competition for business gains is backed by an increased pressure of competitive spending for purposes of a reputable appearance. All this applies in retail trade and in such lines of industry and public service as partakes of the nature of retail trade, in the respect that salesmanship and the costs of salesmanship enter into their case in an appreciable measure; this is an extensive field, it is true, and incontinently growing more extensive with the later changes in the customary methods of marketing products; but it is by no means anything like the whole domain of industrial business, and by no means a field in which business is carried on without interference of a higher control from outside its own immediate limits.

All this generously large and highly expensive and profitable field of trade and of trade-like industry, in which the businessmen in charge deal somewhat directly with a large body of customers, is always subject to limitations imposed by the condition of the market; and the condition of the market is in part not under the control of these businessmen, but is also in part controlled by large concerns in the background; which in their turn are after all also not precisely free agents; in fact not much more so than their cousins in the retail trade, being confined in all their motions by the constraint of the price-system that dominates the whole and gathers them all in its impersonal and inexorable net.

There is a colloquial saying among businessmen, that they are not doing business for their health; which being interpreted means that they are doing business for a price. It is out of a discrepancy in price, between purchase and sale, or between transactions which come to the same result as purchase and sale, that the gains of business are drawn; and it is in terms of price that these gains are rated, amassed and funded. It is necessary, for a business concern to achieve a favorable balance in terms of price; and the larger the balance in terms of price the more successful the enterprise. Such a balance can not be achieved except by due regard to the conditions of the market, to the effect that dealings must not go on beyond what will yield a favorable balance in terms of price between income and outgo. As has already been remarked above, the prescriptive and indispensable recourse in all this conduct of business is sabotage, limitation of supply to bring a remunerative price result.

The new dispensation offers two new factors bearing on this businesslike need of a sagacious sabotage, or rather it brings a change of coefficients in two factors already familiar in business management: a greater need, for gainful business, of resorting to such limitation of traffic; and a greater facility of ways and means for enforcing the needed restriction. So, it is confidently to be expected that in the prospective piping time of peace the advance in the industrial arts will continue at an accelerated rate; which may confidently be expected to affect the practicable increased production of merchantable goods; from which it follows that it will act to depress the prices of these goods; from which it follows that if a profitable business is to be done in the conduct of productive industry a greater degree of continence than before will have to be exercised in order not to let prices fall to an unprofitable figure; that is to say, the permissible output must be held short of the productive capacity of such industry by a wider margin than before. On the other hand, it is well known out of the experience of the past few decades that a larger coalition of invested capital, controlling a larger proportion of the output, can more effectually limit the supply to a salutary maximum, such as will afford reasonable profits. And with the new dispensation affording a freer scope for business enterprise on conditions of greater security, larger coalitions than before are due to come into bearing. So that the means will be at hand competently to meet this more urgent need of a stricter limitation of the output, in spite of any increased productive capacity conferred on the industrial community by any conceivable advance in the industrial arts. The outcome to be looked for should apparently be such an effectual recourse to capitalistic sabotage as will neutralise any added advantage that might otherwise accrue to the community from its continued improvements in technology.

In spite of this singularly untoward conjuncture of circumstances to be looked for, there need be no serious apprehension that capitalistic sabotage, with a view to maintaining prices and the rate of profits, will go all the way, to the result indicated, at least not on the grounds so indicated alone. There is in the modern development of technology, and confidently to be counted on, a continued flow of new contrivances and expedients designed to supersede the old; and these are in fact successful, in greater or less measure, in finding their way into profitable use, on such terms as to displace older appliances, underbid them in the market, and render them obsolete or subject to recapitalisation on a lowered earning-capacity. So far as this unremitting flow of innovations has its effect, that is to say so far as it can not be hindered from having an effect, it acts to lower the effectual cost of products to the consumer. This effect is but a partial and somewhat uncertain one, but it is always to be counted in as a persistent factor, of uncertain magnitude, that will affect the results in the long run.

As has just been spoken of above, large coalitions of invested wealth are more competent to maintain, or if need be to advance, prices than smaller coalitions acting in severalty, or even when acting in collusion. This state of the case has been well illustrated by the very successful conduct of such large business organisations during the past few decades; successful, that is, in earning large returns on the investments engaged. Under the new dispensation, as has already been remarked, coalitions should reasonably be expected to grow to a larger size and achieve a greater efficiency for the same purpose.

The large gains of the large corporate coalitions are commonly ascribed by their promoters, and by sympathetic theoreticians of the ancient line, to economies of production made practicable by a larger scale of production; an explanation which is disingenuous only so far as it needs be. What is more visibly true on looking into the workings of these coalitions in detail is that they are enabled to maintain prices at a profitable, indeed at a strikingly profitable, level by such a control of the output as would be called sabotage if it were put in practice by interested workmen with a view to maintain wages. The effects of this sagacious sabotage become visible in the large earnings of these investments and the large gains which, now and again, accrue to their managers. Large fortunes commonly are of this derivation.

In cases where no recapitalisation has been effected for a considerable series of years the yearly earnings of such businesslike coalitions have been known to approach fifty percent on the capitalised value. Commonly, however, when earnings rise to a striking figure, the business will be recapitalised on the basis of its earning-capacity, by issue of a stock dividend, by reincorporation in a new combination with an increased capitalisation, and the like. Such augmentation of capital not unusually has been spoken of by theoretical writers and publicists as an increase of the community's wealth, due to savings; an analysis of any given case is likely to show that its increased capital value represents an increasingly profitable procedure for securing a high price above cost, by stopping the available output short of the productive capacity of the industries involved. Loosely speaking, and within the limits of what the traffic will bear, the gains in such a case are proportioned to the deficiency by which the production or supply under control falls short of productive capacity. So that the capitalisation in the case comes to bear a rough proportion to the material loss which this organisation of sabotage is enabled to inflict on the community at large; and instead of its being a capitalisation of serviceable means of production it may, now and again, come to little else than a capitalisation of chartered sabotage.

Under the new dispensation of peace and security at large this manner of capitalisation and business enterprise might reasonably be expected to gain something in scope and security of operation. Indeed, there are few things within the range of human interest on which an opinion may more confidently be formed beforehand. If the rights of property, in their extent and amplitude, are maintained intact as they are before the law today, the hold which business enterprise on the large scale now has on the affairs and fortunes of the community at large is bound to grow firmer and to be used more unreservedly for private advantage under the new conditions contemplated.

The logical result should be an accelerated rate of accumulation of the country's wealth in the hands of a relatively very small class of wealthy owners, with a relatively inconsiderable semi-dependent middle class of the well-to-do, and with the mass of the population even more nearly destitute than they are today. At the same time it is scarcely to be avoided that this wholly dependent and impecunious mass of the population must be given an appreciably better education than they have today. The argument will return to the difficulties that are liable to arise out of this conjuncture of facts, in the way of discontent and possible disturbance.

* * * * *

Meantime, looking to the promise of the pacific future in the light of the pacific past, certain further consequences, particularly consequences of the economic order, that may reasonably be expected to follow will also merit attention. The experience of the Victorian peace is almost as pointed in its suggestion on this head as if it had been an experiment made ***ad hoc***; but with the reservation that the scale of economic life, after all, was small in the Victorian era, and its pace was slack, compared with what the twentieth century should have to offer under suitable conditions of peace and pecuniary security. In the light of this most instructive modern instance, there should appear to be in prospect a growth of well-bred families resting on invested wealth and so living on unearned incomes; larger incomes and consequently a more imposingly well-bred body of gentlefolk, sustained and vouched for by a more munificent expenditure on superfluities, than the modern world has witnessed hitherto. Doubtless the resulting growth of gentlemen and gentlewomen would be as perfect after their kind as these unexampled opportunities of gentle breeding might be expected to engender; so that even their British precursors on the trail of respectability would fall somewhat into insignificance by comparison, whether in respect of gentlemanly qualities or in point of cost per unit.

The moral, and even more particularly the aesthetic, value of such a line of gentlefolk, and of the culture which they may be expected to place on view,--this cultural side of the case, of course, is what one would prefer to dwell on, and on the spiritual gains that might be expected to accrue to humanity at large from the steady contemplation of this meritorious respectability so displayed at such a cost.

But the prosaic necessity of the argument turns back to the economic and civil bearing of this prospective development, this virtual bifurcation of the pacified nation into a small number of gentlemen who own the community's wealth and consume its net product in the pursuit of gentility, on the one hand, and an unblest mass of the populace who do the community's work on a meager livelihood tapering down toward the subsistence minimum, on the other hand. Evidently, this prospective posture of affairs may seem "fraught with danger to the common weal," as a public spirited citizen might phrase it. Or, as it would be expressed in less eloquent words, it appears to comprise elements that should make for a change. At the same time it should be recalled, and the statement will command assent on slight reflection, that there is no avoiding substantially such a posture of affairs under the promised regime of peace and security, provided only that the price-system stands over intact, and the current rights of property continue to be held inviolate. If the known principles of competitive gain and competitive spending should need enforcement to that effect by an illustrative instance, the familiar history of the Victorian peace is sufficient to quiet all doubts.

Of course, the resulting articulation of classes in the community will not be expected to fall into such simple lines of sheer contrast as this scheme would indicate. The class of gentlefolk, the legally constituted wasters, as they would be rated from the economic point of view, can not be expected personally to take care of so large a consumption of superfluities as this posture of affairs requires at their hands. They would, as the Victorian peace teaches, necessarily have the assistance of a trained corps of experts in unproductive consumption, the first and most immediate of whom would be those whom the genial phrasing of Adam Smith designates "menial servants." Beyond these would come the purveyors of superfluities, properly speaking, and the large, indeed redundant, class of tradespeople of high and low degree,--dependent in fact but with an illusion of semi-dependence; and farther out again the legal and other professional classes of the order of stewards, whose duty it will be to administer the sources of income and receive, apportion and disburse the revenues so devoted to a traceless extinguishment.

There would, in other words, be something of a "substantial middle class," dependent on the wealthy and on their expenditure of wealth, but presumably imbued with the Victorian middle-class illusion that they are of some account in their own right. Under the due legal forms and sanctions this, somewhat voluminous, middle-class population would engage in the traffic which is their perquisite, and would continue to believe, in some passable fashion, that they touch the substance of things at something nearer than the second remove. They would in great part appear to be people of "independent means," and more particularly would they continue in the hope of so appearing and of some time making good the appearance. Hence their fancied, and therefore their sentimental, interest would fall out on the side of the established law and order; and they would accordingly be an element of stability in the commonwealth, and would throw in their weight, and their voice, to safeguard that private property and that fabric of prices and credit through which the "income stream" flows to the owners of preponderant invested wealth.

Judged on the state of the situation as it runs in our time, and allowing for the heightened efficiency of large-scale investment and consolidated management under the prospective conditions of added pecuniary security, it is to be expected that the middle-class population with "independent means" should come in for a somewhat meager livelihood, provided that they work faithfully at their business of managing pecuniary traffic to the advantage of their pecuniary betters,--meager, that is to say, when allowance is made for the conventionally large expenditure on reputable appearances which is necessarily to be included in their standard of living. It lies in the nature of this system of large-scale investment and enterprise that the (pecuniarily) minor agencies engaged on a footing of ostensible independence will come in for only such a share in the aggregate gains of the community as it is expedient for the greater business interests to allow them as an incentive to go on with their work as purveyors of traffic to these greater business interests.

The current, and still more this prospective, case of the quasi-self-directing middle class may fairly be illustrated by the case of the American farmers, of the past and present. The American farmer rejoices to be called "The Independent Farmer." He once was independent, in a meager and toil-worn fashion, in the days before the price-system had brought him and all his works into the compass of the market; but that was some time ago. He now works for the market, ordinarily at something like what is called a "living wage," provided he has "independent means" enough to enable him by steady application to earn a living wage; and of course, the market being controlled by the paramount investment interests in the background, his work, in effect, inures to their benefit; except so much as it may seem necessary to allow him as incentive to go on. Also of course, these paramount investment interests are in turn controlled in all their manoeuvres by the impersonal exigencies of the price-system, which permits no vagaries in violation of the rule that all traffic must show a balance of profit in terms of price.

The Independent Farmer still continues to believe that in some occult sense he still is independent in what he will do and what not; or perhaps rather that he can by shrewd management retain or regain a tolerable measure of such independence, after the fashion of what is held to have been the posture of affairs in the days before the coming of corporation finance; or at least he believes that he ought to have, or to regain or reclaim, some appreciable measure of such independence; which ought then, by help of the "independent means" which he still treasures, to procure him an honest and assured livelihood in return for an honest year's work. Latterly he, that is the common run of the farmers, has been taking note of the fact that he is, as he apprehends it, at a disadvantage in the market; and he is now taking recourse to concerted action for the purpose of what might be called "rigging the market" to his own advantage. In this he overlooks the impregnable position which the party of the second part, the great investment interests, occupy; in fact, he is counting without his host. Hitherto he has not been convinced of his own helplessness. And with a fine fancy he still imagines that his own interest is on the side of the propertied and privileged classes; so that the farmer constituency is the chief pillar of conservative law and order, particularly in all that touches the inviolable rights of property and at every juncture where a division comes on between those who live by investment and those who live by work. In pecuniary effect, the ordinary American farmer, who legally owns a moderate farm of the common sort, belongs among those who work for a livelihood; such a livelihood as the investment interests find it worth while to allow him under the rule of what the traffic will bear; but in point of sentiment and class consciousness he clings to a belated stand on the side of those who draw a profit from his work.

So it is also with the menial servants and the middle-class people of "independent means," who are, however, in a position to see more clearly their dependence on the owners of predominant wealth. And such, with a further accentuation of the anomaly, may reasonably be expected to be the further run of these relations under the promised regime of peace and security. The class of well-kept gentlefolk will scarcely be called on to stand alone, in case of a division between those who live by investment and those who live by work; inasmuch as, for the calculable future, it should seem a reasonable expectation that this very considerable fringe of dependents and pseudo-independents will abide by their time-tried principles of right and honest living, through good days and evil, and cast in their lot unreservedly with that reputable body to whom the control of trade and industry by investment assigns the usufruct of the community's productive powers.

* * * * *

Something has already been said of the prospective breeding of pedigreed gentlefolk under the projected regime of peace. Pedigree, for the purpose in hand, is a pecuniary attribute and is, of course, a product of funded wealth, more or less ancient. Virtually ancient pedigree can be procured by well-advised expenditure on the conspicuous amenities; that is to say pedigree effectually competent as a background of current gentility. Gentlefolk of such syncopated pedigree may have to walk circumspectly, of course; but their being in this manner put on their good behavior should tend to heighten their effectual serviceability as gentlefolk, by inducing a single-mindedness of gentility beyond what can fairly be expected of those who are already secure in their tenure.

Except conventionally, there is no hereditary difference between the standard gentlefolk and, say, their "menial servants," or the general population of the farms and the industrial towns. This is a well-established commonplace among ethnological students; which has, of course, nothing to say with respect to the conventionally distinct lines of descent of the "Best Families." These Best Families are nowise distinguishable from the common run in point of hereditary traits; the difference that makes the gentleman and the gentlewoman being wholly a matter of habituation during the individual's life-time. It is something of a distasteful necessity to call attention to this total absence of native difference between the well-born and the common, but it is a necessity of the argument in hand, and the recalling of it may, therefore, be overlooked for once in a way. There is no harm and no annoyance intended. The point of it all is that, on the premises which this state of the case affords, the body of gentlefolk created by such an accumulation of invested wealth will have no less of an effectual cultural value than they would have had if their virtually ancient pedigree had been actual.

At this point, again, the experience of the Victorian peace and the functioning of its gentlefolk come in to indicate what may fairly be hoped for in this way under this prospective regime of peace at large. But with the difference that the scale of things is to be larger, the pace swifter, and the volume and dispersion of this prospective leisure class somewhat wider. The work of this leisure class--and there is neither paradox nor inconsistency in the phrase--should be patterned on the lines worked out by their prototypes of the Victorian time, but with some appreciable accentuation in the direction of what chiefly characterised the leisure class of that era of tranquility. The characteristic feature to which attention naturally turns at this suggestion is the tranquility that has marked that body of gentlefolk and their code of clean and honest living. Another word than "tranquility" might be hit upon to designate this characteristic animus, but any other word that should at all adequately serve the turn would carry a less felicitous suggestion of those upper-class virtues that have constituted the substantial worth of the Victorian gentleman. The conscious worth of these gentlefolk has been a beautifully complete achievement. It has been an achievement of "faith without works," of course; but, needless to say, that is as it should be, also of course. The place of gentlefolk in the economy of Nature is tracelessly to consume the community's net product, and in doing so to set a standard of decent expenditure for the others emulatively to work up to as near as may be. It is scarcely conceivable that this could have been done in a more unobtrusively efficient manner, or with a more austerely virtuous conviction of well-doing, than by the gentlefolk bred of the Victorian peace. So also, in turn, it is not to be believed that the prospective breed of gentlefolk derivable from the net product of the pacific nations under the promised regime of peace at large will prove in any degree less effective for the like ends. More will be required of them in the way of a traceless consumption of superfluities and an unexampled expensive standard of living. But this situation that so faces them may be construed as a larger opportunity, quite as well as a more difficult task.

A theoretical exposition of the place and cultural value of a leisure class in modern life would scarcely be in place here; and it has also been set out in some detail elsewhere.[10] For the purpose in hand it may be sufficient to recall that the canons of taste and the standards of valuation worked out and inculcated by leisure-class life have in all ages run, with unbroken consistency, to pecuniary waste and personal futility. In its economic bearing, and particularly in its immediate bearing on the material well-being of the community at large, the leadership of the leisure class can scarcely be called by a less derogatory epithet than "untoward." But that is not the whole of the case, and the other side should be heard. The leisure-class

---

10 Cf. *The Theory of the Leisure Class*, especially ch. v.-ix. and xiv.

life of tranquility, running detached as it does above the turmoil out of which the material of their sustenance is derived, enables a growth of all those virtues that mark, or make, the gentleman; and that affect the life of the underlying community throughout, pervasively, by imitation; leading to a standardisation of the everyday proprieties on a presumably, higher level of urbanity and integrity than might be expected to result in the absence of this prescriptive model.

Integer vitae scelerisque purus, the gentleman of assured station turns a placid countenance to all those petty vexations of breadwinning that touch him not. Serenely and with an impassive fortitude he faces those common vicissitudes of life that are impotent to make or mar his material fortunes and that can neither impair his creature comforts nor put a slur on his good repute. So that without afterthought he deals fairly in all everyday conjunctures of give and take; for they are at the most inconsequential episodes to him, although the like might spell irremediable disaster to his impecunious counterfoil among the common men who have the community's work to do. In short, he is a gentleman, in the best acceptation of the word,--unavoidably, by force of circumstance. As such his example is of invaluable consequence to the underlying community of common folk, in that it keeps before their eyes an object lesson in habitual fortitude and visible integrity such as could scarcely have been created except under such shelter from those disturbances that would go to mar habitual fortitude and integrity. There can be little doubt but the high example of the Victorian gentlefolk has had much to do with stabilising the animus of the British common man on lines of integrity and fair play. What else and more in the way of habitual preconceptions he may, by competitive imitation, owe to the same high source is not immediately in question here.

*   *   *   *   *

Recalling once more that the canon of life whereby folk are gentlefolk sums itself up in the requirements of pecuniary waste and personal futility, and that these requirements are indefinitely extensible, at the same time that the management of the community's industry by investment for a profit enables the owners of invested wealth to divert to their own use the community's net product, wherewith to meet these requirements, it follows that the community at large which provides this output of product will be allowed so much as is required by their necessary standard of living,--with an unstable margin of error in the adjustment. This margin of error should tend continually to grow narrower as the businesslike management of industry grows more efficient with experience; but it will also continually be disturbed in the contrary sense by innovations of a technological nature that require continual readjustment. This margin is probably not to be got rid of, though it may be expected to become less considerable under more settled conditions.

It should also not be overlooked that the standard of living here spoken of as necessarily to be allowed the working population by no means coincides with the "physical subsistence minimum," from which in fact it always departs by something appreciable. The necessary standard of living of the working community is in fact made up of two distinguishable factors: the subsistence minimum, and the requirements of decorously wasteful consumption--the "decencies of life." These decencies are no less requisite than the physical necessaries, in point of workday urgency, and their amount is a matter of use and wont. This composite standard of living is a practical minimum, below which consumption will not fall, except by a fluctuating margin of error; the effect being the same, in point of necessary consumption, as if it were all of the nature of a physical subsistence minimum.

Loosely speaking, the arrangement should leave nothing appreciable over, after the requirements of genteel waste and of the workday standard of consumption have been met. From which in turn it should follow that the rest of what is comprised under the general caption of "culture" will find a place only in the interstices of leisure-class expenditure and only at the hands of aberrant members of the class of the gently-bred. The working population should have no effectual margin of time, energy or means for other pursuits than the day's work in the service of the price-system; so that aberrant individuals in this class, who might by native propensity incline, e.g., to pursue the sciences or the fine arts, should have (virtually) no chance to make good. It would be a virtual suppression of such native gifts among the common folk, not a definitive and all-inclusive suppression. The state of the case under the Victorian peace may, again, be taken in illustration of the point; although under the presumably more effectual control to be looked for in the pacific future the margin might reasonably be expected to run somewhat narrower, so that this virtual suppression of cultural talent among the common men should come nearer a complete suppression.

The working of that free initiative that makes the advance of civilisation, and also the greater part of its conservation, would in effect be allowed only in the erratic members of the kept classes; where at the same time it would have to work against the side-draught of conventional usage, which discountenances any pursuit that is not visibly futile according to some accepted manner of futility. Now under the prospective perfect working of the price-system, bearers of the banners of civilisation could effectually be drawn only from the kept classes, the gentlefolk who alone would have the disposal of such free income as is required for work that has no pecuniary value. And numerically the gentlefolk are an inconsiderable fraction of the population. The supply of competently gifted bearers of the community's culture would accordingly be limited to such as could be drawn by self-selection from among this inconsiderable proportion of the community at large.

It may be recalled that in point of heredity, and therefore in point of native fitness for the maintenance and advance of civilisation, there is no difference between the gentlefolk and the populace at large; or at least there is no difference of such a nature as to count in abatement of the proposition set down above. Some slight, but after all inconsequential, difference there may be, but such difference as there is, if any, rather counts against the gentlefolk as keepers of the cultural advance. The gentlefolk are derived from business; the gentleman represents a filial generation of the businessman; and if the class typically is gifted with any peculiar hereditary traits, therefore, they should presumably be such as typically mark the successful businessman--astute, prehensile, unscrupulous. For a generation or two, perhaps to the scriptural third and fourth generation, it is possible that a diluted rapacity and cunning may continue to mark the businessman's well-born descendants; but these are not serviceable traits for the conservation and advancement of the community's cultural heritage. So that no consideration of special hereditary fitness in the well-born need be entertained in this connection.

As to the limitation imposed by the price-system on the supply of candidates suited by native gift for the human work of civilisation; it would no doubt, be putting the figure extravagantly high to say that the gentlefolk, properly speaking, comprise as much as ten percent of the total population; perhaps something less than one-half of that percentage would still seem a gross overstatement. But, to cover loose ends and vagrant cases, the gentlefolk may for the purpose be credited with so high a percentage of the total population. If ten percent be allowed, as an outside figure, it follows that the community's scientists, artists, scholars, and the like individuals given over to the workday pursuits of the human spirit, are by conventional restriction to be drawn from one-tenth of the current supply of persons suited by native gift for these pursuits. Or as it may also be expressed, in so far as the projected scheme takes effect it should result in the suppression of nine (or more) out of every ten persons available for the constructive work of civilisation. The cultural consequences to be looked for, therefore, should be quite markedly of the conservative order.

Of course, in actual effect, the retardation or repression of civilisation by this means, as calculated on these premises, should reasonably be expected to count up to something appreciably more than nine-tenths of the gains that might presumably be achieved in the conceivable absence of the price-system and the regime of investment. All work of this kind has much of the character of teamwork; so that the efforts of isolated individuals count for little, and a few working in more or less of concert and understanding will count for proportionally much less than many working in concert. The endeavours of the individuals engaged count cumulatively, to such effect that doubling their forces will more than double the aggregate efficiency; and conversely, reducing the number will reduce the effectiveness of their work by something more than the simple numerical proportion. Indeed, an undue reduction of numbers in such a case may lead to the total defeat of the few that are left, and the best endeavours of a dwindling remnant may be wholly nugatory. There is needed a sense of community and solidarity, without which the assurance necessary to the work is bound to falter and dwindle out; and there is also needed a degree of popular countenance, not to be had by isolated individuals engaged in an unconventional pursuit of things that are neither to be classed as spendthrift decorum nor as merchantable goods. In this connection an isolated one does not count for one, and more than the critical minimum will count for several per capita. It is a case where the "minimal dose" is wholly inoperative.

There is not a little reason to believe that consequent upon the installation of the projected regime of peace at large and secure investment the critical point in the repression of talent will very shortly be reached and passed, so that the principle of the "minimal dose" will come to apply. The point may readily be illustrated by the case of many British and American towns and neighbourhoods during the past few decades; where the dominant price-system and its commercial standards of truth and beauty have over-ruled all inclination to cultural sanity and put it definitively in abeyance. The cultural, or perhaps the conventional, residue left over in these cases where civilisation has gone stale through inefficiency of the minimal dose is not properly to be found fault with; it is of a blameless character, conventionally; nor is there any intention here to cast aspersion on the desolate. The like effects of the like causes are to be seen in the American colleges and universities, where business principles have supplanted the pursuit of learning, and where the commercialisation of aims, ideals, tastes, occupations and personnel is following much the same lines that have led so many of the country towns effectually outside the cultural pale. The American university or college is coming to be an outlier of the price-system, in point of aims, standards and personnel; hitherto the tradition of learning as a trait of civilisation, as distinct from business, has not been fully displaced, although it is now coming to face the passage of the minimal dose. The like, in a degree, is apparently true latterly for many English, and still more evidently for many German schools.

In these various instances of what may be called dry-rot or local blight on the civilised world's culture the decline appears to be due not to a positive infection of a malignant sort, so much as to a failure of the active cultural ferment, which has fallen below the critical point of efficacy; perhaps through an unintended refusal of a livelihood to persons given over to cultivating the elements of civilisation; perhaps through the conventional disallowance of the pursuit of any other ends than competitive gain and competitive spending. Evidently it is something much more comprehensive in this nature that is reasonably to be looked for under the prospective regime of peace, in case the price-system gains that farther impetus and warrant which it should come in for if the rights of ownership and investment stand over intact, and so come to enjoy the benefit of a further improved state of the industrial arts and a further enlarged scale of operation and enhanced rate of turnover.

* * * * *

To turn back to the point from which this excursion branched off. It has been presumed all the while that the technological equipment, or the state of the industrial arts, must continue to advance under the conditions offered by this regime of peace at large. But the last few paragraphs will doubtless suggest that such a single-minded addiction to competitive gain and competitive spending as the stabilised and amplified price-system would enjoin, must lead to an effectual retardation, perhaps to a decline, of those material sciences on which modern technology draws; and that the state of the industrial arts should therefore cease to advance, if only the scheme of investment and businesslike sabotage can be made sufficiently secure. That such may be the outcome is a contingency which the argument will have to meet and to allow for; but it is after all a contingency that need not be expected to derange the sequence of events, except in the way of retardation. Even without further advance in technological expedients or in the relevant material sciences, there will still necessarily ensue an effectual advance in the industrial arts, in the sense that further organisation and enlargement of the material equipment and industrial processes on lines already securely known and not to be forgotten must bring an effectually enhanced efficiency of the industrial process as a whole.

In illustration, it is scarcely to be assumed even as a tentative hypothesis that the system of transport and communication will not undergo extension and improvement on the lines already familiar, even in the absence of new technological contrivances. At the same time a continued increase of population is to be counted on; which has, for the purpose in hand, much the same effect as an advance in the industrial arts. Human contact and mutual understanding will necessarily grow wider and closer, and will have its effect on the habits of thought prevalent in the communities that are to live under the promised regime of peace. The system of transport and communication having to handle a more voluminous and exacting traffic, in the service of a larger and more compact population, will have to be organised and administered on mechanically drawn schedules of time, place, volume, velocity, and price, of a still more exacting accuracy than hitherto. The like will necessarily apply throughout the industrial occupations that employ extensive plant or processes, or that articulate with industrial processes of that nature; which will necessarily comprise a larger proportion of the industrial process at large than hitherto.

As has already been remarked more than once in the course of the argument, a population that lives and does its work, and such play as is allowed it, in and by an exactingly articulate mechanical system of this kind will necessarily be an "intelligent" people, in the colloquial sense of the word; that is to say it will necessarily be a people that uses printed matter freely and that has some familiarity with the elements of those material sciences that underlie this mechanically organised system of appliances and processes. Such a population lives by and within the framework of the mechanistic logic, and is in a fair way to lose faith in any proposition that can not be stated convincingly in terms of this mechanistic logic. Superstitions are liable to lapse by neglect or disuse in such a community; that is to say propositions of a non-mechanistic complexion are liable to insensible disestablishment in such a case; "superstition" in these premises coming to signify whatever is not of this mechanistic, or "materialistic" character. An exception to this broad characterisation of non-mechanistic propositions as "superstition" would be matters that are of the nature of an immediate deliverance of the senses or of the aesthetic sensibilities.

By a simile it might be said that what so falls under the caption of "superstition" in such a case is subject to decay by inanition. It should not be difficult to conceive the general course of such a decay of superstitions under this unremitting discipline of mechanistic habits of life. The recent past offers an illustration, in the unemotional progress of decay that has overtaken religious beliefs in the more civilised countries, and more particularly among the intellectually trained workmen of the mechanical industries. The elimination of such non-mechanistic propositions of the faith has been visibly going on, but it has not worked out on any uniform plan, nor has it overtaken any large or compact body of people consistently or abruptly, being of the nature of obsolescence rather than of set repudiation. But in a slack and unreflecting fashion the divestment has gone on until the aggregate effect is unmistakable.

A similar divestment of superstitions is reasonably to be looked for also in that domain of preconceptions that lies between the supernatural and the mechanistic. Chief among these time-warped preconceptions--or superstitions--that so stand over out of the alien past among these democratic peoples is the institution of property. As is true of preconceptions touching the supernatural verities, so here too the article of use and wont in question will not bear formulation in mechanistic terms and is not congruous with that mechanistic logic that is incontinently bending the habits of thought of the common man more and more consistently to its own bent. There is, of course, the difference that while no class--apart from the servants of the church--have a material interest in the continued integrity of the articles of the supernatural faith, there is a strong and stubborn material interest bound up with the maintenance of this article of the pecuniary faith; and the class in whom this material interest vests are also, in effect, invested with the coercive powers of the law.

The law, and the popular preconceptions that give the law its binding force, go to uphold the established usage and the established prerogatives on this head; and the disestablishment of the rights of property and investment therefore is not a simple matter of obsolescence through neglect. It may confidently be counted on that all the apparatus of the law and all the coercive agencies of law and order, will be brought in requisition to uphold the ancient rights of ownership, whenever any move is made toward their disallowance or restriction. But then, on the other hand, the movement to disallow or diminish the prerogatives of ownership is also not to take the innocuous shape of unstudied neglect. So soon, or rather so far, as the common man comes to realise that these rights of ownership and investment uniformly work to his material detriment, at the same time that he has lost the "will to believe" in any argument that does not run in terms of the mechanistic logic, it is reasonable to expect that he will take a stand on this matter; and it is more than likely that the stand taken will be of an uncompromising kind,--presumably something in the nature of the stand once taken by recalcitrant Englishmen in protest against the irresponsible rule of the Stuart sovereign. It is also not likely that the beneficiaries under these proprietary rights will yield their ground at all amicably; all the more since they are patently within their authentic rights in insisting on full discretion in the disposal of their own possessions; very much as Charles I or James II once were within their prescriptive right,--which had little to say in the outcome.

Even apart from "time immemorial" and the patent authenticity of the institution, there were and are many cogent arguments to be alleged in favor of the position for which the Stuart sovereigns and their spokesmen contended. So there are and will be many, perhaps more, cogent reasons to be alleged for the maintenance of the established law and order in respect of the rights of ownership and investment. Not least urgent, nor least real, among these arguments is the puzzling question of what to put in the place of these rights and of the methods of control based on them, very much as the analogous question puzzled the public-spirited men of the Stuart times. All of which goes to argue that there may be expected to arise a conjuncture of perplexities and complications, as well as a division of interests and claims. To which should be added that the division is likely to come to a head so soon as the balance of forces between the two parties in interest becomes doubtful, so that either party comes to surmise that the success of its own aims may depend on its own efforts. And as happens where two antagonistic parties are each convinced of the justice of its cause, and in the absence of an umpire, the logical recourse is the wager of battle.

Granting the premises, there should be no reasonable doubt as to this eventual cleavage between those who own and those who do not; and of the premises the only item that is not already an accomplished fact is the installation of peace at large. The rest of what goes into the argument is the well-known modern state of the industrial arts, and the equally well-known price-system; which, in combination, give its character to the modern state of business enterprise. It is only an unusually broad instance of an institutional arrangement which has in the course of time and changing conditions come to work at cross purposes with that underlying ground of institutional arrangements that takes form in the commonplace aphorism, Live and let live. With change setting in the direction familiar to all men today, it is only a question of limited time when the discrepancy will reach a critical pass, and the installation of peace may be counted on to hasten this course of things.

That a decision will be sought by recourse to forcible measures, is also scarcely open to question; since the established law and order provides for a resort to coercion in the enforcement of these prescriptive rights, and since both parties in interest, in this as in other cases, are persuaded of the justice of their claims. A decision either way is an intolerable iniquity in the eyes of the losing side. History teaches that in such a quarrel the recourse has always been to force.

History teaches also, but with an inflection of doubt, that the outworn institution in such a conjuncture faces disestablishment. At least, so men like to believe. What the experience of history does not leave in doubt is the grave damage, discomfort and shame incident to the displacement of such an institutional discrepancy by such recourse to force. What further appears to be clear in the premises, at least to the point of a strong presumption, is that in the present case the decision, or the choice, lies between two alternatives: either the price-system and its attendant business enterprise will yield and pass out; or the pacific nations will conserve their pecuniary scheme of law and order at the cost of returning to a war footing and letting their owners preserve the rights of ownership by force of arms.

The reflection obviously suggests itself that this prospect of consequences to follow from the installation of peace at large might well be taken into account beforehand by those who are aiming to work out an enduring peace. It has appeared in the course of the argument that the preservation of the present pecuniary law and order, with all its incidents of ownership and investment, is incompatible with an unwarlike state of peace and security. This current scheme of investment, business, and sabotage, should have an appreciably better chance of survival in the long run if the present conditions of warlike preparation and national insecurity were maintained, or if the projected peace were left in a somewhat problematical state, sufficiently precarious to keep national animosities alert, and thereby to the neglect of domestic interests, particularly of such interests as touch the popular well-being. On the other hand, it has also appeared that the cause of peace and its perpetuation might be materially advanced if precautions were taken beforehand to put out of the way as much as may be of those discrepancies of interest and sentiment between nations and between classes which make for dissension and eventual hostilities.

So, if the projectors of this peace at large are in any degree inclined to seek concessive terms on which the peace might hopefully be made enduring, it should evidently be part of their endeavours from the outset to put events in train for the present abatement and eventual abrogation of the rights of ownership and of the price-system in which these rights take effect. A hopeful beginning along this line would manifestly be the neutralisation of all pecuniary rights of citizenship, as has been indicated in an earlier passage. On the other hand, if peace is not desired at the cost of relinquishing the scheme of competitive gain and competitive spending, the promoters of peace should logically observe due precaution and move only so far in the direction of a peaceable settlement as would result in a sufficiently unstable equilibrium of mutual jealousies; such as might expeditiously be upset whenever discontent with pecuniary affairs should come to threaten this established scheme of pecuniary prerogatives.

www.bookjungle.com email: sales@bookjungle.com fax: 630-214-0564 mail: Book Jungle PO Box 2226 Champaign, IL 61825

The Codes Of Hammurabi And Moses
W. W. Davies

QTY

The discovery of the Hammurabi Code is one of the greatest achievements of archaeology, and is of paramount interest, not only to the student of the Bible, but also to all those interested in ancient history...

Religion   **ISBN:** *1-59462-338-4*   Pages:132
MSRP $12.95

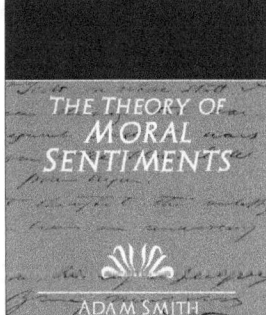

The Theory of Moral Sentiments
Adam Smith

QTY

This work from 1749. contains original theories of conscience amd moral judgment and it is the foundation for systemof morals.

Philosophy   **ISBN:** *1-59462-777-0*   Pages:536
MSRP $19.95

Jessica's First Prayer
Hesba Stretton

QTY

In a screened and secluded corner of one of the many railway-bridges which span the streets of London there could be seen a few years ago, from five o'clock every morning until half past eight, a tidily set-out coffee-stall, consisting of a trestle and board, upon which stood two large tin cans, with a small fire of charcoal burning under each so as to keep the coffee boiling during the early hours of the morning when the work-people were thronging into the city on their way to their daily toil...

Childrens   **ISBN:** *1-59462-373-2*

Pages:84
MSRP $9.95

My Life and Work
Henry Ford

QTY

Henry Ford revolutionized the world with his implementation of mass production for the Model T automobile. Gain valuable business insight into his life and work with his own auto-biography... "We have only started on our development of our country we have not as yet, with all our talk of wonderful progress, done more than scratch the surface. The progress has been wonderful enough but..."

Pages:300

Biographies/   **ISBN:** *1-59462-198-5*   MSRP $21.95

www.bookjungle.com *email: sales@bookjungle.com fax: 630-214-0564 mail: Book Jungle PO Box 2226 Champaign, IL 61825*

The Art of Cross-Examination
Francis Wellman

QTY

I presume it is the experience of every author, after his first book is published upon an important subject, to be almost overwhelmed with a wealth of ideas and illustrations which could readily have been included in his book, and which to his own mind, at least, seem to make a second edition inevitable. Such certainly was the case with me; and when the first edition had reached its sixth impression in five months, I rejoiced to learn that it seemed to my publishers that the book had met with a sufficiently favorable reception to justify a second and considerably enlarged edition. ..

Reference   ISBN: *1-59462-647-2*   Pages:412   MSRP $19.95

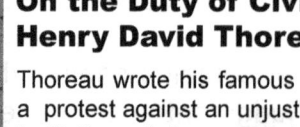

On the Duty of Civil Disobedience
Henry David Thoreau

QTY

Thoreau wrote his famous essay, On the Duty of Civil Disobedience, as a protest against an unjust but popular war and the immoral but popular institution of slave-owning. He did more than write—he declined to pay his taxes, and was hauled off to gaol in consequence. Who can say how much this refusal of his hastened the end of the war and of slavery ?

Law   ISBN: *1-59462-747-9*   Pages:48   MSRP $7.45

Dream Psychology Psychoanalysis for Beginners
Sigmund Freud

QTY

Sigmund Freud, born Sigismund Schlomo Freud (May 6, 1856 - September 23, 1939), was a Jewish-Austrian neurologist and psychiatrist who co-founded the psychoanalytic school of psychology. Freud is best known for his theories of the unconscious mind, especially involving the mechanism of repression; his redefinition of sexual desire as mobile and directed towards a wide variety of objects; and his therapeutic techniques, especially his understanding of transference in the therapeutic relationship and the presumed value of dreams as sources of insight into unconscious desires.

Psychology   ISBN: *1-59462-905-6*   Pages:196   MSRP $15.45

The Miracle of Right Thought
Orison Swett Marden

QTY

Believe with all of your heart that you will do what you were made to do. When the mind has once formed the habit of holding cheerful, happy, prosperous pictures, it will not be easy to form the opposite habit. It does not matter how improbable or how far away this realization may see, or how dark the prospects may be, if we visualize them as best we can, as vividly as possible, hold tenaciously to them and vigorously struggle to attain them, they will gradually become actualized, realized in the life. But a desire, a longing without endeavor, a yearning abandoned or held indifferently will vanish without realization.

Self Help   ISBN: *1-59462-644-8*   Pages:360   MSRP $25.45

www.bookjungle.com email: sales@bookjungle.com fax: 630-214-0564 mail: Book Jungle PO Box 2226 Champaign, IL 61825

QTY

	Title	ISBN	Price
☐	**The Rosicrucian Cosmo-Conception Mystic Christianity** *by Max Heindel* *The Rosicrucian Cosmo-conception is not dogmatic, neither does it appeal to any other authority than the reason of the student. It is: not controversial, but is: sent forth in the, hope that it may help to clear...* New Age/Religion Pages 646	ISBN: 1-59462-188-8	$38.95
☐	**Abandonment To Divine Providence** *by Jean-Pierre de Caussade* *"The Rev. Jean Pierre de Caussade was one of the most remarkable spiritual writers of the Society of Jesus in France in the 18th Century. His death took place at Toulouse in 1751. His works have gone through many editions and have been republished...* Inspirational/Religion Pages 400	ISBN: 1-59462-228-0	$25.95
☐	**Mental Chemistry** *by Charles Haanel* *Mental Chemistry allows the change of material conditions by combining and appropriately utilizing the power of the mind. Much like applied chemistry creates something new and unique out of careful combinations of chemicals the mastery of mental chemistry...* New Age Pages 354	ISBN: 1-59462-192-6	$23.95
☐	**The Letters of Robert Browning and Elizabeth Barret Barrett 1845-1846 vol II** *by Robert Browning and Elizabeth Barrett* Biographies Pages 596	ISBN: 1-59462-193-4	$35.95
☐	**Gleanings In Genesis (volume I)** *by Arthur W. Pink* *Appropriately has Genesis been termed "the seed plot of the Bible" for in it we have, in germ form, almost all of the great doctrines which are afterwards fully developed in the books of Scripture which follow...* Religion/Inspirational Pages 420	ISBN: 1-59462-130-6	$27.45
☐	**The Master Key** *by L. W. de Laurence* *In no branch of human knowledge has there been a more lively increase of the spirit of research during the past few years than in the study of Psychology, Concentration and Mental Discipline. The requests for authentic lessons in Thought Control, Mental Discipline and...* New Age/Business Pages 422	ISBN: 1-59462-001-6	$30.95
☐	**The Lesser Key Of Solomon Goetia** *by L. W. de Laurence* *This translation of the first book of the "Lernegton" which is now for the first time made accessible to students of Talismanic Magic was done, after careful collation and edition, from numerous Ancient Manuscripts in Hebrew, Latin, and French...* New Age/Occult Pages 92	ISBN: 1-59462-092-X	$9.95
☐	**Rubaiyat Of Omar Khayyam** *by Edward Fitzgerald* *Edward Fitzgerald, whom the world has already learned, in spite of his own efforts to remain within the shadow of anonymity, to look upon as one of the rarest poets of the century, was born at Bredfield, in Suffolk, on the 31st of March, 1809. He was the third son of John Purcell...* Music Pages 172	ISBN: 1-59462-332-5	$13.95
☐	**Ancient Law** *by Henry Maine* *The chief object of the following pages is to indicate some of the earliest ideas of mankind, as they are reflected in Ancient Law, and to point out the relation of those ideas to modern thought.* Religiom/History Pages 452	ISBN: 1-59462-128-4	$29.95
☐	**Far-Away Stories** *by William J. Locke* *"Good wine needs no bush, but a collection of mixed vintages does. And this book is just such a collection. Some of the stories I do not want to remain buried for ever in the museum files of dead magazine-numbers an author's not unpardonable vanity,..."* Fiction Pages 272	ISBN: 1-59462-129-2	$19.45
☐	**Life of David Crockett** *by David Crockett* *"Colonel David Crockett was one of the most remarkable men of the times in which he lived. Born in humble life, but gifted with a strong will, an indomitable courage, and unremitting perseverance...* Biographies/New Age Pages 424	ISBN: 1-59462-250-7	$27.45
☐	**Lip-Reading** *by Edward Nitchie* *Edward B. Nitchie, founder of the New York School for the Hard of Hearing, now the Nitchie School of Lip-Reading, Inc, wrote "LIP-READING Principles and Practice". The development and perfecting of this meritorious work on lip-reading was an undertaking...* How-to Pages 400	ISBN: 1-59462-206-X	$25.95
☐	**A Handbook of Suggestive Therapeutics, Applied Hypnotism, Psychic Science** *by Henry Munro* Health/New Age/Health/Self-help Pages 376	ISBN: 1-59462-214-0	$24.95
☐	**A Doll's House: and Two Other Plays** *by Henrik Ibsen* *Henrik Ibsen created this classic when in revolutionary 1848 Rome. Introducing some striking concepts in playwriting for the realist genre, this play has been studied the world over.* Fiction/Classics/Plays 308	ISBN: 1-59462-112-8	$19.95
☐	**The Light of Asia** *by sir Edwin Arnold* *In this poetic masterpiece, Edwin Arnold describes the life and teachings of Buddha. The man who was to become known as Buddha to the world was born as Prince Gautama of India but he rejected the worldly riches and abandoned the reigns of power when... Religion/History/Biographies Pages 170*	ISBN: 1-59462-204-3	$13.95
☐	**The Complete Works of Guy de Maupassant** *by Guy de Maupassant* *"For days and days, nights and nights, I had dreamed of that first kiss which was to consecrate our engagement, and I knew not on what spot I should put my lips..."* Fiction/Classics Pages 240	ISBN: 1-59462-157-8	$16.95
☐	**The Art of Cross-Examination** *by Francis L. Wellman* *Written by a renowned trial lawyer, Wellman imparts his experience and uses case studies to explain how to use psychology to extract desired information through questioning.* How-to/Science/Reference Pages 408	ISBN: 1-59462-309-0	$26.95
☐	**Answered or Unanswered?** *by Louisa Vaughan* *Miracles of Faith in China* Religion Pages 112	ISBN: 1-59462-248-5	$10.95
☐	**The Edinburgh Lectures on Mental Science (1909)** *by Thomas* *This book contains the substance of a course of lectures recently given by the writer in the Queen Street Hall, Edinburgh. Its purpose is to indicate the Natural Principles governing the relation between Mental Action and Material Conditions...* New Age/Psychology Pages 148	ISBN: 1-59462-008-3	$11.95
☐	**Ayesha** *by H. Rider Haggard* *Verily and indeed it is the unexpected that happens! Probably if there was one person upon the earth from whom the Editor of this, and of a certain previous history, did not expect to hear again...* Classics Pages 380	ISBN: 1-59462-301-5	$24.95
☐	**Ayala's Angel** *by Anthony Trollope* *The two girls were both pretty, but Lucy who was twenty-one who supposed to be simple and comparatively unattractive, whereas Ayala was credited, as her Bombwhat romantic name might show, with poetic charm and a taste for romance. Ayala when her father died was nineteen...* Fiction Pages 484	ISBN: 1-59462-352-X	$29.95
☐	**The American Commonwealth** *by James Bryce* *An interpretation of American democratic political theory. It examines political mechanics and society from the perspective of Scotsman James Bryce* Politics Pages 572	ISBN: 1-59462-286-8	$34.45
☐	**Stories of the Pilgrims** *by Margaret P. Pumphrey* *This book explores pilgrims religious oppression in England as well as their escape to Holland and eventual crossing to America on the Mayflower, and their early days in New England...* History Pages 268	ISBN: 1-59462-116-0	$17.95

www.bookjungle.com *email:* sales@bookjungle.com *fax:* 630-214-0564 *mail:* Book Jungle PO Box 2226 Champaign, IL 61825

QTY

The Fasting Cure *by Sinclair Upton* ISBN: *1-59462-222-1* **$13.95**
In the Cosmopolitan Magazine for May, 1910, and in the Contemporary Review (London) for April, 1910, I published an article dealing with my experiences in fasting. I have written a great many magazine articles, but never one which attracted so much attention... New Age/Self Help/Health Pages 164

Hebrew Astrology *by Sepharial* ISBN: *1-59462-308-2* **$13.45**
In these days of advanced thinking it is a matter of common observation that we have left many of the old landmarks behind and that we are now pressing forward to greater heights and to a wider horizon than that which represented the mind-content of our progenitors... Astrology Pages 144

Thought Vibration or The Law of Attraction in the Thought World ISBN: *1-59462-127-6* **$12.95**
by William Walker Atkinson Psychology/Religion Pages 144

Optimism *by Helen Keller* ISBN: *1-59462-108-X* **$15.95**
Helen Keller was blind, deaf, and mute since 19 months old, yet famously learned how to overcome these handicaps, communicate with the world, and spread her lectures promoting optimism. An inspiring read for everyone... Biographies/Inspirational Pages 84

Sara Crewe *by Frances Burnett* ISBN: *1-59462-360-0* **$9.45**
In the first place, Miss Minchin lived in London. Her home was a large, dull, tall one, in a large, dull square, where all the houses were alike, and all the sparrows were alike, and where all the door-knockers made the same heavy sound... Childrens/Classic Pages 88

The Autobiography of Benjamin Franklin *by Benjamin Franklin* ISBN: *1-59462-135-7* **$24.95**
The Autobiography of Benjamin Franklin has probably been more extensively read than any other American historical work, and no other book of its kind has had such ups and downs of fortune. Franklin lived for many years in England, where he was agent... Biographies/History Pages 332

Name	
Email	
Telephone	
Address	
City, State ZIP	

☐ Credit Card   ☐ Check / Money Order

Credit Card Number	
Expiration Date	
Signature	

Please Mail to: Book Jungle
PO Box 2226
Champaign, IL 61825
or Fax to: 630-214-0564

ORDERING INFORMATION

web: www.bookjungle.com
email: sales@bookjungle.com
fax: 630-214-0564
mail: Book Jungle PO Box 2226 Champaign, IL 61825
or PayPal to sales@bookjungle.com

Please contact us for bulk discounts

DIRECT-ORDER TERMS

**20% Discount if You Order
Two or More Books**
Free Domestic Shipping!
Accepted: Master Card, Visa,
Discover, American Express

www.ingramcontent.com/pod-product-compliance
Lightning Source LLC
Chambersburg PA
CBHW080240170426
43192CB00014BA/2509